Praise for the Southbound World Heritage series

"These are fantastically comprehensive guides ... packed full of information and beautiful photographs and small enough to slip inside a backpack"
—**Jane Strode, *Daily Sun***

"Dit is gebruikersvriendelik, nuttig en omvattend en het 'n groot opvoedkundige waarde"—***Die Beeld***

"Handy travel companions ... these guides may be small but they're literally jam-packed with information ... making these guides holiday must-haves for an informed and more enjoyable trip"
—***Longevity* magazine**

"These handy books are accessible to everyone from the lay person to geologists and scientists, answering all your questions regarding these sites"
—***Saturday Dispatch***

"... compact pocket guides packed with info, maps and colourful pictures"
—***50/50***

"They are a celebration of various aspects of South African culture, including our historical inheritance and the land on which we live"
—**Diane de Beer, *Pretoria News***

"There's this marvellous new collection of pocket guides by Southbound, each highlighting a specific World Heritage Site in South Africa ... Easy to use and fun to read, the pocket guides are a must for anyone remotely interested in our country's heritage"—***Independent on Saturday***

"These books reveal fascinating parts of our country that many of us aren't properly aware of. They'd make excellent gifts, singly or collectively, and are great primers for planning a holiday"—**Bruce Dennill, *The Citizen***

"All [eight] of South Africa's World Heritage Sites are covered, each in a manageable pocket guide which provides a remarkable amount of information for the edification of the serious ecotourist ... comprehensive contents ... an extensive amount of information ..."—**Carol Knoll, *Environmental Management***

"... intensely practical ... fantastic series to buy ..."
—**Jenny Crwys-Williams, *Talk Radio 702***

"... these are among the best we have—opinionated and full of personality"
—**Patricia McCracken, *Farmer's Weekly***

Southbound Travel Guides

Swaziland

David Fleminger

Also by David Fleminger:
Back Roads of the Cape (Jacana 2005)
Robben Island (Southbound 2006)
The Cradle of Humankind (Southbound 2006)
Vredefort Dome (Southbound 2006)
Mapungubwe Cultural Landscape (Southbound 2006)
*The Richtersveld Cultural and Botanical Landscape
  including Namaqualand* (Southbound 2008)
Lesotho (Southbound 2009)

Published in 2009 by Southbound
an imprint of 30° South Publishers (Pty) Ltd.
28, Ninth Street, Newlands
Johannesburg 2092, South Africa
www.30degreessouth.co.za
info@30degreessouth.co.za

Design and origination by 30° South Publishers (Pty) Ltd.

Printed and bound by Pinetown Printers, Durban

ISBN 978-1-920143-27-5

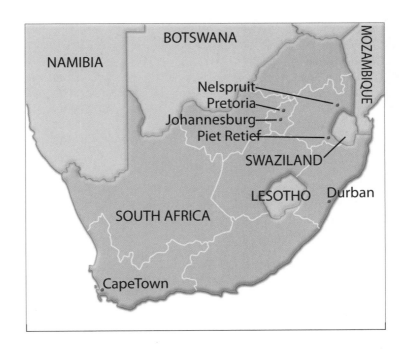

For my uncle Morris Bay—a remarkable man who never let reality get in the way of a good story. He is deeply missed

Contents

Getting started

Introduction

I love Swaziland. From the first time I ventured into this tiny tranquil kingdom back in the early 1990s, I immediately felt comfortable, relaxed, and at peace with the world. I have been back many times since; usually only for a few days at a stretch, but it's always a pleasure; just like visiting an old friend or slipping on a favourite pair of jeans.

You'll have to forgive me if I am overstating the case, but Swaziland has a way of getting inside your soul. It's a dreamy, sleepy, beautiful country that enchants visitors with its scenery and laid-back atmosphere. It is also a proud country, with a fascinating history and a strong cultural identity. Above all, it is a place of continuity where traditions stretching back hundreds of years are still very much a part of everyday life. Swaziland, in fact, is the domain of the last absolute monarch in the world—and even though this political dispensation may seem downright medieval in today's terms, it undoubtedly represents a big part of Swaziland's timeless charm.

One reason for this unbroken continuum is that, rather uniquely, there have been no wars or armed conflicts on Swazi soil for well over 100 years. Even though it is surrounded by countries that have been riven by civil war and racial tension, this tiny landlocked territory has somehow avoided many of the traumas that have characterized the turbulent 20th century in southern Africa. It has not been invaded, conquered, usurped or dominated by any oppressive regimes; even the usually fraught British colonial era in the country was established and then dismantled with remarkable amicability.

The other thing that strikes most visitors to Swaziland is the unhurried pace of life. Just like Aesop's tortoise who won the race against the rushing rabbit, time in Swaziland moves at a snail's pace; steady and slow. In fact, you could say that everything in Swaziland happens at walking pace—the same speed at which people stroll up and down the endless hills. Predictably, this means that Swaziland isn't exactly at the top of the world's productivity ratings, and industry struggles to find a firm footing in this chilled-out corner of the world. But that's largely what makes it a perfect destination for anyone who needs to relax and recharge. So, all in all, Swaziland seems to be a happy country. The people are very friendly, there's very little crime, and the wider community appears to function effectively. However, there are several challenges facing this idyllic spot on the map as it barrels into the 21st century: tragically, the HIV and AIDS infection rate is among the highest in the world; economic development is limited; the majority of the population are very poor, and unemployment is rampant.

Even the usually sacrosanct authority of the monarchy is under attack with a small minority of Swazis pointing fingers at what they perceive to be extravagant spending by the current king. Others have a problem with the king's polygamy, even though this is in accordance with Swazi tradition. Cries for a multi-party democracy from activists, who interestingly do *not* want the monarchy abolished, are often in conflict with the greater majority of rural monarchists.

Nevertheless, for all its troubles, Swaziland gives us a tempting glimpse of how Africa might have turned out if the last 100 years or so of colonial and political turmoil had been handled in a more responsible manner by the powers-that-were. As such, it is a telling example of what can happen when an African country is allowed to find its own solutions. One day, perhaps, the entire continent will be as pleasant as Swaziland.

So, Swaziland is beautiful, compact and peaceful. It also offers a range of leisure activities that range from hiking to horse riding, to white water rafting, to cultural events, to gambling, to big game spotting, to shopping. All in all, it's a great place to be and every time I visit, I come away with the half-serious notion that I should emigrate there.

In the pages that follow, you will find out more about the fascinating history of this remarkable little country. We will also explore the various attractions and destinations that might appeal to the traveller, and suggest several itineraries to help you plan your trip.

The 'Exploring Swaziland' section is divided into five sections: the Centre (Mbabane/Ezulwini/Manzini); the Northwest; the Southwest; the Northeast and the Southeast. Phone numbers for hotels and attractions are found under their relevant headings. Every attempt has been made to assemble accurate and up-to-date information but, for a country where nothing seems to change, contact details seem to be in a constant state of flux.

My hope is that this guidebook, the first of its kind in many years, will enhance both your Swazi tourism experience and your understanding of the nation's history. Ideally, after reading this book, you will be encouraged to either plan a trip if you haven't been before, or be stimulated go back and discover more about the wonderful Kingdom of Swaziland.

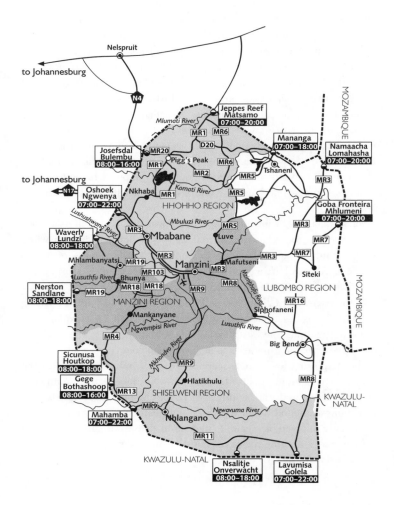

The basics

Size

Swaziland covers a roughly circular area of just over 17,000 square kilometres. That's about the same size as Wales or Kuwait—making it the third smallest country in Africa (after the Seychelles and Gambia). The kingdom measures roughly 175km from north to south and 115km from east to west.

Population

Until recently, he kingdom had an official population of 1.1 million. However, the latest estimates put it at 930,000, a negative growth rate caused by HIV/AIDS. Many Swazis also migrate to neighbouring South Africa every year in search of employment opportunities. There are about a million Swazi-speaking people living across the border in South Africa, although many of them are native South Africans who were cut off from their brethren during the colonial border adjustments of previous centuries. The average age of the population is around 18 with 40% of the population under 15, and the average life expectancy is a rather dismal 37 years, projected to worsen to 33 by 2015. About 75% of the population lives in the rural area

Climate

Swaziland has a pleasant subtropical climate, with most of the rain falling during the summer months. Average summer temperatures range from 15 to 25 degrees Celsius, while winter tends to offer mild days with peaks between 15 and 19 degrees. This will vary depending on the altitude, however, and it can get chilly in the western mountains, especially in the evening; so bring something warm. Conversely, the eastern Lowveld can get unpleasantly hot and humid during summer. Malaria is endemic to the eastern part of Swaziland (basically anywhere east of Manzini), but this is not a problem in the lofty climes of the western region.

Rainfall also varies with the altitude; from 1,000 to 1,600mm in the high-lying western region to between 500 and 600mm in the east. The country's highest point, at 1,862 metres, is Emlembe/Mlembu Mountain near Pigg's Peak, and the lowest point is on the Great Usuthu River, which bottoms out at only 21m above sea level.

Language

Demographically speaking, Swaziland is a relatively cohesive place. The majority of the population are members of a single cultural group with a common language, tradition and king. This unity makes the Swazi nation justifiably proud. The official languages are SiSwati (an Nguni language, similar to Zulu) and English. Both are taught in the schools, where English is often the medium of instruction. As a result, English is widely spoken, especially by the youth.

Religion

About 80 per cent of the population is Christian; the rest subscribe to traditional belief systems, although boundaries between the two faiths are not distinct. For example, many Swazis find no contradiction between going to church and consulting with traditional diviners (*sangomas*) who communicate with ancestors. Modern visitors who wish to have their future told by the ritual of 'throwing the bones' can visit a practising *sangoma* as part of a cultural tour.

The first Christian mission was established at Mahamba in 1844, but these hardy Wesleyans were soon forced out of the territory by political trouble and only returned several decades later. Today, most Christian denominations are represented. Charismatic and evangelical congregations are becoming increasingly popular.

The missionary zeal of some churches is still evident in Swaziland. Recently, the educational syllabus was amended whereby students would be taught about other religions of the world. This decision was strongly opposed by fundamentalist church leaders, which I found rather benighted.

Borders

Swaziland is land-locked. In the east it is bordered by Mozambique, while South Africa surrounds it in the north, west and south. Traditionally, the Swazi domain was much bigger than it is now, extending from the Phongolo River in the south to the Crocodile River in the north and from Kosi Bay in the east to beyond the western escarpment. However, towards the end of the 19th century, the present-day borders of Swaziland were controversially pushed back as part of the contemporary political wrangling between the South African Boer republics, the Swazi monarchy and the British. There are still persistent complaints from the Swazis regarding their diminished boundaries, especially in the north and southeast, but this is unlikely to be resolved any time soon.

As Swaziland is an independent country, entry is only permitted through one of the official border posts it shares with its two neighbours, South Africa and Mozambique. Thankfully, the border process is now computerized and waiting times have been greatly improved. There still isn't a Duty Free, though.

Currency

The official Swazi unit of currency is the Lilangeni (plural: Emalangeni), which translates as 'royal person'. This is directly pegged to the South African Rand at 1:1. You can use South African currency as legal tender throughout Swaziland. Note, though, that you can't spend your Emalangeni in South Africa, so don't accumulate too much change.

The flag

The current Swazi flag was first flown on 30 October 1967. It has a central horizontal band of crimson—signifying royalty and the battles of the past. This is bordered on either side by a thin strip of yellow, symbolising the natural resources of the nation. All this is sandwiched between two outer bands of blue that stand for peace and stability. In the middle of the flag are the shield, spear and staff of the king's regiment, the *Inyatsi*. It is said that the shield is black and white to show that all races live together peacefully in Swaziland.

Economy

In terms of Gross Domestic Product the main economic activities in Swaziland are agriculture (12%), industry (45%) and services (43%). Farming is focused on sugar, citrus, cattle, pineapples and, to a lesser degree, cotton. Forestry, manufacturing and tourism are also important contributors. Mining used to play a significant role, but most mining activity has now ceased, with only one coal mine still operational.

Swaziland also has a neat little sideline in the production of Coca-Cola concentrate, and exports significant quantities of the sticky sweet stuff annually. This is a legacy of the previous century, when apartheid-era sanctions forced the Coca-Cola Company to move its manufacturing facilities out of South Africa in 1987. Coke is now one of Swaziland's biggest earners of foreign exchange. The king even spoke at the company's 20th anniversary party. Unsurprisingly, South Africa snaps up most of Swaziland's exports, and supplies about 90% of its imported goods. South Africa also supplies Swaziland with most of its electricity. Receipts from the Southern African Customs Union make up about two-thirds of the government's revenue, with the rest coming from taxes. The nearest harbour is at Maputo, about 200km from Matsapha, the industrial hub.

Unemployment sits at around 40%, with 70% of the population living below the poverty datum line, however most of these people practise successful subsistence farming so these statistics are perhaps misleading.

Tibiyo Taka Ngwane, the national fund, is a development agency that facilitates investment and owns many of the country's assets—which are generally held in trust for the nation by the king. This complicated relationship between king and country means that many big businesses operate with Tibiyo as a partner.

Healthcare

There are several public clinics and hospitals located around Swaziland. There are also a couple of privately-run healthcare facilities for those who can afford them. Nevertheless, about 80 per cent of the population will visit a traditional healer (inyanga) before they see a western doctor. It is therefore crucial that this ancient form of healthcare be embraced by organizations trying to combat the scourge of HIV and AIDS.

HIV and AIDS

Swaziland has one of the highest HIV-infection rates in the world. Despite a recent reduction of several percent, prevalance is still estimated at between 26% and 40%, with 15% of households headed by children under 18. There are currently around 80,000 AIDS orphans, projected to increase to 120,000 by 2010. As such AIDS is a national disaster, having nullified a large chunk of the productive population.

To try and combat the pandemic, several international agencies and NGOs have set up operations in Swaziland. Their activities range from education to orphan care to health services. The churches are also involved, but I felt that a prominent church-sponsored billboard which advised 'All sex that leads to hell is unsafe' was rather unhelpful.

Politics

The Swazi king is an absolute monarch —the last in the world. There is a parliament, however, which consists of a House of Assembly and a Senate.

Political parties were banned by Sobhuza II, the current king's father, in 1973 and are still technically illegal. Sobhuza felt that the concept of a political opposition was inimical to the African experience, and rejected democracy as an alien concept. He also stated that all parties belonged to the king, so it was inappropriate to make people choose one over the other. Instead, the *tinkhundla* system is used to advise the king and nominate candidates for parliament. Under *tinkhundla*, the nation is split into 55 *inkhundla*: 14 in Hhohho district, eleven in Lubombo district, 16 in Manzini district and 14 in Shiselweni district. The boundaries of these *tinkhundla* are revised every five years.Each *inkhundla* comprises a number of local chiefdoms under the leadership of an *indvuna*, who is chosen by the king. In election years, each *inkhundla* uses a secret ballot to nominate three local members to stand as candidates for the House of Assembly. During this stage, no campaigning is allowed.

In the secondary phase, the nominated candidates are permitted to campaign and, on election day, each *inkhundla* votes one member to the House of Assembly through a secret ballot.

The House of Assembly therefore consists of members elected by the *tinkhundla*, as well as ten members appointed directly by the king. There is also an attorney-general (who does not have a vote) and four women elected by a joint sitting of parliament from a shortlist supplied by the Election and Boundaries Commission. The Senate consists of ten members elected by the House of Assembly and 20 members appointed by the king. At least half the senators must be women.

Parliament is supplemented by a traditional government that consists of the *libandla* (national council) and the *liqoqo* (royal inner council). The *libandla* represents every male in the land, irrespective of age or status. The *libandla* usually meets once a year inside the national *sibaya* (cattle kraal), but can be called up for emergency meetings. The *liqoqo* deals with the day-to-day matters of state and is selected by the king.

The king also chooses his prime minister from the House of Assembly, with advice from his *liqoqo*. The king and the PM then select a cabinet. The PM, cabinet and parliament can be dismissed by the king if he considers them to be incompetent. A somewhat nebulous collection of 'elders' (senior princes of the royal Dlamini clan) also play a role in the traditional and political life of the kingdom. Although I'm certainly no expert on this intricate system of government, suffice it to say that although the parliament may debate issues and put forward policy decisions, the king is the supreme head of state and always has the final say. As such, the king is never wrong, and you may not criticize *umlomo longacalimanga* (the mouth that never lies). However, you can criticize the government; this strange duality is something the Swazis embrace.

Although most Swazis profess to being satisfied by the *tinkhundla* system, a few pro-democracy advocates are now demanding a change in the *status quo*. They insist that the problems facing the country are better met by a government elected by the people, and several technically-illegal opposition parties have started working together to push for far-reaching reforms. The king, for his part, shows no indication that he is ready to become a purely ceremonial monarch.

To make matters worse, there are some radicals who support integration with their more powerful neighbour, South Africa. There are a couple of other reasons for this uncharacteristic position: a stronger economy, more jobs, better infrastructure, potential for increased development and improved welfare structures (pensions in Swaziland are only R80 per month, about a tenth of the South African figure). Nevertheless, it is highly unlikely that the proud people of Swaziland would ever countenance any abdication of their sovereignty.

- www.eisa.org.za – Electoral Institute of Southern Africa

Education

Swaziland has a highly functioning educational system and children will spend an average of ten years in school. Literacy rates are impressive, between 75% and 90%, depending on the age group. Even though the government spends a significant amount on education, schooling is not free and you must buy your own school uniform—no uniform, no schooling. Recently, however, plans have been announced to make schooling free (and compulsory) up to the end of primary school by 2015. Secondary education, at this stage, is still for the parent's account, but girls may be offered half-rates to encourage greater participation in economy. Swaziland has only one university with several campuses (including an agricultural school). As such, there are a very limited number of places available and many school-leavers do not have the opportunity of receiving a tertiary education.

Traditional life

Swaziland is the embodiment of 'living heritage'. Ancient cultural and spiritual rituals are still vital to the lives of many ordinary Swazis, and are not merely performed for the benefit of tourists. Apart from attending the annual *umhlanga* reed dance or the royal *incwala* harvest festival, the best way to experience the vibrant customs of the people is to go on a guided 'cultural tour'. A list of guides can be found at the end of this book. The traditional outfit, still worn by many Swazis, is called *emahiya*, and consists of a number of components, depending on the person's age, status and the occasion. *Emahiya* can include a sarong, an animal skin loincloth, a knee-length skin apron, necklaces, headdress, tassels and an ornamental rope that is tied around the upper body.

The requirements of *emahiya* are quite exacting, and it is considered bad form to transgress these codes. For example, if you are a man, you may wear the skins without the sarong, but if you wear the sarong without the skins, you can be fined a cow (or six goats—an exchange rate that has remained constant for many years). Furthermore, if you are wearing an upper-body tie without the sarong and skins, you are 'just a drunkard'. The cloth can be in blue or yellow or orange or red, but has to consist of the correct patterns to be official. Tourists can buy their own Swazi sarongs at most craft markets (usually with a picture of a young King Mswati emblazoned across the centre).

The traditional Swazi greeting is 'Sanibonani' which is a plural form and also indicates respect, so you won't offend anyone. Failing that, I've always found that a smile and wave does a pretty good job too.

In the rural areas, most people still live in traditional Swazi homesteads, called *umuti (imiti* in the plural). These family compounds can consist of mud huts, grass 'beehives', modern brick-built structures, or a combination of all three. According to custom, the first house to be constructed is the grandmother's house. This is the central meeting place, and is seen as the home of the family's ancestral spirits. It is always a round house, because evil spirits can hide in the corners of a room. Next to the grandmother's house is a kitchen or cooking area. A number of additional dwellings are then built to accommodate the rest of the extended family.

The area around a homestead is usually cleared of grass and the sand is regularly swept clean. This is makes it easy to see snakes, and also reveals the footprints of any intruders who may sneak into the compound while the family is away.

Many homesteads will also have a place where the women sit and weave long stalks of grass into ropes, thatch, clothing, ornaments or handicrafts. The most popular kind of grass comes from Mdzimba Mountain, as it is very fine. Weavers also use Baboon Tail grass, which is more coarse. Bushels of grass are sold by traders in the markets, usually on a Thursday.

Marriage is an important part of Swazi life; people are encouraged to marry young. Small girls often sing a traditional song which warns that 'the bus has gone and left me behind'. As Mandla, my guide, told me, the Swazis like their tomatoes pink and firm. They don't like them red and ripe.

The Swazi marriage ceremony is similar to those of many other Nguni cultures, such as the Zulu or the Xhosa. It requires, among other things, the payment of *lobola* (a dowry paid to the bride's father as compensation for losing a productive daughter). *Lobola* is usually priced in cows, which is one reason why cattle have played such a major role in the traditional economy of southern Africa. Today, many men are unable to raise enough money to buy the necessary cows, and this has lead to a weakening of the institution. Others are forced to pay off the *lobola* in instalments, but I'm not sure if interest is charged in these cases.

Another component of the marriage ceremony is the application of ochre soil to the bodies of the bride and groom. This is because the couple are saying that they will be together until they see ochre again, which is a touching variation on 'till death us do part'.

Finally, the seven to ten per cent of the population who are left-handed should be aware that being a southpaw is considered unlucky in Swaziland. The king can never be left-handed and many teachers will still bandage up a student's left hand so that they learn to write with their right. Women, however, traditionally walk on the left-hand side of a man—but this is for their own protection because, in years past, men would carry a shield in their left hand and a spear in their right.

Orientation

The landlocked kingdom of Swaziland is located in the northeastern part of southern Africa, and also borders on Mozambique. The country is divided into four administrative regions: Hhohho, Manzini, Shiselweni and Lubombo. The high-lying western part of the country (Hhohho and Manzini regions) is mountainous and lush, with dramatic peaks and enchanting valleys. It is characterized by Highveld vegetation, consisting of tall grasslands with isolated trees and bushes. The major plantations of the forestry industry are located in this part of the country, specifically around the town of Pigg's Peak in the northwest corner of the country and Bhunya in the southwest.

The eastern and southern parts (Shiselweni and Lubombo) are much flatter and drier. This Lowveld region is characterized by thorn trees and grassland, much like the bushveld vegetation around the Kruger Park in South Africa, which lies just to the north. Many of the country's sugar plantations are found around the small town of Simunye (in the northeast) and Big Bend (in the southeast). Big Bend also has large cattle farms which sprawl across the plains.

About 60 per cent of the country is given over to communal Swazi National Land, dotted with rural villages and subsistence farms. The eastern boundary of the country (with Mozambique) is demarcated by the Lubombo mountain range, which runs in a straight line from north to south.

The administrative capital of Swaziland is the modest city of Mbabane, located in the mountainous western part of the country. It has a population of around 100,000 people. The major industrial centre is Manzini, located about 35km to the southeast of Mbabane on the main MR3 freeway. It has a population of around 80 000 and is adjacent to the Matsapha Industrial Estate, where most of the manufacturing takes place. The legislative capital is at Lobamba, close to several royal palaces and located halfway between Mbabane and Manzini.

Conveniently, many of the major tourist attractions and accommodation options are also located between Mbabane and Manzini; either in the Ezulwini Valley (meaning Valley of Heaven) or the adjacent Malkerns Valley. This compact region therefore functions as both an economic and leisure hub and is the perfect place to begin your explorations.

Geology

As is usually the case, the rocks of Swaziland do not follow petty political boundaries, and should be seen in a wider context that spills over into the neighbouring regions of South Africa and Mozambique. As such, the geology of the kingdom offers an attractive snapshot of the transition between the mountainous African highveld in the west (which is part of the central African plateau) and the evocative bushveld lowlands in the east. These two regions are separated by a steep-edged escarpment which extends through the western part of the country. This is part of the Great Escarpment, which runs unbroken from the Drakensberg in KwaZulu-Natal to Mpumalanga in the north

In the northwestern part of the country, the Swaziland Supergroup (also known as the Barberton Supergroup) dominates the topography. This sequence of rocks contains traces of ancient granite/greenstone belts that date back 3.5 billion years to the Archaean epoch, and are among the oldest identifiable rocks on Earth. Fossils of single-celled organisms have been found within the finely grained *chert* of the Onverwacht Group, and these have been dated back 3.3 to 3.4 billion years ago; making them some of the earliest forms of life yet found on the planet.

The Supergroup also harbours valuable mineral deposits such as iron, gold and asbestos. These ores have been extensively mined in years past, especially at Ngwenya Mountain, where there is a mammoth excavation from a now-dormant iron ore mine. Pigg's Peak is also home to several defunct mining operations. Both sites have visitors' centres.

This part of the country is heavily folded, creating an expanse of marvellous mountains. These sublime peaks are best explored in the Malolotja Nature Reserve and along the MR1 highway that runs from Ngwenya to Pigg's Peak. The mountains continue on the South African side of the border, in the Songimvelo Nature Reserve near Barberton. The plans to unite Malolotja and Songimvelo into a transfrontier conservation area (TFCA) are far advanced, and will help protect this rugged section of so-called Barberton Mountain Land.

Granite batholiths are common in the northwest. These are large domes formed by molten rock which was pushed up from the Earth's mantle into underground chambers, where it cooled before eventually being exposed on the surface by erosion. The Swaziland batholiths range in size from a few hundred metres to several kilometres, and this type of formation is best evidenced by the enormous Sibebe rock just outside Mbabane. The smooth dome of Sibebe is said to be the largest batholith in the world, and can be climbed as part of a guided tour.

Moving eastwards, the granite rocks have decomposed to form a series of rolling *koppies* (hills) and curving ridges, known as whalebacks, which are studded with golden boulders. These formations extend from the Highveld into the transitional middleveld, and even pop up occasionally in the Lowveld.

Over the millennia, a number of rivers have cut deep valleys through the landscape. These watercourses generally flow from west to east, running from the western highlands to meet the sea along the Mozambican coast. As such, Swaziland is one of the best-watered territories in the region, with an annual discharge measured at 5,000 cusecs—that's nine million litres of water a minute. Listed from north to south, the main river systems include the Mlumati, Komati, Mbuluzi, Usushwana, Ngwempisi, Mkhondvo, Ngwavuma and the Great Usuthu (or Lusutfu) which flows into the Phongolo River to reach the sea at the port of Maputo. The Komati and Great Usuthu rivers are two of the most impressive waterways in Swaziland, and both offer visitors a variety of water sports.

The rivers of Swaziland were (and still are) instrumental in eroding away the high plateau to create the flat, savannah-like plains of the Lowveld that dominate the eastern part of the country. This low-lying area of sedimentary and volcanic rocks is part of the Karoo Supergroup, which was laid down between the Permian and Jurassic periods (between 145 and 300 million years ago). The Lowveld environment extends beyond Swaziland's eastern border into Mozambique.

On Swaziland's eastern boundary, however, the sprawling savannah of the Lowveld is rudely interrupted by a straight line of mountains called the Lubombo. This range was formed when molten basalts and rhyolites spilled out of the earth and split apart, filling up a north-south rift that was created as the supercontinent of Gondwanaland about 180 million years ago. Much of the basalt has now eroded away, leaving behind a narrow strip of towering rhyolite that runs about 800km from KwaZulu-Natal into Mpumalanga.

The Lubombo range acts as both a physical and political barrier between Swaziland and Mozambique. The Lubombo are virtually impossible to traverse by vehicle, and access between the two countries is limited to several *poorts* where rivers have punctured a passage through the rocks. The Lubombo offers a number of interesting tourist activities, which are now being marketed as the Lubombo Tourism Route. A project that seeks to unite several conservation areas along the Lubombo is also underway.

Ecology

Since Swaziland straddles the central African plateau, the escarpment and Lowveld, this tiny country is home to a wide range of plant, animal and bird species. According to the comprehensive book *Wild Swaziland* (which is the source of most of the information in this section), this has created a number of bio-diversity hotspots that include the Drakensberg Escarpment Endemic Birding Area and the Barberton Centre of Plant Endemism in the west, and the Maputaland Centre of Plant Diversity in the east.

All told, the kingdom has six major habitats: montane grasslands, sour bushveld, lowveld bushveld, Lubombo bushveld, forests and wetlands. These distinct environments can also be grouped into four ecosystems; namely grasslands, savannah, forest and aquatic.

The grassland ecosystem occurs in the west of the country, at altitudes above 900 metres. This montane environment contains many species of grass, shrubs and herbs, but few trees. Patches of indigenous forest can also be found along watercourses and around rocky outcrops. The grasslands are home to many species of reptiles, birds and some mammals. Several large species of antelope previously hunted to local extinction are being re-introduced into the Malolotja Nature Reserve.

The savannah (or bushveld) ecosystem is characterized by a mixture of grasses and trees. The density of tree cover varies with the altitude, ranging from isolated thickets to a dense canopy.

Roughly speaking, this environment includes the sour bushveld in the middle of the country (occurring between 900 and 400m above sea level); the Lowveld bushveld (400 to 200m) and Lubombo bushveld in the east (200 to 800m). Each of these vegetation types offers a variety of characteristic combinations of trees, shrubs and grasses.

The Lowveld bushveld is associated with the big game of Swaziland—elephant, rhino, lion, zebra, wildebeest and various antelope species. The birding is particularly good in this part of the country and the region also contains the kingdom's highest bio-diversity of reptiles, fish and amphibians.

The Lubombo bushveld, found along the slopes of the Lubombo Mountains, is similar to the Lowveld bushveld, although it does include some high-lying grasslands that occur at the top of the range. It contains fewer mammal species, but game spotters will be encouraged to find grey duiker, impala, kudu and nyala. Amphibians, birds and reptiles are plentiful and several endangered plant species, such as cycads and aloes, can be found in the rhyolitic soil of the Lubombo.

The forest ecosystem is found in patches across the country, mainly along watercourses or in deep valleys. This is characterized by woody plants and a continuous canopy. This ecosystem can be divided up into three types: Afromontane forests (above 1,000m), riverine forests (below 800m) and the Lubombo forests. While these forest areas are generally rich in invertebrate life forms (such as butterflies, moths, scorpions and spiders), they do not contain a wide range of mammal species (although birds, reptiles and amphibians are quite well represented).

The aquatic ecosystem (or wetlands) comprises rivers, streams, marshes, human-made dams and other areas that are prone to seasonal flooding. It is estimated that about 160 square kilometres of Swaziland's total area can be classified as wetlands crucial to the healthy functioning of the wider ecosystem. Many species of fish, amphibians, reptiles, water birds and some mammals make their home here.

All the ecosystems described above are currently under threat from overgrazing, human development, pollution, excessive burning, soil erosion and cultivation of monocultures (such as sugar or pine plantations). This has led to a decrease in bio-diversity and a number of bird, reptile and amphibian species are currently under threat. Alien tree species (such as wattle and lantana) are another problem, as they drink up too much water from the soil and choke the river valleys. Thankfully, there are currently a number of conservation projects underway which seek to protect the precious natural resources of the country.

And now, for all those ecological accountants out there, here is an approximate tally of the different plant and animal species identified in Swaziland thus far.

There are an estimated 131 mammal species, 43 of which are rodents, shrews and bats. Centuries of hunting have severely depleted the country's once plentiful herds of game, although this is slowly being addressed through the efforts of the privately owned Big Game Parks organization and to a degree Swaziland National Trust Commission , which collectively administer the main conservation areas in the kingdom.

Over 500 species of birds have been spotted, representing over half the species found in southern Africa. Although there are no nationally endemic birds, 52 species are endemic to the wider region. Sadly, many bird species are on the decline and 40 species are now considered to be threatened. Chief among these is the highly endangered blue swallow, which can only be spotted in the Malolotja Nature Reserve.

The Komati, Mbuluzi and Usuthu river systems are home to 54 indigenous species of freshwater fish, accounting for about one-fifth of all the species found in southern Africa. There are also several alien species, such as largemouth bass and rainbow trout, which were introduced from the early part of the twentieth century for the benefit of sports fishermen. There are currently about a dozen dams across the country that are suitable for angling. These contain both alien and indigenous species, and are accessible to the public as long as you have a permit. Unfortunately, as a result of water pollution, decreased runoff, irrigation and dam construction, the waterways of Swaziland are not always in the best of health.

There are 44 recorded amphibian species in Swaziland, which is about one-third of all species found in southern Africa. Sadly, habitat loss and industrial pollution is putting the frogs under pressure. The giant bullfrog is already extinct in the Highveld, and the yellow-striped tree frog is also facing local extinction. Nevertheless, there are a number of interesting frog species, including tree frogs, burrowing frogs, reed frogs, grass frogs, noisy toads and the rare Natal ghost frog.

With 111 species on record, reptiles are well represented in Swaziland. These include one type of crocodile, five species of tortoise and terrapin, 44 lizards and 61 snakes. Collectively, this amounts to a quarter of all the reptile species found in southern Africa. Thirty-five species are endemic to the sub-continent and three are narrowly endemic to Swaziland: the giant Swazi flat gecko, the Barberton girdled lizard and the Swazi rock snake. For those who are ophidiophobic, rest assured that only seven of the 61 species of snake are poisonous, but these 'Big Seven' are pretty potent. So watch out for the puff adder, Mozambique spitting cobra, snouted cobra, *rinkhals*, black mamba, *boomslang* and vine snake. The southern African python can also be found in the kingdom.

Finally, there are about 700 tree and shrub species in Swaziland, 56 of which are listed in the *Red Data Book* of endangered plants. Several endemic tree species are found only in the Lubombo Mountains. There are also huge numbers of wild flowers and other flora types, which number around 3,678 taxa. Three thousand of these are small shrubs, herbs and grasses, and a dozen are endemic. Malolotja is the best place to spot the wildflowers.

For a full listing of all the flora and fauna found in the kingdom, including those which are listed as threatened, refer to the Swaziland National Trust Commission's website: www.sntc.org.sz

Conservation in Swaziland

Historically, Swaziland had substantial stocks of wild animals, including the legendary 'Big Five'. Unfortunately, over the years, hunting and other developmental pressures took their toll on the herds, especially the larger animals, and by the start of the 20th century, some people began to realize that something had to be done to protect the remaining game before it disappeared forever.

Swaziland's first reserve, Hlatikulu, was subsequently proclaimed in 1905, and Ubombo in 1907. Amazingly, these two reserves covered ten per cent of the country's surface area and things started looking up for the kingdom's fauna. Unfortunately, in 1917, there was an outbreak of nagana (sleeping sickness) and the wild animals were incorrectly blamed for spreading the disease to livestock. As a result, most of the protected areas were de-proclaimed; by 1922 both reserves had vanished entirely.

Game numbers continued to decline during the next four decades, until a man named Ted Reilly stepped in and made it his mission to save the wildlife of the kingdom. Reilly came from a colonial family that lived on a large farm called Mlilwane (Little Fire), in the Ezulwini Valley. Mickey Reilly, Ted's father, started out by mining tin on the land and was instrumental in bringing electricity to Swaziland. Later, the farm was used to grow rice, maize and citrus crops.

By 1960 the family farm was doing nicely, but Ted Reilly noticed that the kingdom's natural fauna wasn't. So he took it upon himself to survey the country and identify conservation-worthy areas. He then approached the British authorities with a proposal to establish two national parks at Hlane and Malolotja. This suggestion was politely turned down on the grounds that Swaziland didn't need a parks system, since the Kruger Park was a couple of hours to the north and Hluhluwe Game Reserve a couple of hours to the south, both within 'easy enough reach of Swaziland to service the people of Swaziland with their wildlife needs'.

Undaunted, Reilly approached King Sobhuza II directly, and presented his case. The king was receptive to the idea of preserving the kingdom's wildlife heritage and gave Reilly permission to go ahead. At the time, most of the remaining game was found at Hlane, the king's private hunting ground, so Reilly and some helpers started capturing the game at Hlane and transported the animals by Land Rover to his farm at Mlilwane.

Since there was no other land available for conservation, Mlilwane was thus converted into a game reserve. Farming was abandoned, fences were erected, dams were built and, by 1961, Mlilwane started admitting visitors. The animals thrived in their new home, and the sanctuary was officially opened to the public in 1964. According to Ann Reilly of Big Game Parks, a representative of the SA Wildlife Society who attended the opening said, "What a wonderful idea. Pity it's never going to work."

But, against the odds, the sanctuary survived. Entrance fees were charged to generate revenue and the Reilly family made up the shortfall so that, from the very beginning, Mlilwane was self-funding. In 1966, Mlilwane was proclaimed a game sanctuary under the Game Act of 1953. In the same year, Reilly was appointed the royal advisor on nature conservation as was gazetted as Swaziland's first game ranger.

In 1967, King Sobhuza II approached Machobane (Reilly's Swazi name) to do with Hlane, what he had done with Mlilwane. Hlane was held in trust by the king for the Swazi nation. Reilly agreed, and sent intrepid rangers to clear poachers out of the newly-declared national park. This caused a big public outcry, as animals were considered *imvelo* (heritage) and were therefore owned by no one.

The king eventually called a meeting to impress on everyone that this was a royal project and that Machobane's men had to be obeyed. When the area was relatively secure, surplus game was sent from Mlilwane back to Hlane.

By now, things were now going so well that Mlilwane needed to expand and King Sobhuza II ordered the relocation of 60 families from an adjoining piece of land. This was then purchased by the World Wildlife Fund and handed to the sanctuary. In 1969, the Reillys formed the non-profit Mlilwane Trust (for the benefit of the people and wildlife of Swaziland), and the entire farm was donated to the trust. Interestingly, Ted Reilly initially felt that the land should be given to the state as a national park, but the king himself suggested keeping it in a private trust.

In 1972, Ted and his wife, Liz, were instrumental in establishing the Swaziland National Trust Commission (SNTC), a government body tasked with safeguarding the kingdom's natural and cultural heritage. The SNTC took a while to find its feet and meetings of the commission weren't well attended (until members started getting a sitting fee). Reilly, while a board member was never the head of the SNTC, as he still ran his own private reserve and wanted to engender a culture of conservation that wasn't based on personalities. Unfortunately, the relationship between Reilly and SNTC proved to be a contentious one.

For the moment, however, things were going well. A survey of the country was undertaken in 1973 by Ted and Liz Reilly, who identified 34 consevation worthy areas. This resulted in the declaration of the beautiful Malolotja Nature Reserve in 1977. Mlilwane was also proclaimed as a nature reserve under the SNTC Act, although it remained in the hands of the private trust.

A second SNTC survey took place in 1978, and 31 areas were identified: 58 per cent as national parks, 13 per cent as nature reserves, 24 per cent as national landscapes and five per cent as national wetlands. This would have placed a total of 9.47 per cent of the entire kingdom under protection. However, only one reserve was proclaimed.

This was Mlawula Nature Reserve, proclaimed in 1980, and situated on what had once been part of the old Ubombo reserve.

The SNTC later declared two additional reserves: Hawane in 1992, and Mantenga in 1994. The SNTC is also responsible for the National Museum and the King Sobhuza Memorial Park, both located in Lobamba.

Meanwhile, in 1978 and 1979, Mkhaya Game Reserve was purchased by the Mlilwane Trust as a refuge for the last remaining herds of pureblood Nguni cattle. It was declared a game reserve in 1985, and is used as a secure holding area for several endangered species before they are sent to one of the kingdom's other protected areas.

Unfortunately, by 1989 Ted Reilly and the SNTC had a major falling-out. The main issue related to the SNTC's budget, which was becoming increasingly skewed towards staff payroll instead of conservation or maintenance. There were also accusations of jealousy, because Reilly was still the royal advisor on conservation. Furthermore, he was successfully managing his three 'private' game parks with no government funding while the SNTC reserves were struggling, even with large subsidies. Whatever the case, Reilly subsequently resigned from the commission and rebranded his organization as Big Game Parks. BGP now administers Mlilwane, Mkhaya and Hlane Royal National Park, and the redoubtable Ted Reilly is still the CEO.

Another factor in the split was the so-called Rhino Wars which raged between 1988 and 1992. During this time, poachers armed with automatic weapons stole across the border and picked off the docile rhinos at Hlane and Mlawula (which had been donated by the Mlilwane Trust). One by one, the valuable animals disappeared and Reilly's rangers were unable to stop the incursions. At one stage, three animals were stolen in one night and not a trace of the missing creatures could be found.

The problem was that the Game Act was being administered by the SNTC, who didn't technically own any rhino, and nothing was being done to enforce the legislation. To make matters worse, any poachers who were apprehended were set free by the courts (presumably in exchange for bribes).

The situation got so bad that Ted Reilly proposed to the king that all the remaining rhinos should be relocated to South Africa for safekeeping. This seemed rather extreme (and expensive), so the king suggested that Reilly amend the Game Act instead. Reilly then consulted with various experts and published the new legislation in 1991. Poachers now faced severe penalties (including the possibility of long prison sentences). Rangers were also given the right to shoot to kill in life-threatening circumstances, without being liable for prosecution. Furthermore, the act made it possible to go after any magistrate thought to be defeating the ends of justice.

The terms of the new act were widely publicized in the papers, on radio and through an extensive poster campaign. This made the Reillys very unpopular in certain circles, but everyone in Swaziland now knew the consequences of poaching.

Matters soon came to a head with the notorious Case of the Brown Rhino. It should have been an open-and-shut trial. The man had been found with a rhino horn, illegally in his possession, which nobody could deny. In a staggering display of hubris, he declared that it was unclear whether the rhino horn had come from a black rhino, a white rhino or a brown rhino, and since the non-existent 'brown rhino' wasn't a protected species, the man was set free.

This caused a big stink in legal circles. King Mswati, however, shared his father's concern for the kingdom's wildlife and was impressed with the Reillys' persistent dedication to conservation. He then took the extraordinary step of taking the running of the Game Act away from the parastatal SNTC and gave it to the privately run Big Game Parks organization to administer, under the auspices of the King's Office. This remarkable arrangement remains in place to this day, much to the annoyance of the SNTC.

Thankfully, the SNTC and BGP currently enjoy a productive working relationship. They consult with each other about new projects and collaborate on important conservation initiatives, such as the Lubombo Conservancy. They are also both involved in various outreach programmes that seek to educate Swazi people, young and old, about their precious heritage. And no rhinos have been poached in Swaziland since 1992.

The future of conservation

The total area of Swaziland's seven existing reserves is currently 64,100 hectares, only 3.7 per cent of the country's total area. In 2000, the SNTC commissioned a new survey of protection-worthy areas (PWAs) through the Forest Policy and Legislation Project. The report identified 44 PWAs either by virtue of being noted in the Reilly's previous 1973 surveys, or because they were areas with virtually no human settlement but considered to have potentially high biodiversity value by local experts. Another twelve areas were subsequently identified.

Sixteen areas of high priority have now been specified. These include nine areas of high overall priority (Mdzimba, Ntungulu, Nyonyane, Ndlotane, Mahuku, Jilobi, Shewula, Manzimnyame and Makhonjwa); two areas of biological priority (Mahamba and Muti Muti) and five areas of socio-economic priority (Sinceni, Maguga, Sibebe, Gebeni and Panata). The SNTC is currently drawing up plans to develop these sites accordingly.

Swaziland, in conjunction with the Peace Parks Foundation, is also actively involved in the establishment of four Transfrontier Conservation Areas. These are the Songimvelo-Malolotja TFCA, the Lubombo Conservancy-Goba TFCA, the Nsubane-Pongola TFCA and the Usuthu-Tembe-Futi TFCA, incorporating the Usuthu Gorge. Fences have already come down between Songimvelo and Malolotja, and development of the other three TFCAs is well advanced.

- www.noboundaries.co.za: Transfrontier Conservation Initiatives in Maputaland
- www.peaceparks.org
- www.sntc.org.sz/programs/tfcas.asp
- www.biggameparks.org
- www.royaljozini.com

A history of Swaziland

Early humans

Swaziland's geology does not contain any limestone (which is an important component for the formation of fossils), so no hominid remains have been found in the kingdom. However, archaeologists have uncovered numerous stone tools and hand axes that attest to human habitation dating back at least 1.5 to two million years. This is not surprising when you consider the relative proximity of the famous hominid fossil sites at Makapansgat, Sterkfontein and Taung, located just a few hundred kilometres to the west.

Most of the stone tools in Swaziland have been found along river banks and in the Lubombo Mountains. These artefacts are similar to those found in other early stone age sites, such as Olduvai Gorge in the Great African Rift Valley. As such, they are representatives of the Olduwan stone tool industry (which has nothing to do with Star Wars, although its name suggests a connection).

More sophisticated stone tools dating back between 250,000 and 1.5 million years have also been found, and these are associated with the Acheulian industry. Based on the evidence gleaned from sites in South Africa and east Africa, the various stone tools of Swaziland are presumed to have been made by our early ancestors, *Homo habilis* and/ or *Homo erectus*.

From 200,000 to 150,000 years ago, early forms of anatomically modern *homo sapiens* started producing a number of relatively sophisticated stone tools that are associated with the middle stone age. Many examples of these artefacts have been found across Swaziland, most notably in the Ngwenya Mountains. These include knife-like blades and stone scrapers.

Then, around 43,000 years ago, some of these wily creatures started excavating minerals from the side of Ngwenya Mountain, near the modern-day Oshoek border post. These ancient diggings, which took the form of short horizontal shafts, are noted as being the earliest 'mines' on the planet. However, the people responsible for the excavations at Lion and Castle caverns were not after gold or iron—knowledge of metalwork was not yet current. Instead, these prehistoric people were extracting sparkling specularite (a black rock that contains glittering specks) and colourful haematite (a brown-red ochre). It is thought that these decorative minerals were crushed up and used for painting, body decoration and other ritual practices. The ancient excavations at Lion Cavern can be visited as part of a guided tour.

Moving forward into the Later Stone Age (in the southern African context, this lasted from around 40,000 to 1,000 years ago), the stone tool kit was expanded to include composite objects that saw stone blades fitted to wooden shafts with leather straps. Transitional examples of these 'hafted' tools have been found at Border Cave in the Lubombo Mountains, close to the Phongolo River. Skeletal remains of very early *Homo sapiens* have also been found in the cave, dating back about 75,000 years (although the precise date is still being debated). Border Cave can be visited from the KwaZulu-Natal side of the mountains and an interpretation centre has been constructed.

Archaeologists have also found fascinating evidence of Later Stone Age habitation at the Siphiso and Nyonyane shelters. According to Bob Forrester, Siphiso (in Mlawula) was occupied from around 13,500 years ago to 350 years ago and Nyonyane (in Mlilwane) from 11,000 to 3,200 years ago. Interestingly, there is evidence that both shelters were unoccupied for a 4,000- to 5,000-year gap; this hiatus corresponds to a cold climatic phase that brought dry conditions to the region. This presumably forced the inhabitants to move to the warmer coastal plains. It is surmised that the people who lived in these shelters were ancestors of the Bushman (or San) cultural group.

The Bushmen

A climatic cold snap is thought to have ended between 2,000 and 3,000 years ago. From this date, the archaeological sequence once again shows signs of human occupation as the proto-Bushmen moved back to their old haunts. The most spectacular evidence of this re-occupation is found in the rock paintings which can still be seen in various rock shelters around Swaziland. Although previous inhabitants may have also painted on the rocks, it is thought that all the rock paintings currently in existence date from the last couple of thousand years, as any earlier artistic expressions would not have survived the wet conditions.

Although rock paintings have been identified across Swaziland, the biggest concentration is found on the granite walls of the western Highveld mountains. These paintings depict animals, people, hunting parties, battle scenes and dances, and are similar in nature to other rock paintings found in Lesotho and the Drakensberg.

There are currently two rock art sites open to the public. The Nsangwini Rock Art Shelter is the largest in the country, and can be accessed as part of a community-run tourism project. It's a very worthwhile excursion that combines a good walk, fantastic scenery and a breathtaking glimpse into the artistry of an ancient culture. The Nsangwini Shelter is discussed in more detail later in this book.

The only other place where members of the public can see rock art is at Sandlane, located about a kilometre from the Sandlane border post. The site is part of the Mntjali family homestead; members of the family act as voluntary guides to the site.

The first Swazis

For thousands of years the nomadic Bushmen were the only people resident in the sub-continent. But all that was about to change. From about 4,000 years ago, a major migration began which saw a number of tribes leave their home in western Africa and move down the west and east coasts of the continent. Modern ethnographers have collectively termed these people the BaNtu, named after their root language, Ntu. This Bantu diaspora may have been caused by climatic change, overpopulation or an innate desire for exploration. In any event, the Bantu were to change the face of Africa forever.

The Bantu were not hunter-gatherers like the Bushmen. While they certainly did hunt for wild game, it was not their bread and butter. Instead, they had adopted an agricultural and stock farming culture which had spread down the Nile valley from the middle east. As such, they planted domesticated crops such as sorghum and millet, and they kept herds of goats and cattle which gave them a steady supply of milk and meat. They had also learnt how to mine and work metal into implements, thus associating themselves with the Iron Age.

It took a long time for the stream of Bantu migrants to reach southern Africa, but their progress was inexorable; driven by the ever-increasing need for new grazing land. As they moved, various groups split off from the main column and set up shop at suitable locations. These offshoots then proceeded to develop their own dialects and cultures, based on the old Bantu traditions. Such early tribal groupings are often distinguished by the distinctive decorated pottery they made, as each new tribe tended to favour certain shapes and designs.

Based on this type of archaeological evidence, it is thought that the first Bantu tribes crossed the Zambezi and then the Limpopo River about 2,000 years ago. Interestingly, there is a traditional story that these pioneers crossed the turbulent Zambezi on rafts made from reeds (*umhlanga*), and there is a Swazi expression, *savela eluhlangeni*, which translates as 'We originated from the reeds'. To this day, reeds play a central role in Swazi iconography.

The earliest Bantu pottery found in Swaziland dates to roughly 450 AD. These tell-tale shards were discovered by modern archaeologists at that prehistoric hotspot, Ngwenya Mountain. This pottery culture is known as 'Silverleaves', but it is not known what language they spoke or to which cultural group they belonged.

Meanwhile, several tribal groups had established themselves between the Zambezi and Limpopo rivers. Some say that this is where the split between the Sotho and Nguni tribes occurred. The Sotho, for their part, kept inland and spread across the southern African plateau, where they became the Sotho, Tswana and Pedi. The Nguni-speaking people would go on to colonize the eastern coast of the subcontinent, where they developed into the Tsonga, Swazi, Zulu and Xhosa.

And so we come to an Nguni tribe called the eMbo, living near Delagoa Bay (modern-day Maputo), between the Lubombo Mountains and the ocean. Around the mid-1300s, a ruler named Nkosi I is said to have been in control of the eMbo. He was succeeded by his son, Ngwane I, who died around 1435. Next in line was Dlamini I—founder of the royal dynasty that would one day rule Swaziland. Today, there are many people in Swaziland who have the surname Dlamini. I once asked a Swazi bus driver if all the Dlaminis are related to the king. He replied, "The king is warm-blooded. I am cold-blooded." So much for blood being thicker than water.

In any case, Dlamini I had two sons: Mswati I ('father' of the Swazi nation) and Mthonga ('father' of the Tsonga nation). Mthonga's people went on to establish the Tembe kingdom that came to control southern Mozambique. Meanwhile, Mswati I begat Ngwane II, who begat Dlamini II, who begat Nkosi II, who begat Mavuso I, who begat Magudulela.

Then something rather ghastly happened. In the Swazi tradition, the Queen Mother holds a very important position, acting as a counter-weight against the power of the king (her son). However, Magudulela's mother did not want to be the Queen Mother, and was looking for a way out. Swazi tradition also states that the king may not be left-handed, as it is seen as an evil sign and 'you cannot use your left hand to rule the kingdom'.

So, the reluctant Queen Mother took her son's right hand and plunged it into a pot of boiling porridge. This injury forced Magudulela to use his left hand, and thus made him forfeit the throne. The son of another wife was subsequently chosen and anointed as King Ludvonga I.

Ludvonga's rightful heir, Hlubi, also had a stroke of bad luck. Swazi custom holds that the king must have no brothers, so any wife who produces two or more sons makes them all ineligible for the throne. Unfortunately, shortly before his coronation, Hlubi's mother popped out an unexpected male sibling and he was forced to cede the title to his half-brother, who became King Dlamini III.

During this time, the eMbo were once again splitting up into a number of migratory groups, probably as a result of expansion by the neighbouring Tembe tribe. Some of these clans gradually moved south of the Phongolo River into present-day Zululand, where they established themselves into a number of new tribes. The most significant of these for the purposes of our story are the Ndwandwe and the Mthethwa.

Subsequently, between 1750 and 1770, Dlamini III also moved away from the ancestral lands and headed west to establish his new ceremonial and administrative centres (which had to be in separate locations). He thus chose two sites on the Lubombo Mountains; the administrative capital was near the Phongolo River and the ceremonial capital was close to the Ngwavuma River. It was at the latter that the Swazis first developed their tradition of *kuluma*, the tasting of the first fruits. Today, this is known today as the *incwala* ceremony, and several herbs necessary for the ritual are still gathered from the Ngwavuma region.

Dlamini III's successor was Ngwane III, who took over around 1770.

Facing increasing pressure from the Tembe to the east, Ngwane initially took his people to the south, where they clashed with the Ndwandwe. He then turned north and crossed the Phongolo River to settle in the Shiselweni region, located in the southern part of the territory now known as Swaziland. Ngwane is therefore acknowledged as the founder of the present-day Swazi nation, and many Swazis still refer to their country as kaNgwane (the place of Ngwane).

At this stage, Ngwane's people were few in number but, as they moved over the Phongolo, they conquered and/or incorporated several smaller Sotho, Nguni and Tswana tribes that they found living in the area. This was the first phase of Swazi expansion, marked by a high degree of assimilation in which the Dlamini clan effectively combined with the new tribes to create a composite cultural group under the strong leadership of Ngwane. This kind of tribal consolidation was occurring throughout the region during this time, most notably with the Mthethwa under Dingiswayo and the Ndwandwe under Zwide.

It is thought that this process was spurred on by a combination of factors. The contemporary Madlatule drought had brought famine to the land. There was also an increasing demand for scarce resources, including cattle, grazing land and the availability of women. Furthermore, the Europeans had just arrived at Delagoa Bay and the local economy was becoming more trade-based and competitive. All of these, Philip Bonner argues, necessitated the development of new political systems that included the establishment of *amabutho*—age-specific battle regiments that reported to a single chief or king.

In any case, Ngwane III built his ceremonial capital, called Zombodze, near what is now the town of Nhlangano. His administrative capital, called Hhohho, was at Mlosheni, a short distance away. This area is in the transitional zone between the middleveld and Lowveld, and it provided good grazing all year round, allowing the emerging *emaNgwane* (people of Ngwane) to prosper.

Interestingly, Ngwane III is said to have killed all his male heirs, giving him the gruesome praise name, 'the mamba that lays twelve eggs and eats them'. However, following some strong words from his advisors, he left one young son alive to continue the bloodline.

Ngwane died around 1780 and was buried in a cave on a hill called eMbilaneni (the hallowed place). This is still a sacred site where several high-ranking members of the royal household have been laid to rest.

After being spared by his considerate father, Nduvungunye became the next king of *emaNgwane*. He built Lobamba as a residence for his mother and established his administrative capital at Shiselweni. He also continued his father's good work by consolidating his power and expanding his territory. Unfortunately, Nduvungunye died suddenly in 1815, after being struck by lightning. This was a shocking turn of events (sorry, couldn't resist), but Nduvungunye did manage to father a suitable heir, Somhlolo, before he died. Somhlolo would go on to become the influential King Sobhuza I.

The Royal Family

The structure of the Swazi monarchy is unusual and, since the royal house is so central to Swazi history, we should take a moment to have a closer look at its traditions so that we may understand the institution more thoroughly. Incidentally, it is claimed that many of these traditions are affiliated with the Sotho culture, and some historians have written that the Swazis are a unique combination of Sotho and Nguni influences.

So, firstly, it should be noted that the heir to the throne is not chosen during the lifetime of the reigning king. This makes good sense, especially when you consider that many royal dynasties around the world have been plagued with messy succession battles that pit fathers, sons and brothers against one another.

Thus, it is only when a king dies that one of his wives is chosen as the new queen mother, or *ndlovukazi* (the great elephant). This decision is made depending on the rank of the wife's father and the nature of her marriage to the late king. For example, the king must always be a Dlamini, and he is not allowed to intermarry (smart thinking), so the Queen Mother can never be a Dlamini by birth.

However, there are several requirements that have to be met before the son can assume the throne. The new king cannot be left-handed, and he cannot have any brothers born of the same mother. The king is also expected to be young and unmarried. If the nominated queen mother does not have a son who meets these conditions, she will have one of the king's other sons 'placed in her womb' (adopted). With all these arduous requirements to be met, it is not surprising that the king needs to have multiple wives. Since the new king will probably be a minor at the time of his father's death, the old king's mother becomes the queen regent who rules the nation with the help of a senior relative of the late king (who is appointed by the Royal Council). This must all be sorted out before the old king can be buried.

After the funeral, the heir is then taken away from his mother and kept in a place known as *umtsangala* for the duration of the national mourning period (usually three years). At the end of this term, the heir is reunited with his mother at a new residence, called *lusasa,* where he will live until he comes of age (usually at 21) and is officially installed as the new king. At this point, the queen regent steps down and the new queen mother assumes the role of *ndlovukazi.*

As such, the apron strings of the Swazi royal family are long and hard to cut. Indeed, the new king and his mother operate as a dual monarchy in which the queen mother *(ndlovukazi)* and the king *(ngwenyama—* the great lion) rule as equals. This is why every king must have two capitals; the administrative capital *(lilawu)* where the king is in control, and the ceremonial capital *(umphakatsi)* where the queen mother reigns supreme. Each capital has its own court, advisors and councils, and the decision of one cannot be overruled by the other.

Hilda Kuper, who spent several years at the court of Sobhuza II, put it like this: "Between the *Ngwenyama* and *Ndlovukazi* there is a delicate balance of powers; legal, economic and ritual. He may take from the royal herd; she may rebuke him if he wastes national wealth. She is the custodian of the sacred objects of the nation, but they are not effective without his co-operation in manipulating them. In all activities they should assist each other, for he is iNkosi and she is also iNkosi. Together they are spoken of as twins.

"I, for one, think it's a great idea, and can think of several democratically elected presidents who would do well to listen to their mothers!"

Sobhuza I (ruled 1815–1839)

After a brief minority, Somhlolo came to power as King Sobhuza I some time after 1815. This was a pivotal time in the history of the region, and

Sobhuza's reign coincides with the rise of the mighty Shaka. Indeed, if Sobhuza had not played his cards so shrewdly, he and his people may well have been swallowed up by the dramatic changes that were about to transform the political landscape of the subcontinent; a period that became known as *Mfecane* (the crushing). That fact that Sobhuza survived and even flourished during this period of tremendous upheaval is testament to his pragmatic and, dare we say, Machiavellian approach to politics.

The turmoil began right at the beginning of Sobhuza's reign when he clashed with Zwide, chief of the powerful Ndwandwe people, who lived immediately to the south. The bone of contention was the ownership of some fertile farmland in the Phongolo Valley, which fell into a grey area between the two kingdoms.

After assessing the situation, however, Sobhuza determined that the Ndwandwe were too strong to defeat, and he chose to stand down. As Dr Matsebula puts it, "He [Sobhuza] believed in avoiding any confrontation he was not sure of winning. To him it was futile to go to war with a powerful opposition. [This was] a policy which was to become a cornerstone for the Swazi people afterwards."

So Sobhuza formulated a cunning plan to reduce tensions with his neighbours by asking for permission to marry one of Zwide's daughters. Zwide agreed reluctantly and a suitable bride, Thandile, was chosen. However, Zwide still warned that this union would not stop him from attacking Sobhuza in the future. Talk about a tough father-in-law!

Fearing the worst, Sobhuza abandoned his capital at Shiselweni and moved to the north. This was just as well, because Zwide soon sent his forces to attack Shiselweni, which was burnt to the ground. The name Shiselweni has now been applied to the southern administrative region of Swaziland, and translates as 'place of burning'.

What happened next is the subject of one of those historical disputes in which two contradictory accounts have to battle it out for veracity.

One version of the story holds that Sobhuza fled as a refugee, and was hotly pursued over the Usuthu River and through the highlands by Zwide until he was forced to seek refuge with a Sotho chief named Magoboyi, who lived in the Dlomodlomo Mountains to the northwest. Here, it is claimed, Sobhuza regrouped and then started conquering the neighbouring tribes—much to his host's dismay.

The other, more Swazi-centric narrative says that Sobhuza was no refugee. Before he and his people decamped, he had sent out scouts into the north to report on conditions there. The scouts duly returned and said that the Sotho (Pedi) tribes living in the north were small and disorganized, making them a perfect target for conquest. And so began Sobhuza's great expedition, in which he defeated and then incorporated several new tribes into his growing Ngwane nation. These new additions were collectively known as *emakhandzambili*—those found ahead.

However you place the emphasis, it's safe to say that Sobhuza spent some time in Dlomodlomo and then withdrew to return to the Shiselweni area. Some say this is because the Sotho tribes in the area revolted against Sobhuza's raids and forced him to retreat. In any event, things were happening back in Shiselweni that demanded his attention.

You see, while he was gone, several Ngwane tribes had remained at Shiselweni, including some members of the royal family. One of these was a brother of Sobhuza, called Magwegwe, who tried to usurp the throne from the absent king. However, the loyal Mamba tribe (under Maloyi) sent word to Sobhuza about his brother's treachery, and the king returned from Dlomodlomo to get rid of Magwegwe. The Mamba were rewarded with special privileges to raise their own regiments and perform their own 'little' version of the sacred *incwala* ceremony, honours which they continue to hold to this day.

This all took place around 1818 and coincided with Zwide's defeat by Shaka Zulu. The absence of Ndwandwe raiders gave Sobhuza a chance to think. He decided that Shiselweni was too close to the volatile Phongolo region, and resolved to move his centre of operations into the highlands, a natural fortress of mountains and valleys to the northwest.

Sobhuza had first visited this region during his peripatetic phase, when he spent some time at the foot of Mdzimba Mountain, where a river had carved a great valley through the rocks. Here, the local inhabitants pointed out a labyrinth of caves that riddled the flanks of Mdzimba. Sobhuza realized immediately that these caves would prove to be a valuable hiding place in times of war.

And so, around 1820, Sobhuza moved his royal residences into this valley and built two new homesteads, Lobamba and Langeni. The area soon became important as the location where rain-making rituals took place. At that time, the word for rain was *izulu*, which can also refer to the concept of 'the heavens', and the valley became known as Ezulwini. To this day, several royal residences are located within this 'valley of heaven'.

The Ezulwini area and its surrounds (in what is now the central part of modern Swaziland) were at that time inhabited by a collection of Sotho, Nguni and Tsonga chiefdoms. Sobhuza knew that he would have to conquer these tribes in order to establish his authority over the region, so he carefully set about breaking their power by any means necessary. First, he married off his daughter to the influential Maseko chief, Mgazi. Then he turned his attention to the feuding Magagula chiefs, Mnjoli and Moyeni. He tried initially to form an allegiance with Mnjoli, but was firmly rebuffed when Mnjoli beat up his messengers. Undeterred, Sobhuza camouflaged his men under cow hides and smuggled them into Mnjoli's enclosure. When they brought in the herds for the night, Sobhuza's men attacked. This 'Trojan cattle' tactic worked beautifully, and Mnjoli was defeated (slit open, in fact, because they thought he had swallowed the tribe's legendary rain-making charms).

Next, Sobhuza besieged Moyeni until the latter was forced to flee. The Mncina also fled before the Ngwane and the Ndzimandze were destroyed. There is also a story that, during this time, a Magagula vassal named Moya rebelled and led a force to attack Sobhuza. The king responded by sending messengers to the Portuguese at Lourenço Marques (modern-day Maputo) to recruit mercenaries. As payment, he offered ten cows to any man who had guns and knew how to use them. Five adventurers took up the offer, becoming the first Europeans to enter kaNgwane. After they had done their job and received their payment, they presented Sobhuza with a sack of maize seeds in return. This is the traditional account of how the mielie crop arrived in Swaziland.

As his confidence and power grew, Sobhuza faced less resistance from the local tribes. The Ngwenya, Dhladhla, Mavimbela, Maziya and Mahlalela all capitulated, and Sobhuza consolidated his hold over the region.

This expansion was aided by Sobhuza's policy of allowing local chiefs to maintain some authority as long as they swore allegiance to the Dlamini-Ngwane. As the historian A. R. Booth puts it: "Like all great figures who prevailed during those troubled times, he did so by a successful mixing of force, political skill, diplomacy, guile and bluster."

This is not to say that Sobhuza's conquests were secure, however. Much of this territory remained in a state of flux and, with regiments stretched thin and a lack of official representatives on the ground, many of the conquered tribes were subjects in name only.

Unlike the first phase of Swazi expansion under Ngwane III, this time there was little assimilation between the various tribes. Rebellions broke out regularly, and the Ngwane kingdom was effectively a nation under arms. To make matters worse, marriages (and wealth) were concentrated within a small group of Ngwane aristocracy, which prevented the establishment of inter-tribal alliances. As such, it would take another generation or so before Ngwane authority was firmly established and a cohesive cultural system set up. Meanwhile, there was trouble brewing in the south.

Sobhuza, Zwide and Shaka

From around 1816, Zwide of the Ndwandwe initiated a series of invasions into Ngwane territory, in which he effectively occupied the Shiselweni region. This conquest was temporary, however, because Zwide was soon forced to turn his attention to an old enemy—the Mthethwa, a powerful tribe living along the Mfolozi River, immediately to the south of Ndwandwe territory.

According to Zulu historian Alan Mountain, Zwide was a cruel and ambitious chief. Popular gossip held that he and his mother, Ntombazi, kept the skulls of defeated enemies so that they could absorb the bones' supernatural power. As such, Zwide had already clashed several times with the Mthethwa. Each time they had fought, Zwide was defeated and forced to swear allegiance to the Mthethwa. But he had not kept his word, and continued to try and expand his territory. This destabilized the entire region and the normally conciliatory Mthethwa chief, Dingiswayo, decided that the treacherous Zwide had to be dealt with once and for all.

Dingiswayo assembled his forces near the present-day village of Nongoma. He also summoned the mighty warrior Shaka, leader of the small Zulu polity, who was at that time a vassal of the Mthethwa. While he waited for Shaka and his regiments to arrive, Dingiswayo took a small escort and went on a reconnaissance mission. He was subsequently captured by an Ndwandwe patrol and taken to Zwide's homestead at kwaDlovunga. Here, Dingiswayo was quickly put to death and his head added to Zwide's skull collection.

With the Mthethwa state literally headless, the militant Shaka took the opportunity to consolidate his power. Within a few years he had effectively absorbed the Mthethwa into his own Zulu tribe, and now he began an aggressive expansion policy that saw him come to dominate the region between the Phongolo and Tugela rivers. Obviously, Zwide was now Shaka's sworn enemy, and their two armies engaged each other at a number of vicious battles (most notably at kwaGqokli Hill in 1818).

By 1819, Shaka had decisively defeated Zwide and the Ndwandwe king fled to the north. According to Matsebula, Zwide did not seek refuge with Sobhuza (his son-in-law), fearing that this would encourage the Zulu armies to invade Swazi territory and put his daughter in danger.

One of Thandile's brothers did seek refuge with Sobhuza, however, and he was allowed to settle north of the Komati River at a place that became known as Ebulandzeni (the place of the in-laws). To this day, some people who live in this area speak a dialect that is marked by Zulu-heavy linguistic forms.

Zwide, for his part, did not go quietly into the night and slowly rebuilt his army in the Delagoa Bay interior. His son, Sikhunyana, continued the quarrel with Shaka and the Ndwandwe remained a thorn in the side of the Zulu nation until their final defeat in 1826.

Meanwhile, Shaka was causing havoc in the south and various tribes were fleeing across the region: Zwangendaba, a headman of Zwide, moved up the Lumbombo range and absorbed several Ngwane tribes who eventually wound up on the shores of Lake Malawi as the aNgoni; Mzilikazi of the Khumalo broke away from Shaka and went up to the Highveld where they rampaged through the region as the Matabele; Soshangane (also of the Ndwandwe) went up to Delagoa Bay and took over the Tembe-Mabhuda territory, creating the Gaza empire that combined the Tsonga with his new 'Shangaan' tribal identity.

These were just some of the marauding tribes moving around Sobhuza's territory between 1820 and 1828, and the king was feeling unnerved. He was also apprehensive of Shaka, the 'Black Napoleon', who now controlled the entire region south of the Phongolo. To make matters worse, there was already a mutual enmity between the two tribes because of Shaka's massacre of the eLangeni clan, who were affiliated to the Ngwane.

The reasons for the attack on the eLangeni date back to Shaka's childhood, which would no doubt please Dr Freud. Shaka's mother, Nandi, was part of the eLangeni. She fell in love with Senzangakona, chief of the small Zulu tribe and fell pregnant. Unfortunately, they were not married at the time, and Shaka was born out of wedlock. He and his mother then returned to the eLangeni, where he was teased and persecuted throughout his childhood. So, after his parents finally married and Shaka assumed control of his father's Zulu tribe, he exacted revenge on the eLangeni by slaughtering them.

Not wanting to bring down a similar fate on his own people, Sobhuza made sure not to offend this powerful warlord and assumed a tacitly subservient position. He sent two of his daughters to Shaka as wives. He made rain for the Zulus. It is even suggested that Sobhuza became a 'tributary' of Shaka, essentially making himself and his people vassals of the Zulu nation—although Swazi sources are mute on this last point. Nevertheless, it does appear that the Ngwane 'several times joined the Zulus and as often revolted'.

Then there is the story of Sobhuza's visit to Shaka. According to Swazi sources, Shaka had come to hear of Sobhuza's virtues and wished to meet the man for himself—perhaps to determine whether the Ngwane king would be an ally or a threat. When the invitation arrived, Sobhuza was uncertain. Shaka was tricky and unpredictable; the invitation could have been a trap. After consulting his advisors, Sobhuza decided to accept and embarked on the ten-day journey down to Shaka's royal kraal, kwaBulawayo, in Zululand.

Once again, we now have two versions of events. Matsebula says that Shaka was impressed by Sobhuza's willingness to have a face-to-face meeting—he entertained the Ngwane king kindly and gave him gifts of cattle. This diplomatic event ensured that the Swazis were not invaded by the Zulu army under Shaka.

Other sources say that, as Sobhuza neared Shaka's homestead, ominous dark clouds filled the sky. When they arrived, Shaka said he was feeling unwell and sent his mother and a governor to greet the

Ngwane king. The welcoming party gave Sobhuza and his men gifts of cattle and assured them of their safety. However, in the background, Shaka's warriors were dancing and singing, asking that Shaka give them permission to kill the visitors. The jittery guests were then shown to a nearby homestead where they would spend the night, with assurances that Shaka may visit them the following day.

During the night, the thunderstorm broke. It was all looking very ominous, and Sobhuza decided to leave immediately. So they took the cattle and went out into the storm, heading north to the Phongolo. By dawn, they had crossed the swiftly flowing river and found a cave in which they prepared to catch up on some lost sleep.

But then, in the distance, they saw a large Zulu army coming after them. Luckily, by this time, the rain-swollen river had risen into a raging torrent and the Zulu warriors couldn't even throw their assegais over the flooded waterway. Soon, another Zulu regiment arrived and encouraged their brethren to try and ford the river. Those who attempted the crossing were swept away to their death, and the Zulus were forced to retreat.

Following this latter narrative, relations between Sobhuza and Shaka deteriorated. Shaka executed his Swazi wives on some spurious charge and several attacks were launched on Sobhuza. Strangely, there is little evidence of these invasions in the Swazi verbal history. The outcome of these invasions is also unclear. Zulu tradition, recounted by a later Zulu king, Cetshwayo, says that the Swazis were soundly defeated and forced to resume the payment of tributes to Shaka—but this account might be biased. Other sources say that the Swazis retreated into the mountains and caves, from where they fought off their attackers with varying degrees of success.

In any event, Shaka could not break the independence of Sobhuza, and his kingdom endured. This was clearly a result of Sobhuza's spirited defence of his territory and convenient timing. You see, in the early years of his reign, Shaka had concentrated on conquering the land to his south and west, and didn't seem too concerned about the remote Ngwane territory. When he was finally ready to concentrate on the north, Shaka's time was nearly up.

Sobhuza and Dingane

In September 1828, while his army was off in the north trying to break the power of Soshangane (and possibly Sobhuza as well), the mighty Shaka found himself caught up in a palace coup. Encouraged by their aunt Mkhabayi, Shaka's half-brothers, Dingane and Mhlangana, walked into the royal kraal at kwaBulawayo and assassinated the increasingly erratic Black Napoleon. This threw the Zulu nation into confusion, and Sobhuza took advantage of the relative peace to push his borders to their farthest extent—up to the Sabie River in the north and to the Steenkampsberg (near Lydenberg) in the west.

Meanwhile, back in Zululand, Dingane assumed the Zulu throne after a bloody succession battle with Mhlangana. He proceeded to launch a number of devastating attacks on Sobhuza, with the intention of taking over the Ngwane territory. In 1834 the Zulu army managed to impose a blockade of Swazi trade with Delagoa Bay. By 1835 it was said that the Swazis were once again tributaries of the Zulu. In 1836 a major raid was mounted, which sought to destroy the Ngwane once and for all. But it didn't quite go according to plan.

Three Zulu divisions were sent up to trap the Ngwane, but one division was delayed en route and Sobhuza managed to slip through the gap left in the cordon. This third division finally arrived after the other Zulu forces had left and, after a pitched battle with the Ngwane rearguard, returned home with a conciliatory booty of 6,000 head of cattle. Dingane was unimpressed with this outcome and Mongo, the leader of the tardy regiment, was stripped of his wives and property as punishment.

Some sources say that Sobhuza died during this turbulent period, but others claim that he died during another Zulu invasion that took place in 1839. For the sake of clarity, I am going to go with the later date so that I can neatly complete the story of Dingane and Sobhuza within this section.

Accordingly, in the months after the unsuccessful Zulu invasion of 1836, several Ngwane clans living on the southern border of the territory grew stroppy and began indulging in some cattle raiding on the Zulu side of the Phongolo River. This infuriated Dingane, who sent out a retaliatory force to reclaim the stolen cows. The Zulu party included some European traders from Natal who had guns and, when faced with the unstoppable firepower of the white men, the Swazi raiders quickly gave up their booty and the Zulu commando returned home.

But the balance of power soon shifted. In 1838 Dingane met his Waterloo at the hands of the Voortrekkers, who defeated the Zulu army at the Battle of Blood River. The Zulu king was then forced to flee the approaching Boer commando and abandoned his kraal at uMgungundlovu in favour of a new refuge in the Hluhluwe region.

The British stepped in at this point and negotiated a treaty between the Zulus and the Boers which saw Dingane give away all his territory south of the Tugela River. This was a big blow and the Zulu king was bowed, but not broken. Now it became even more imperative for Dingane to expand his territory north of the Phongolo River, into Swazi territory.

By 1839 he felt ready to mount another invasion and sent four regiments to establish a military village at Lubuya, near the source of the Ingwavuma River. Here the Zulu army were ordered to prepare for the upcoming battle and to await further instructions. Based on his previous experiences Dingane was confident that the Ngwane would not make the first move, and so took his time in preparing his strategy. But the Swazis decided that they would not sit idly by and wait for the invasion. Instead, the whole country rose to a man and launched an unprecedented attack on the Zulu army.

The now-famous battle at Lubuya raged for two days and both sides incurred heavy losses. Then, on the third day, the exhausted Swazi warriors arrived at the battlefield to find that the Zulus had disappeared. It was the last major battle to be fought on Swazi soil. Dingane had been defeated and his troops were severely depleted.

But the Zulu king was a determined man and ordered his half-brother, Mpande, to send his warriors to the battle zone. Mpande was understandably suspicious of his fratricidal sibling and refused to send his men away in case this made him vulnerable. Mpande's insubordination infuriated Dingane and, fearful of reprisals, Mpande decided to jump ship—so he took 17,000 followers and moved across the Tugela River, into Boer territory.

After convincing the suspicious boers that he could be trusted, Mpande joined forces with the white men and, in January 1840, a joint invasion was mounted to overthrow Dingane. A decisive battle ensued at Maqonqo and Dingane suffered another major defeat. Under the watchful eye of the Boers, Mpande was declared king, and Dingane had no choice but to flee once again. This time he took his remaining followers and crossed over the Phongolo River into Sobhuza's territory.

Not wanting any trouble, Dingane kept a low profile and set up a small homestead at Esankoleni in the sacred Hlathikhulu forest, near present-day Lavumisa/Golela. This area was controlled by the Nyawo clan, which was then being ruled by a regent named Silevana. Obviously, a bunch of noisy Zulus messing about in the forbidden forest did not go unnoticed by Silevana; he informed a military patrol under Sonyezane Dlamini about the presence of the wanted fugitive.

Seizing the initiative, Sonyezane, Silevana and their men crept into the forest to find Dingane's poorly-defended hideaway. Then, in the pre-dawn light, they launched an attack and Silevana Nyawo thrust an assegai into Dingane. The once-proud Zulu monarch slowly bled to death and was quietly buried among the thick trees. Fearing reprisals, Dingane's fate at the hands of the Nyawo was kept a secret for 150 years. The location of his grave was only revealed in recent times, and today it is marked by an official tombstone.

It was around this time that Sobhuza, too, died. Interestingly, a short time before he passed on, Sobhuza is said to have had a vision in which white-skinned people with 'hair like the tails of cattle' arrived in the country. They carried with them *umculu* (a scroll or book—taken to refer to the Bible) and *indilinga* (round metal—understood as money).

Sobhuza apparently advised his councillors to accept the former but refuse the latter—which is easier said than done. He then went on to say that these white-skinned people must never be harmed because 'if [you spill] a drop of white man's blood, [our] country would be destroyed and [we] would disappear as a nation'. The Swazi people seem to have taken Sobhuza's warning to heart; this royal prophecy is said to be one reason why there has never been an outright war between the Europeans and the Swazi.

This stands in stark contrast to a prophecy made by Shaka Zulu as he lay dying in the arms of his murderous brothers. It too referred to the white man, albeit in much darker terms: 'The whole land will be white with the light of the stars. It will be overrun by swallows'. Shaka's vision

Southbound Travel Guides

proved to be a chilling foretelling of the colonial invasion that would destroy the independence of the Zulu nation within the next 60 years.

The nation forged by Sobhuza I endured, however, partly due to the shrewd king's understanding of a rapidly changing political landscape. His conciliatory attitude to the white settlers crowding around his territory is particularly significant. He traded with the Portuguese. He sent emissaries to the Voortrekkers after their victory at Blood River, and he made treaties with the Boers against Dingane. It is even said that he showed Dingane's scalp to the Boers to prove that the Zulu king was dead, whereupon the white Volksraad of Natal signed a treaty of friendship with the Swazi and gave them a gift of 20 head of cattle.

It is therefore thanks to Sobhuza that the threats posed by formidable opponents, such as Zwide, Shaka, Dingane and the Boers, were surmounted. Historian Philip Bonner is unequivocal in his praise of the king's accomplishments: "Sobhuza showed himself to be one of the *Mfecane's* great survivors ... more importantly, it was he who laid the foundations of the pre-colonial Swazi state. Its administration might be sketchy and its settlements sparse, but its basic structure and composition can be traced back to him. In the end, then, modern Swaziland must be seen as Sobhuza's creation, and one need look no further that this for a lasting monument to his reign."

Mswati II (ruled 1840–1865)

Sobhuza's heir was Mswati II, and it would fall to him to unite and integrate the various divisions within Sobhuza's Ngwane nation into a single political unit. It is from this king's name that Europeans first derived the term 'Swazi'. The territorial name 'Swaziland' also came into use around the same time. Ironically, both these words are corruptions of the traditional term *emaSwati* and are actually derived from the Zulu pronunciation of 'Mswati'. Nevertheless, the names stuck; from here on in I will refer to the Ngwane as the Swazi, although the terms can still be used interchangeably.

But despite his eponymity, Mswati II didn't have an easy succession. The problem was that Sobhuza had nominated Mswati as his heir but, as he got older, he became afraid that he would die while Mswati was still very young. This would mean an extended minority period, during which time the nation would be vulnerable to attack. So Sobhuza was persuaded to nominate a number of his older sons as heirs, including Malambule, Thekwane and Fokoti.

However, the council of elders wanted Mswati and refused all the other candidates. Luckily, Sobhuza managed to hang on until Mswati II was in his teens. And so, after a short regency period, Mswati reached the age of majority and was duly sworn in as king around 1839 or 1840. He built his ceremonial capital at Ludzidzini, in the Ezulwini Valley, and his administrative centre at Hhohho (said to be named after the sound of baboons barking in the surrounding forests).

The nation that he now inherited consisted of around 75 separate clans. Over the years that followed, this rather ragtag group would consolidate their different dialects and cultures into a unified whole that would become the Swazi nation as we know it today.

But it wasn't going to be easy. From the start, Mswati II was derided as the 'herd-boy king' and his ambitious brothers, who had been teased with the promise of power, constantly tried to usurp his power. To counter this threat the elders decided to send the most dangerous brothers away from the royal centre of Ezulwini into the outlying 'provinces' of the territory. This may not have been the best idea because, even before Mswati officially assumed the throne, Fokoti put together an army and launched a coup attempt. This rebellion quickly failed when many of Fokoti's supporters abandoned him on the eve of a battle at Mahamba hill, and the outnumbered rebels were quickly defeated.

In light of this and other disruptions, the authorities realized that something had to be done to unite the fragmented 'conquest society' inherited by Mswati into a cohesive nation under a single king. So, to encourage loyalty to the new monarch, a number of cultural, administrative and ritualistic devices were set up to make the king more central to his subjects' lives.

For example, the annual *incwala* harvest ceremony (which had been practised for generations in many Nguni cultures) was entrenched to make the link between the welfare of the king and the welfare of the nation more explicit. The military system was also reorganized into a series of age-specific regiments that operated from a network of royal villages that extended across the territory.

However, to keep the regional chiefdoms happy, a number of concessions were made whereby the local authorities enjoyed a small degree of independence, and this kept the whole system in balance. Interestingly, many of these developments were inspired by *ndlovukazi* Thandile, Mswati's mother, who adapted them from the old Ndwandwe traditions as practised by her father Zwide—the nemesis of Sobhuza and Shaka Zulu.

Meanwhile, down in the south, the Zulus were once again becoming restless. Now under the leadership of Mpande, the Zulu nation was still in a tricky position. They had lost most of their territory to the Boers at Port Natal; their cattle herds were severely depleted and they lived in constant threat of annexation. So, just as Dingane had done, Mpande looked towards the north for a solution.

Thus, in 1841, Mpande asked the Swazis for permission to set up a military outpost on the north bank of the Phongolo. This disingenuous request was refused, understandably, and Mpande responded by asking his Boer 'allies' in Natal for permission to send a commando into Swaziland so that he could retrieve some cattle supposedly stolen from Dingane. It was an obviously spurious excuse for a raiding party; the Volksraad in Port Natal refused the application as they had already signed a treaty with the Swazis. But the Boers never ignored an opportunity to get hold of some free cattle, and they cunningly declared that any cattle stolen from Dingane belonged to them, by right of conquest, and proposed sending their own commando to meet Mswati and 'negotiate' a settlement.

Nothing came of this idea, however, as the Boers and the British suddenly got into a colossal fight over the ownership of Port Natal (now Durban), and the issue of Swazi cattle became decidedly moot. When the dust settled, the British had seized control of Natal and most of the Boers left the area in a huff. They eventually re-settled across the interior and on the eastern part of the Transvaal Highveld, close to the western border of Swaziland. This rambunctious group of whites would soon become an important dynamic in Swazi politics.

Back in Natal, Mpande was still angling for a way to invade Swaziland. On several occasions he asked the new British rulers for permission to go into Swaziland on one pretext or another, but his appeals were consistently refused by a colonial authority that wanted to maintain the status quo. They were afraid of letting the Zulu nation become too powerful, and didn't want Mpande to expand his territory or herds.

In the years that followed, the balance of power would tip back and forth between the Swazis, the Zulu, the British, the Boers and a couple of other regional players. All in all, it was a complicated time in southeastern Africa and, throughout his reign, Mswati had to constantly manoeuvre his nation through a bewildering series of political challenges.

Unfortunately, as is often the case with Swazi history, there are several radically different accounts of the proceeding events. There is also a general lack of contemporary documentation. So, to keep things consistent, I will be following the findings of respected historian Philip Bonner and apologize in advance for any oversights. With this disclaimer out of the way, let's get started ...

Mswati and the Boers

The Boers (literally translated as 'farmers') were a group of hunter-pastoralists who originated from the Dutch-run settlement at the Cape of Good Hope. Over the course of 150 years they multiplied and spread out over the western and eastern Cape, where they started asserting a distinct identity (which eventually consolidated into the Afrikaans culture during the early 1900s).

When the British took over the Dutch colony at the Cape after 1806, the Boers were uncomfortable with the new 'foreign' regime and, after several decades of increasingly vociferous grumbling, many Boers decided it was time to leave. The catalyst for this decision was the British announcement that slavery was about to be abolished in the Empire.

And so, starting in the 1830s, groups of Voortrekkers loaded up their wagons and, in search of a homeland of their own, embarked on a Great Trek into the interior of South Africa. They soon established themselves around the Bloemfontein area, which would later become the Orange Free State. They also tried settling in Natal, where they defeated the Zulu king Dingane at Blood River, but were subsequently overtaken by the British annexation of 1843.

After this undesirable turn of events, the iconoclastic Voortrekker leader, Andries Hendrik Potgieter, left Natal and set up a new town on the Highveld, close the Vaal River, which he eponymously named Potchefstroom. But the dictatorial Potgieter didn't get on with some of the more democratically inclined trekkers so, in 1845, he decided to leave Potchefstroom with his followers and establish a new settlement closer to the Portuguese port of Lourenço Marques at Delagoa Bay.

The site he chose lay between Swazi and Pedi territory (close to what is today Pilgrim's Rest). According to Swazi tradition it was technically part of Mswati's sphere of influence, but Potgieter was probably unaware of this nuance and approached Sekwati, the paramount chief of the Pedi, for permission to settle in his realm. This was duly granted, on condition that the Boers provide protection against any Swazi assaults, and a new town was established with the cumbersome name, Andries-Ohrigstad (a combination of Potgieter's first name and the surname of a sympathetic Dutch merchant who supported the trekkers' cause).

Now, by and large, the Voortrekkers were a fractious and argumentative bunch, and the politics of the new 'Republic' of Ohrigstad were *vrot* with tension. The main bone of contention was the Volksraad (or parliament). Simply put, the autocratic Potgieter didn't want one, and his opponents did. During the months of haggling that followed Potgieter used his personal relationship with Sekwati as a trump card since, without the chief's permission, the trekkers would have been out on their ears.

It was around this time that Malambule (Mswati's older brother) started causing trouble in Swaziland. During Mswati's minority, Malambule had acted as principal regent. However, after he handed over power, Malambule and Mswati fell out—some say because Mswati uncovered an assassination plot by Malambule; others claim that Malambule decided to keep some royal cattle for himself, a treasonable offence.

In any case, Mswati had his circumcision in 1845 and finally assumed full control over the Swazi throne. Malambule now began actively planning a hostile takeover of the nation, and approached Mpande for support. The Zulu king seized the opportunity and the two conspirators appear to have cooked up a cunning plan to lure Mswati into a trap that would finally give Mpande an excuse to invade the Swazi territory, with the ultimate goal of establishing Malambule as the new ruler under Zulu control.

Mswati must have gotten wind of this plot and desperately scouted around for allies. Luckily, the gun-toting Boers had just moved into the neighbourhood and Mswati decided to send up a welcome wagon to establish diplomatic relations with the people who were now living on what he considered to be his territory.

However, Potgieter didn't want his opponents in the Volksraad to realize that the treaty with Sekwati might be invalidated by a rival Swazi claim over the same land, and so swiftly rebuffed Mswati's overtures. Nevertheless, news of the Swazi delegation leaked out and Potgieter's rivals took the opportunity to cosy up to Mswati.

By the middle of June 1846, Mpande had started assembling his forces in anticipation of an attack on Swaziland. Malambule simultaneously moved his headquarters to Mahamba, near the Phongolo River. It was obvious that something was up, and Mswati thought it prudent to secure the support of his new allies.

Although it is still unclear who initially approached whom, in July 1846 the Ohrigstad Boers signed a treaty with Mswati's brother Somcuba, who was noted as 'ruling in place of the king'. This document gave the white settlers the right to occupy land between the Crocodile and Olifants rivers, although the specific borders of the grant were kept rather vague.

In exchange for the land, the Boers gave Mswati a promise of protection against a possible Zulu invasion and agreed to pay over 110 head of cattle, which were to be paid out in instalments. Since Mswati only had nominal control over the territory he was giving away, it sounded like a good deal. As it turned out, however, the impoverished Boer Republic could not settle the debt in full until 1871, and this failure to produce the necessary cows was to have unforeseen consequences.

For the moment, however, the treaty was concluded and not a moment too soon. Within a few weeks, Mswati and Malambule's forces engaged in a skirmish at Mahamba, and Malambule retreated to his chiefdom at Lavumisa (named after his mother). At the same time, Mpande sent a message to the British in Natal, saying that he was preparing his troops because 'he judged it prudent to be prepared for any emergency'.

It seems clear, judging by the neat timing, that this was all part of Malambule and Mpande's plan.

Before we continue, however, we must take a moment to meet another group of Europeans who would become embroiled in what was about to follow: enter the Missionaries.

Mswati and the missionaries

Soon after he assumed the throne, Mswati sought to honour his father's dream by inviting the missionaries to bring *umculu*—the good book—into the country. Sobhuza had already pleaded with the Reverend William Shaw of the Wesleyan Missionary Society, back in the mid-1830s, to establish a mission in the territory. It has been suggested that Sobhuza's motivation for this was to create some kind of buffer between his people and the ever-aggressive Zulus but, whatever the reason, the missionaries failed to materialize.

The request was repeated several times by Mswati until finally, in 1844, the Wesleyans gave in and despatched the Reverends James Allison and Richard Giddy to the wilds of Swaziland. They were accompanied by two Basotho converts, known only as Job and Barnabas.

Armed with the Bible, and a couple of guns of course, this small party made its way from the Caledon River in the Free State to the southern border of Swaziland. After a long and occasionally dangerous journey, the travellers crossed the Mkhondvo River in June of that year, where they were met by enthusiastic messengers from the king.

They left their wagons at the homestead of Chief Nyamayenja and continued on horseback to the king's residence at Ludzidzini, some 80km away. When they arrived, they were impressed with the young monarch—Reverend Allision wrote that he was "about 19 years of age, well made, stout and active; his features were regular and pleasing; his hair long, at a distance appearing like an immense wig, his skin of a light bronze colour".

After several welcoming speeches, in which the missionaries were hailed as 'teachers' and 'fathers', the king sent the party back to their wagons and instructed them to build a mission station at an allocated spot in the south of the territory. This was done at a village called Dlovunga, where the local chief was ordered to supply men and materials. A crude chapel and housing were quickly built and the first service saw 400 people in attendance.

Flush with success, the two white missionaries returned to South Africa, leaving Job and Barnabas in charge. Things seemed to be going well and, encouraged by the enthusiastic reception, the Wesleyans decided to send a larger party back to Swaziland in 1845. This group of 15 preachers, under Reverend Allison, soon established a larger mission station a few kilometres away from Dlovunga and proceeded to preach to a growing crowd. Allison also pioneered the writing of the SiSwati language and translated the catechism, which was printed in 1846. Soon the congregation numbered some 1,300.

It was around this time (September 1846) that Malambule emerged from his homestead at Lavumisa and headed with his men to the Mkhondvo River—close to where the missionaries had set up shop. A substantial battle between Malambule and Mswati's troops then took place. The skirmish enveloped the mission station and several native converts were killed. The missionaries were so alarmed by this unexpected turn of events that they decided to abandon their post and move back to Natal. About 1,000 converts decided to follow.

After this unceremonious departure, the area was given a new name: Mahamba (the runaways). In time, and with Mswati's permission, many of the refugees returned to Swaziland; but several decades would pass before any missionaries felt brave enough to return to the territory.

Malambule, for his part, fled south to the headwaters of the Phongolo River, into Zulu territory. The trap was now sprung, as Mswati's armies eagerly pursued the rebellious royal deep into an area of 'dubious sovereignty'. They also, supposedly, raided several small chiefdoms they found along the way. The Zulu king finally had his excuse to invade Swaziland.

Mpande quickly notified the British governor that he was going to invade Swaziland and "follow the enemy as far as [we] may go to recover cattle". In the face of the Swazis' apparently unprovoked raid into Zulu territory, the British had no choice but to allow Mpande to proceed.

And so, in early 1847, the Zulu invasion began. Mpande's forces swept across the Phongolo and marched all the way through Swaziland to the Crocodile River. But the Swazis had been prepared for such an eventuality; many of them had already taken their cattle and retreated to the safety of Boer territory (allegedly in exchange for hefty 'refuge' fees). As such, the anticipated haul of cattle wealth was not realized but, nevertheless, the Zulus now occupied much of Swaziland.

By July, however, the Zulu army had withdrawn, possibly as a result of Boer pressure. Ironically, Potgieter had tried to support the Zulus in defiance of the Volksraad, but the Boer allegiance with the Swazis had won out and the invasion was over.

Making friends with Shepstone

After the Zulu invasion of 1847 was over, Mswati turned his attention to domestic matters; the most important of which was his increasingly rebellious brother, Somcuba. After Malambule had turned traitor, Somcuba assumed many of Malambule's responsibilities and soon began to want more. Then, when Somcuba refused to part with some royal cattle that he was holding for the king, Mswati decided that it was time to clip Somcuba's wings.

The problem was that Somcuba had already established himself as the leading Swazi representative among the Boers, signing the treaty as 'ruling in place of the king', and Mswati ran the risk of offending his new allies if he removed Somcuba from his position. However, the Boers were proving to be less valuable than the Swazis had originally thought. The northern Pedi tribes were already making life difficult for the white settlers and there was a possibility that the Swazis would be called in to protect the Boers, instead of the other way round.

To make matters worse, Potgieter decided in the middle of 1848 that he had had enough of the troublesome Volksraad, and left Ohrigstad with 6,000 followers to establish a new town on the Soutpansberg Mountains, far to the north. This prompted the remaining boers to consider establishing a new town further to the west, beyond the fever zone.

They argued so much about the location of their new settlement that the mountains around Ohrigstad became known as the Strydpoort (Conflict Mountains). Finally, in September 1849, Ohrigstad was abandoned and the Boers established a new capital named Lydenburg (place of suffering—a testimony to the troubles that had plagued them in Ohrigstad).

About this time, Mswati finally became *gatvol* and sent a force to defeat Somcuba. The two sides engaged in battle on the banks of the Komati River and Somcuba was forced to flee to Lydenburg, where he lived among the Boers for the next five years, all the while gathering allies in anticipation of a rematch with Mswati.

The Swazis, for their part, sent emissaries to Natal and informed the British about what was going on between Somcuba and the Boers. They also expressed their concern about the potential for another Zulu attack and asked the Brits for protection should any of their enemies try to invade.

With so much going on, the British didn't want to get involved. Instead, they suggested that Mswati make peace with Mpande, even if this meant that the Swazis become a tributary state of the Zulu. With few other options available to him, Mswati seems to have done just that (although some Swazi historians do not agree with this last point).

The fragile truce between the Swazis and the Zulus didn't last long, however. Mpande kept trying to consolidate his power in Swaziland, while the Swazis wanted to retain as much independence as possible. And so, in July 1852, two Zulu divisions thundered into Swaziland and caught the Swazis unprepared.

Many Swazis were killed; a large number of cattle were stolen and the caves that had previously sheltered the Swazis from previous Zulu incursions were extensively smoked out. It was during this invasion that Mpande's son, Cetshwayo, made a name for himself and his Tulwana regiment, so much so that the campaign came to be called *Ukufunda ka Tulwana* (the teaching of the Tulwana).

British observers soon reported that Swazis were fleeing in all directions. Within a month or two, Swazis were flooding into Natal. This prompted the Native Commissioner in Natal, Sir Theophilus Shepstone, to comment that "the Amaswazi are destroyed as a tribe, and are a needy, destitute, starving people'. This may have been an exaggeration, but at the end of September Mswati himself sent messengers to the Lieutenant-Governor of Natal asking for refuge, saying 'Our tribe is fast dispersing and seeking asylum from the Zulu ... Umswazi begs the government to receive him and the last remnant of the Swazi tribe".

Mswati may have been overstating the case to prompt the British into action. And it worked. The last thing the authorities in Natal wanted was a bunch of desperate refugees hanging around the place. The

British sent increasingly urgent messages to Mpande to desist, but to no avail.

Then, Mpande got distracted by his own domestic problems. Unlike his predecessors, Shaka and Dingane, Mpande had not taken the precaution of eliminating his sons and the young Cetshwayo was becoming increasingly covetous of his father's throne. To counter this threat, Mpande started grooming another son, Mbuyazi, as his heir.

This effectively split the Zulu nation into two camps—those who supported Cetshwayo and those who backed Mbuyazi. The Swazis were quick to capitalize on this divisive succession issue through a cunning piece of native diplomacy, in which they approached Shepstone and suggested that he marry one of Mswati's sisters, Tifokati.

It may seem that the Swazis were a bit naïve to think that the mighty Shepstone would take a second wife, and a native to boot, but the offer was not meant in such a literal fashion. Instead, the Swazis suggested that Tifokati actually marry a proxy in the form of Shepstone's chief *induna,* Ngoza, thus creating a symbolic union between the two houses. This would open a direct line of communication between the British and the Swazis and help ensure that the British would try to stop the Zulu attacks.

Shepstone tactfully refused his Swazi bride, but was flattered by the offer. As a token of thanks he sent two wagonloads of blankets through Zululand to the Swazis, with express instructions that the gift should reach its recipients intact. The Zulu now realized that the Swazis had made a friend of Shepstone and neither Mpande, Cetshwayo or Mbuyazi wanted to anger the British for fear that they might start supporting a rival.

Soon the Zulu armies withdrew from Swaziland, and Mswati's kingdom was once again at peace. The gambit had worked, and a relationship between Swaziland and the Shepstone family was established which was to have major repercussions in the years to come.

Mswati now turned his attention to some much-needed administrative reforms. He tightened up control over his outlying chiefdoms. He also embarked on an aggressive expansion policy, declaring that he wanted to enlarge his territory to the same size as it had been during Sobhuza's time. Finally, Mswati turned his attention to Somcuba, who was still proving to be a thorn in his side.

By this time Somcuba was openly rebelling against his former king by holding his own *incwala* ceremony and killing messengers that Mswati sent to the Boers. It was all too much, and Mswati insisted to the Boers that Somcuba be killed or handed over. This was a demand with which the Boers could not comply.

So, in September 1853, Mswati invaded the Boer territories and laid siege to Lydenburg for seven days. With the Boers holed up in town, another group of warriors attacked Somcuba's homestead, but failed to penetrate his defences and were forced to retreat.

In the face of this drastic action the Volksraad argued about which side to support, Mswati or Somcuba. It wasn't an easy decision to make. By this time the various Boer settlements dotted around the Transvaal were united into the 'South African Republic' (established by the Sand River Convention of 1852). This meant that Potchefstroom, Pretoria, Lydenburg and the Soutpansberg were now all part of a single political entity.

However, since the distances between the various outposts were so vast (it took 80 hours to get from Potchefstroom to Lydenburg by wagon) a national government was simply not effective. Furthermore, each community had its own specific problems and Boers living in one part of the Republic were reluctant to ride out to help those living in another region. This meant that the isolated Boer settlements relied on neighbouring African tribes to supply them with labour, defence and expertise, such as hunting skills. However, since the Boers often used coercion (or even outright force) to recruit native workers, they were often in a state of low-grade war with any number of the surrounding tribes while, at the same time, working to form alliances with others.

As such, the Volksraad couldn't decide whether to curry favour with Mswati (an unknown quantity as far as they were concerned), or maintain links with Somcuba and his 500 men who lived within arm's reach. As the saying goes, 'better a bird in the hand' …

So, after the Swazi raid on Lydenburg, the Boers spent several tense months waiting for a repeat attack. Some wanted to reaffirm the 1846 treaty, with Somcuba still acting as the Swazi signatory. Others wanted to renegotiate a new treaty with Mswati, even if it meant giving up Somcuba. And all the while, rumours about an imminent Swazi invasion swirled through the town.

Then, around the end of 1854, Somcuba was finally killed in a

Swazi raid. This probably came as a relief to everyone (except perhaps Somcuba), and Boer-Swazi relations began to thaw. A few months later, in July 1855, another treaty between the Boers and the Swazis was signed, whereby a 16-kilometre-wide corridor along the north bank of the Phongolo River was ceded to Lydenburg on condition that white farmers settle in the area.

The circumstances that gave rise to this treaty are somewhat mysterious, but it is assumed that the Swazis wanted to create a buffer zone between themselves and the ever-threatening Zulus. It is also suggested that the Boers had in fact given Somcuba over to the Swazis, and that this cession of land was part of that deal.

In any case, the cession soon lapsed from a Swazi perspective, as no Boers moved into the territory once the Swazis had vacated the land. Instead, a number of Zulus moved in and established homesteads right on the border of Mswati's kingdom. This greatly annoyed the Swazis, who came to the conclusion that the Boers were simply too weak to help them fight the Zulu menace. Henceforth, Swaziland turned to the British as their primary European ally and kept up a regular correspondence with their old friend, Theophilus Shepstone.

The Shaka of the North

Over the next ten years, Mswati embarked on an aggressive expansion phase that earned him the encomiums 'the greatest of the Swazi fighting kings' and 'the Shaka of the North'. Following his father's example, Mswati focused on conquering smaller tribes that offered little in the way of defences and absorbed them into the swelling ranks of the Swazi people.

Nevertheless, it was a violent and war-torn time for the Swazis. Fields were often left untilled and the regiments (numbering up to 6,000 troops) were kept very busy. But, by the end of the extended campaign, Mswati's domain is said to have stretched from the Phongolo River in the south to beyond the Olifants River in the north, and from east of the Lubombo to beyond the mountains in the west. Reports show that his forces even occasionally crossed the Limpopo River into Zimbabwe.

However, in some of these far-flung regions Mswati's authority was not absolute. As soon as the Swazi regiments withdrew, many of the

Sotho, Venda and Pedi tribes living in these outlying areas simply went back to their old habits and chiefs. To counter this recidivism, Mswati constructed a number of military outposts along the Crocodile River. At each post he installed soldiers under the dual authority of a female and male leader.

Mswati also started centralising power around himself and his capital. He had had enough of the semi-autonomous chiefdoms on the edges of his realm who continued to give him grief, and sought to strengthen his position as the heart of the nation. To accomplish this, he assumed a central role in many rituals and increasingly blurred the distinction between politics and religion (the same things had been done by many 'divine' European kings).

As such, any chiefs found practising unauthorized ceremonies were swiftly dealt with. Sometimes exile was used as a deterrent for rebellious behaviour, but transgressors were more often killed outright. Royal wives and princes were given control over previously autonomous chiefdoms and physical force was used to stamp out the remnants of any stubborn chief's independence. This consolidation of the royal ruling class created both the capacity and the need for aggressive expansion, as ever-increasing volumes of cattle and tributes were required to keep the whole system going.

Mswati also abolished circumcision and allowed certain regiments to marry without paying lobola. This ensured the loyalty of his troops, which was important, as they were constantly pushed to take part in long and gruelling campaigns across the region. Furthermore, Mswati embraced a Swazi tradition whereby the king took wives from many different chiefdoms, thus entrenching the ties between the king and his subjects. This tradition is still practised by modern Swazi kings, often to the dismay of contemporary observers.

Mswati even got involved in foreign affairs when the Shangaan king, Soshangane, died in 1858. The Shangaan ruled over southern Mozambique, an area that was rich in elephants and ivory; so the stakes were high and, as was often the case, the death of Soshangane caused a succession battle between two of his sons, Mawewe and Mzila. The Nguni elite supported Mawewe (who was married to one of Mswati's sisters) while the Portuguese authorities at Lourenço Marques supported Mzila.

At first, Mzila (with Portuguese backing) defeated Mawewe, who was forced to flee to his brother-in-law, Mswati, for protection. Then, in 1862, Mswati sent a force under Mawewe back into Mozambique to regain the throne. Mzila was defeated, and scarpered north of the Save River with his troops. This was a dry and inhospitable country and, when Mawewe followed, he found the land picked clean by Mzila's men. As a result, many of Mawewe's troops died along the way and he was soundly defeated by Mzila when they eventually engaged in battle.

Mzila took the advantage and pushed Mawewe south of Bilene before Mawewe fled once again to Mswati. Several subsequent attempts were made to defeat Mzila but, despite one sortie in which the Portuguese were pushed back to 'within cannon range' of their fort, Mswati found it impossible to effectively control his army over such large distances.

Nevertheless, the Swazi forces did manage to establish control over a large piece of land in southern Mozambique. This gave them access to ivory, cattle and human captives. In fact, it was during this time that Swaziland became, in the words of Philip Bonner, "the principal captive-trading state in southeastern Africa".

The exact number of captives traded during this time is hard to determine, but they probably numbered in the hundreds, if not thousands. Even a young Paul Kruger is said to have visited Swaziland to hunt elephants and buy a couple of captives for his farms.

Since this involvement in the slave trade is a little-known aspect of Swazi history, it deserves an explanation: there were two kinds of captives, those who came from outside the kingdom's boundaries (titfunjwa) and those who came from within the kingdom (tigcili). The titfunjwa were essentially non-Swazi prisoners of war, often members of the Tsonga tribe, and trade in this human cargo probably began before Sobhuza's time. Titfunjwa were either used by the Swazis as a cheap labour force or sold to the Boers and other tribes in exchange for cattle or guns.

The tigcili, on the other hand, were usually Swazi children. As a Swazi source said in 1898, "it often happened that when a person was killed for some crime or other and his cattle and children seized, those children were taken by the Swazis and sold to the boers in the Transvaal". Only children were useful in this regard because the laws of the South African Republic stated that only children under a certain age could become *inboekselings*—technically apprentices, who could be kept as unpaid labour until they turned 25 (21 for girls).

In 1860, the Berlin missionary Alexander Merensky visited Swaziland and made the situation even more apparent, writing in his diary that "Even now, if a man of his [Mswati's] people has many daughters or good cattle his soldiers come, surround the kraal, murder the old, and take the young people and cattle as booty. Children are being sold or given to the great of the realm".

Incidentally, Merensky and his partner, Grutzner, were in Swaziland to try to get permission to establish a mission station. Mswati was encouraging, saying that he could use the missionaries' secretarial skills, and even suggesting that his children be taught at the school they proposed establishing. Then, Mswati asked for the gun they were carrying as a gift and gave them several captives to trade in Lydenburg for a horse. Merensky and Grutzner refused and were kicked out of the kingdom.

On the plus side, if one can venture to find a positive aspect to all this, the captives were not slaves in the traditional sense. In Swaziland they had rights, and could lodge a complaint against their masters. They could also marry (if they had enough cattle for lobola) and could even rise through the ranks to gain some kind of social standing. Nevertheless, at the risk of imposing a modern perspective on a historical practice, the Swazi involvement in this deplorable trade is not something of which they can be proud.

King Ludvonga

In 1865, King Mswati died, aged around 40. He left behind a powerful state, organized along class lines, but no acknowledged heir. Mbilini, the impetuous son of Mswati's first wife, declared that the king had given him the throne on his deathbed, but the Royal Council didn't support the claim. Instead, they preferred another candidate, a young boy named Ludvonga.

The reasons behind the selection of the pre-teen Ludvonga as the next king of Swaziland are somewhat obscure, but it is surmised that the council favoured a long regency period, during which time they would have control over the kingdom. Additionally, rumours of an imminent

Zulu invasion were bubbling up from Zululand once again and the well-established councillors based in the south didn't want to give their enemies any excuse to attack.

Mbilini was furious with the Royal Council and threatened to rebel. He was backed by the younger regiments stationed at Hhohho, who wanted to maintain the impetus of conquest they had enjoyed under Mswati and bristled at the thought of the conservative council taking over the running of the kingdom.

Nevertheless, Ludvonga was appointed the heir apparent with the important approval of Thandile, former *ndlovukazi* and now the queen regent. It should be noted, however, that Matsebula claims that Thandile died during Mswati's reign and that the position of *ndlovukazi* was taken over by her sister, File.

In any case, Mbilini decided against an outright coup attempt and instead decamped to Lydenburg, where the Boers protected him from a pursuing Swazi regiment. Here he attempted to win the support of the Boers while he waited for his followers to join him. But the Boers didn't want to antagonize the Swazis, and Mbilini's anticipated Swazi supporters failed to show up. So he moved into the northern stretches of Zululand, where he would continue to harass his former allies for the next 13 years.

After Mswati's death, the South African Republic (ZAR) decided it was a good time to reopen the border issue with Swaziland. According to Bonner, this was the first time that the Boers had initiated such a discussion, and they outlined a new frontier that reduced the size of Swazi territory. This treaty was signed by members of the Royal Council in 1866.

It does seem strange that the Swazis would agree to such an unfavourable treaty when they were involved in an aggressive expansionist policy just a few months before. Mswati's death obviously had something to do with it, but there must have been other reasons. Bonner rejects the notion that the council was merely weak in the face of Boer demands. Instead, he points out the council was being cautious because both the Zulu and Boer nations had strengthened considerably in the last few years.

Cetshwayo had finally defeated his challenger, Mbuyazi, at the bloody battle of Ndondakasuka, back in 1856, and was by now the effective leader of a reinvigorated Zulu nation. The Boers had likewise grown in number and organizational unity, and were now capable of mounting a real challenge against the Swazi state. As such, the council may have believed that having a clearly demarcated boundary might be a good thing, because if anyone tried to invade the territory, at least there would be a clear line that could not be crossed.

As it turned out, the 1866 treaty was moot because the Boers had still not paid the cattle owing on the old 1855 treaty and, until that debt was paid, the Swazis could easily refuse to accept the new borders. The biggest sticking point was the valuable winter grazing along the Komati River, south of its junction with the Crocodile, and ownership of this 'winterveld' would continue to be a bone of contention between the Boers and the Swazis for many years to come.

Despite their apparent capitulation to Boer demands, the Swazi were still on the offensive in other parts of the region. In 1866, they invaded the eastern Transvaal and attacked the Phalaborwa, Lovedu (under Queen Modjadji) and the Nkuna. These missions were such a success that the Hhohho regiments decided to support Mampuru, the rightful heir to the Pedi throne who was deposed by his brother Sekhukhune after the death of their father, Sekwati, in 1860.

Thandile advised against this campaign, but the regiments marched off anyway and suffered a terrible defeat when they were surrounded by Sekhukhune's rifles at the Battle of Ewulu. As a Swazi observer noted, "the princes fell like leaves in autumn, and the country mourned the unsupportable loss, poor and rich; noble and common; valiant and villains fell alike".

To make up for this setback, the regiments went on to attack Bilene (in Mozambique) and the Soutpansberg before being forced to retreat by Maghato (the arch villain of the Soutpansberg Boers) in 1869. To make matters worse, as the demoralized troops were returning home, they were set upon by a combined force of several Lowveld tribes at Tsulamedi Hill by the Makundwe River.

With the Swazi military reputation in tatters, two old enemies took the opportunity to attack. First Msuthfu, the son of Somcuba, destroyed the village of Eshanweni with the help of Sekhukhune's Pedi army. Then Mbilini led an incursion into the southwest of the country, with the apparent co-operation of Cetshwayo.

Things weren't looking good on the Boer front either. In 1867, Alexander McCorkindale founded New Scotland, a farming district right on the western border of Swaziland (around the modern Chrissiesmeer area). He then proceeded to badger the Swazis for more land in an attempt to establish a route through their territory to the sea. This prompted the Swazis to send a distinguished delegation to the British where, for the first time, they explicitly complained about the ZAR as opposed to the Zulus.

Then, in 1869, Marthinus Wessels Pretorius (the first President of the ZAR) unilaterally proclaimed that the republic was annexing Swaziland. This wasn't as serious as it sounded because the republic really had no way of enforcing its annexation. Boer commandos were hard to raise due to lack of funds and official ZAR delegations to the Swazis were poorly organized, so nothing was signed. Nevertheless, it was a chilling portent of things to come.

The ZAR's increasing interest in Swaziland continued to be apparent during the early 1870s. First, the Royal Council was coerced into granting permission for a project that sought to link the ZAR to the sea, as part of the Boers' long-standing plan to create a harbour beyond British control. After this agreement was signed, several missionaries and concession hunters entered the country, with limited success.

A short while later, the ZAR got permission to establish roads and postal links across Swaziland, as well as an ambiguous undertaking from Swaziland not to invade any chiefdoms in the Transvaal. In 1872, the field cornet of the Wakkerstroom district went so far as to tell Pretoria that Swaziland actually wanted to become part of the ZAR and was prepared to pay taxes, but this flagrantly false story was ignored by all parties concerned.

Things came to something of a head when, in 1873, T. F. Burgers (the new president of the ZAR) visited Swaziland in person. His short stay in the kingdom didn't achieve much, but the Swazis were concerned by the surprise visit and appealed to the British, saying that the president had demanded that Swaziland accept ZAR control. They went on to say that Swaziland had been a loyal tributary of Britain since Mswati's time and asked for something in writing to that effect.

Even though Natal did not want the ZAR to expand their territory towards the sea, it didn't want to commit itself to any direct involvement and fobbed off the Swazi delegation. Instead, they put pressure on the ZAR to stop making such aggressive overtures towards Swaziland and the matter was dropped, for a while.

By this time, Ludvonga was finally ready to assume the throne, and everyone hoped that the new king would be able to establish some kind of authority over a situation that was rapidly spiralling out of control. Unfortunately, in 1874, Ludvonga suddenly died.

The belief was that the king's beer had been poisoned, and the royal kraal was thrown into turmoil. Ndwandwa Dlamini, the chief regent, was summarily executed because it was his job to keep the king safe (and some even directly accused him of murdering Ludvonga so that he could assume the throne under Zulu patronage). Many other councillors were also killed in the fracas. But no matter who got persecuted for Ludvonga's death, the fact remained that Swaziland was without a king at a perilous time when several powerful enemies of the state were conspiring to destroy the country for good.

King Mbandzeni (ruled 1874–1889)

After Ludvonga's unexpected death, a bloody succession struggle broke out. Several of Mswati's sons stepped forward to take over, most notably Giba, but all were rejected for one reason or another. The nation found itself split into a number of warring factions; many people lost their lives in the conflict that ensued.

Subsequent chroniclers, such as the sensationalist (and unreliable) Allister Miller, claimed that the interregnum period was a bloodbath, but this seems to be an overstatement. Still, there were certainly a number of gruesome battles between rival groups and the face of the ruling council was dramatically changed as a result.

Thankfully, the most senior regents were quick to act and reigned in the violence after a couple of chaotic months. But the question still remained, who was going to be the next king?

Thandile and her most trusted councillors (including Malunge, Maloyi and Sandlane) pondered this thorny issue. One of the problems they had to face related to the role of Sisile, Ludvonga's mother. She was already well advanced in her preparations to become the next *ndlovukazi*, and was not prepared to go away quietly.

In fact, it was the formidable Sisile (a sister of the Zulu renegade Mzilikazi) who came up with a solution. She suggested a son of Mswati named Mbandzeni. His mother had already died, so Sisile could adopt the young man as her own and maintain her position as the Queen Mother. Furthermore, Mbandzeni was known to be placid and pliable, unlike most of the other candidates, and this would allow the regency council to retain much of their power. It seemed to be the perfect solution and Mbandzeni was chosen as the new king. It was a decision that would come to haunt Swaziland for generations to come.

Despite opposition from Giba and several other princes, Mbandzeni was installed on the throne three months after Ludvonga's death. He was now king, but he was isolated and dominated by the council who had been effectively in control of Swaziland since Mswati died.

Soon after the coronation, Mabhedla (a brother of Mbandzeni) attempted to raise up a coup from his base in the Hhohho Mountains. He failed to find much support, however, and fled to Sekhukhune for refuge. The Swazi army pursued the rebel but they were ambushed by the Pedi at Mosega Kop. It was the second major defeat at the hands of the Pedi in five years.

The declining military fortunes of the Swazi regiments had a number of knock-on effects. Supplies of cattle and other valuable tributes began to dry up and people started demanding that the regiments pay over the lobola that had been waived under Mswati's rule. Furthermore, since there were fewer battles to fight, the regiments weren't called up as often as before and Swazi control over their territory began to wane. As such, outlying chiefdoms began to assume greater independence and the royal house started losing its lustre.

Meanwhile, by the mid-1870s, Cetshwayo was preparing for his imminent assumption of the Zulu throne (Mpande would die in 1876). The thing was that the Zulu nation was enjoying a population explosion as a result of fewer wars, and there was a shortage of resources. Poor rainfall during this time made the need for additional food and cattle even more pressing, and the formidable Cetshwayo fixed his sights on conquering the Swazi nation once and for all. This would not only give Cetshwayo more space for his people, it would also give the Zulu control of the valuable ivory trade in eastern Mozambique, which was currently dominated by Swaziland.

Accordingly, Cetshwayo sent a request to the British, asking for permission to send troops into Swaziland so that he could avenge the death of Ludvonga and 'wash the spears' in honour of his new kingship. The British refused, naturally, but at the same time, the reckless rebel Mbilini mounted a series of 'unauthorized' raids into Swaziland.

The true nature of the links between Mbilini and Cetshwayo are hard to determine. Mbilini was living in Zulu territory, so it is unlikely that he was operating without some kind of Zulu complicity. However, Cetshwayo denied any responsibility for Mbilini's activities and repeatedly told the Boers that they had a free hand to enter the region and capture Mbilini, if they so desired. Despite this apparent lack of loyalty, it seems safe to assume that the two men were working in collusion with one another, even if Cetshwayo wasn't directly involved in the specifics of Mbilini's adventures.

As if the threats from Cetshwayo, Mbilini and the Boers weren't enough, the British now also became a potential risk to Swazi independence. Since the 1850s, Shepstone and other imperialists had been talking about plans for a confederation of southern African states (under British control, of course). This would give the region a degree of political stability, and would also allow the British to access pools of tribal labour who were sitting 'idle' in Zululand and the Transvaal.

The discovery of diamonds in Kimberley in 1867 made the case for confederation even more compelling, and by the 1870s the issue was being openly discussed in newspapers and parlours across the country. Obviously, the ZAR was totally opposed to the plan, but they were soothed with promises that they would be allowed to take over Zululand and Swaziland in exchange for their co-operation. Even that wasn't enough to get the support of the fiercely independent Boers.

Finally, in 1875, Cetshwayo announced that he was going to invade Swaziland, no matter what anybody said. The assegais of his army needed washing. This time it was the ZAR who came to the rescue. They didn't want to see the strategically located Swazi territory fall into Zulu hands instead of their own. So, the Boers mounted a huge force that marched off to 'protect' Swaziland.

Faced with a military force that stretched for over 3km, consisting of 350 men, four mountain guns and 58 wagons, Cetshwayo stood down. The Zulu threat had evaporated, but the Boers weren't going to let a little thing like that stop them. Instead, they kept going until they reached Mbandzeni's capital, where they put on an impressive display of cannon and gun fire. The Swazis' reciprocal military display was puny by comparison, and the kingdom grew worried for its future.

These misgivings were justified. Soon after they had shown off their superior strength, the Boers boldly announced that they wanted to sign a new treaty, and the Swazis had little choice but to concede. The terms of this document were somewhat one-sided: Swazis now accepted the status of subjects of the ZAR. As such, they guaranteed military aid to the ZAR, promised to not to wage war without the prior permission of the ZAR, undertook to promote commerce with the ZAR, agreed to keep trade routes and roads open and in good condition, granted permission to build a railway through the country, and "in the event of the government of the South African Republic deeming it necessary to appoint in their midst a supervising official [to enforce the provisions of the treaty, the Swazis would] engage themselves to abide by his decision". The borders were also clarified, although the dispute over the Komati winterveld was not resolved.

In return, the Swazis got the promise of protection against their enemies, the right of possession of their lands, "and the guarantee of self-government, though only as far as it was humanly just and defensible". All in all, it wasn't much of a deal for the Swazis. But without an on-going military presence in the kingdom, the Boers would find it difficult to implement their shiny new treaty. The ZAR delegates had also squabbled amongst themselves while at the royal kraal, when Boers and *uitlanders* (foreigners) openly brawled in a fist fight, so it was clear that there were cracks in the republic's 'united' front.

Accordingly, after the delegation had left, the Swazis quickly turned around and complained to the British that they had been misled in to signing the treaty. The grounds for this appeal were a bit shaky as the Swazis claimed that they thought they were signing the treaty with the British. Admittedly, one of the leaders of the ZAR party was a former British agent named Rudolph. However, he had been the magistrate of the nearby district of Utrecht for three years, and the Swazis are unlikely to have been labouring under this particular misapprehension.

Nevertheless, the British were still pursuing their plans for confederation, and didn't want the ZAR to become too powerful. So, in

January 1876, they sent a stern warning to the ZAR not to proceed with any form of territorial expansion.

In May of that year, war broke out between the ZAR and the Pedi, under Sekhukhune. The obstreperous Pedi had been a thorn in the side of the Boers for many years. They had refused to hand over land, jeopardized important railway loans and created a labour shortage in the Transvaal by their reluctance to work on Boer farms. It was time to put them in their place.

However, the Boers realized that they couldn't complete the campaign without the help of the Swazi army, and appealed for military aid. The request was granted, perhaps because the Swazis were eager for revenge against their old enemies. However, the Royal Council was worried that by sending the troops away they would be left vulnerable to a joint attack by Cetshwayo and Sekhukhune (who had formed a loose alliance based on their mutual dislike of the Swazis and the Boers). Furthermore, the Shangaan king, Mzila, also wanted to invade in order to exterminate his brother, Mawewe, who was still living in Swaziland.

With the risks outweighing the rewards, the Swazi army pulled out at the last minute. A furious Boer delegation scurried down to Swaziland and forced the Royal Council to make good on their offer. Finally, with no more outs available to them, 2,000 Swazi warriors were sent to the ZAR in July 1876.

The plan was for the Swazis (under Matsafeni, called Mataffin by the whites) and Lydenburg regiments (under Commandant Coetzer) to attack the fortress of Johannes Dinkwanyane, one of Sekhukhune's brothers. At the same time, another Boer commando would go after Sekhukhune himself. The raid on Dinkwanyane's fort went well, but the sly Boers held back and allowed the Swazis to take the brunt of the action. After losing more than 50 men, the enraged Swazis immediately withdrew from the campaign and returned home

Without any Swazi involvement, the Boer raid on Sekhukhune wasn't a great success and the poorly organized commando retreated after some desultory burning of huts at the foot of the Pedi king's mountain fortress. However, the Boers did leave behind some irregulars (under C. H. von Schlikkeman), who harassed Sekhukhune so much that the chief negotiated a truce in order to buy himself enough time to plant crops for the upcoming season.

The truce with the Pedi was bad news for Britain. They were hoping that the Boers would get a good thumping so that they would be more amenable to confederation. The Swazis, however, were probably quite happy. They had redeemed something of their military reputation and had been able to withdraw from the war honourably, without offending the potentially dangerous ZAR.

This was just as well because, in August 1876, Cetshwayo once again asked for permission to attack a semi-independent Swazi chief who lived at the point where the Lusutfu River cuts through the Lubombo range. From this strategically important location the Zulus would be able to exert control over both Swaziland and southern Mozambique. As such, the British and the ZAR objected. This prompted poor Cetshwayo to bemoan the fact that "I am no king but sit in a heap. I cannot be a king until I have washed my assegais". Despite this rather whiny plea, Cetshwayo's ambitions for Swaziland were thwarted for the umpteenth time.

The British go to war

Then, in April 1877, Theophilus Shepstone took the radical step of annexing the ZAR on behalf of Britain. His reasons for doing this included the shambolic Boer government, ongoing troubles with the unbowed Pedi and the impending bankruptcy of the republic. His confederation of southern Africa was finally coming together.

As the new administrator of the Transvaal, Shepstone honoured all treaties between the ZAR and Swaziland. This strengthened the Swazis position against the Zulu, as not even Cetshwayo was foolhardy enough to bring down the might of the British army on his head. However, Shepstone used his new position to try and formalize relations with the Swazis saying that they must make up their minds whether they were "adjoining neighbours or subjects ... because both the obligations and privileges of living inside the enclosure differed from and were greater than residence without".

Nevertheless, the Swazis maintained that they were tributaries of Britain, not direct subjects. This position could have become problematic if the British had not become embroiled in a battle with Sekhukhune, whereupon they were forced to ask the Swazis for military aid. With the shoe now on the other foot, the Swazis denied the request on the grounds that the British were doing nothing to get rid of the ever-increasing number of Zulus living along the northern bank of the Phongolo.

The Swazis' concerns were well founded and in July 1878, Zulus began occupying Swazi territory in Mahamba and Ngwavuma. Then, in September, Mbilini launched another attack on the kingdom.

For this and several other reasons, Shepstone and Bartle Frere (the new British High Commissioner) decided that an independent Zululand could no longer be countenanced. They quickly set about finding an excuse for war with Cetshwayo and sent MacLeod, the Swazi border commissioner, to find out if Mbandzeni would be prepared to get involved. Mbandzeni's rather cheeky response was that he would be happy to help, if he had any proof that the British could actually fight instead of just talking about it.

Meanwhile, in December 1878, Shepstone seized on a number of minor border infractions and issued the Zulu king with an impossible ultimatum, demanding that the Zulu army be disbanded within a matter of weeks or else face war with the British. MacLeod then returned to Mbandzeni and told him about the ultimatum, this time asking for concrete promises of military assistance.

Faced with the real thing, Mbandzeni stalled, as he did not want his army to be used as a pawn in the imminent conflict. Although he was authorized to bribe Mbandzeni in exchange for support, MacLeod skipped straight to blackmail and threatened Mbandzeni with a new set of unfavourable borders once the war was over. The Swazi king was outplayed and promised to send troops, as long as British forces were sent to protect his people.

The Anglo-Zulu War officially began in January 1879 when British regiments were sent over the Tugela River from Natal. Soon, Mbandzeni got the order to send Swazi troops to protect Wakkerstroom and Utrecht. But Mbandzeni was still not keen on getting involved; he refused to send any men until he got a definite description of the borders for which they were about to die. Instead of a reply, the British sent another order for the Swazi army to go to the Phongolo. This time, Mbandzeni asked for more time to convene the Royal Council so that he could get the proper permission for such an action.

Then, on January 22, the Zulus dealt the British a colossal blow at the Battle of Isandlwana. With 1,329 men lost, this was the worst military defeat for the proud British army since the Indian Mutiny of 1857, and all military action was suspended. While the debacle at Isandlwana caused a huge stink with the British public, the Swazis were surprisingly heartened by the unexpected turn of events. They now knew that the British were truly committed to the war, and they were also impressed by the subsequent stand at Rorke's Drift, where a handful of British soldiers managed to kill an estimated 2,500 Zulus.

Mbandzeni now reiterated his promise of military assistance under the same condition of British protection for his territory. However, it was impossible for Britain to fulfil this obligation, because it could not afford to send troops away from the conflict zone. This was probably just as well, because it appears that Mbandzeni was totally unwilling to launch a full-scale attack on Zululand under any circumstances.

It was only after the British finally defeated Cetshwayo at the Battle of Ulundi, in July 1879, that Mbandzeni changed his tune. With the Zulus put to flight, the Swazi king now practically demanded that his men be let loose on the Zulu settlers who had been living along the Phongolo River since Mswati's time.

But the British weren't quite ready to let Mbandzeni off the hook. Cetshwayo was still hiding in the Ngome Forest and MacLeod asked Mbandzeni to help capture the fugitive king. Mbandzeni tried to wriggle out of the request and was finally forced to admit that he was too frightened to send his troops so deep into Zulu territory.

MacLeod kept this confession a secret, as he was fearful of losing his rank as a British Agent. Instead, he merely reported that 5,000 Swazi warriors were assembled, awaiting further instruction. A short time later, the British authorities replied that they favoured killing Cetshwayo, as opposed to capturing him alive. But, by this time, Mbandzeni had demobbed the regiments and said they couldn't be reassembled in less that several weeks. Before the regiments could be recalled, however, Cetshwayo had been captured and Mbandzeni was freed from his obligations.

According to Philip Bonner: "The Swazi performance during the war had been a truly masterful display of fence-sitting. Without actually doing anything they had managed to project an image of loyalty, which won them tributes from all sides once the fighting ceased."

However, with the fighting over, MacLeod started drafting letters that painted the Swazis in a less positive light. Luckily, these communications became irrelevant when the Swazi were once again called up to participate in yet another campaign against their old enemy, Sekhukhune.

So it was, in October 1879, that Sir Garnet Wolseley asked MacLeod to assemble a Swazi force that would finally defeat the intractable Pedi. This time the Swazis were more than happy to oblige, and quickly gathered between 8,000 and 8,500 troops, 500 of them with guns. While their performance during the Anglo-Zulu War may have relied on procrastination, their campaign against Sekhukhune would be exemplary.

Although some historians have credited the success of the attack on Sekhukhune's hideout to a Boer commando led by Ferreira, others have asserted that it was the Swazis who won the day. Following this version of events, at the final attack on the Sekhukhune's mountain fortress, the Swazis waited patiently until first light. Then, under covering fire, they stormed the rear of the mountains, capturing Sekhukhune well before the acclaimed Ferreira commando arrived.

The Swazi force lost more that 500 men during the battle, and about the same number were wounded. But they were victorious and a song was written about the battle: *iNqaba kaNqofula*—the fort of Sekhukhune. This little ditty has now become something of an anthem for the Swazis, and is often sung at national events.

After this impressive display, Wolseley's chief of staff wrote: "It is difficult to overestimate the political value of the Swazi factor in our future relations with the northern native tribes". Swaziland was now Britain's principal collaborator in southeastern Africa, and the British authorities felt a large debt of gratitude which the Swazis were able to exploit over the next 25 years. Even so, historians such as Bonner point out that the Swazis never fully understood the strength of their position after the Sekhukhune campaign, and suggest that they could have probably got a lot more out of the British in subsequent negotiations.

A case in point was the Transvaal-Swazi Boundary Commission, which took place in early 1880. With the ever-efficient British now in control of the ZAR, it was decided that the messy border issue had to be properly sorted out. However, the British now considered the Swazis to be more important allies than the Boers, and wanted to keep them on-side. As such, the delegation were prepared to consider three potential northern boundaries: one along the Komati River to Mananga; one from Kamhlubana peak to Mananga; and one from the Kamhlubana peak to the junction of the Crocodile and Komati, which would have given a large slice of the ZAR, including the hotly disputed Komati winterveld, to Swaziland.

In the event, Swazis got the second option (which is roughly the same as the current border), and did score some extra territory from the treaty, but they might have bargained for a lot more if they had fully understood their enviable position. Nevertheless, the commission gave the Swazis a guarantee of independence and freedom from taxation, provided they give the British military aid whenever requested to do so.

But there was no time for looking back. In December 1880, the Boers rebelled against the British annexation of the ZAR and the First Anglo-Boer War broke out. Based on past practice, you might have expected the Swazis to wait and see who won before choosing sides, but this time they fully expected the British to cream the opposition and rejected an alliance with the Boers.

However, the British General Colley's defeat at Majuba Hill took everyone by surprise, and by March 1881 the Boers had won the war. In August, the Pretoria Convention was signed and the Transvaal Republic regained its independence. However, there were several clauses in the convention that rankled with the Boers (including the issue of native rights and the disputed border with Swaziland).

And so, in 1884, the new president of the Transvaal, Paul Kruger, set off for Britain. The London Convention that resulted did resolve some of the Boers' issues, but the border with Swaziland remained somewhat fuzzy. The only protection for Swaziland was a formal recognition of its independence and a stipulation that the territory could only be annexed with the express permission of the British, the Boers and the Swazis. Furthermore, in an attempt to resolve the border impasse, a clause was inserted that allowed for the appointment of a British Resident and the establishment of an Imperial Police Force in Swaziland to oversee border relations. As it turned out, these were all unworkable solutions.

The concessions era begins

After the Anglo-Zulu War, Zululand was split up into a number of chiefdoms that operated under British control. The power of the Zulu nation had been splintered and, for the first time in living memory, the Swazi nation didn't have to worry about the threat of a Zulu invasion.

Mbandzeni took the opportunity to develop his domestic policy and assert his political authority. He was the king, after all, and he felt that it was high time he started behaving like one. His growing confidence was bolstered by the deaths of his powerful councillor Malunge and the even more powerful queen regent, Thandile, who died around 1875 after 25 years in politics. Rudolph, the magistrate at Utrecht, was less than charitable when he celebrated the passing of 'that old Jezebel', but his feelings probably reflect Mbanzeni's desire for increased respect in his kingship.

Although he was chosen for his amiable nature, Mbandzeni now started earning an equivocal reputation as 'the quiet puff adder'. However, he still had several powerful councillors to deal with, including Maloyi, Sandlane, Sobandla and his adoptive mother, the powerful *ndlovukazi*, Sisile.

In an effort to placate the increasingly ambitious king, the Royal Council gave Mbandzeni the right to grant grazing, hunting and woodcutting concessions in the kingdom. These were considered second-rate functions, but the king seemed to like his new portfolios and especially enjoyed the gifts and flattery heaped on him by the white men seeking concessions. Around this time, the first Anglican missionaries also got a toehold in the southern part of the country.

To explain what the concessions entailed, allow me to quote from A. G. Marwick, a district commissioner in Swaziland: "the private ownership of land was unknown amongst [the Swazis], and indeed throughout the Bantu world before the advent of the white man ... The land was vested in the whole nation and belonged to the generation also to follow: only the control of the use of it was in the hand of their ruler. Such use might be given to anybody so long as the land was not needed by the members of the tribe, and it was in the power of the ruler to vary his grants of land and even to cancel them for a good cause arising from the behaviour of the grantees and from the needs of his people".

Archdeacon Christopher Watts emphasizes the point that "in granting land concessions, Mbandzeni had always been under the impression that he granted the land only for the lifetime of the actual petitioner … the idea of a 'grant in perpetuity' was quite beyond his comprehension".

As such, most of the concessions granted by Mbandzeni in these early days received little comment from the Royal Council, but some were overly extravagant and caused consternation. One of the most egregious was a grazing concession over 36,000 acres of land in southern Swaziland that Mbandzeni gave to Joachim Ferreira and Ignatius Maritz shortly after he officially received his royal headring in 1876.

This extensive grant was opposed by his councillors, but Mbandzeni refused to back down. In a show of disapproval, Sandlane refused to visit the king for several weeks, until a violent conflict erupted and several of Sandlane's men were killed.

As Bonner succinctly puts it, for the next ten years a pattern was established whereby Mbandzeni's "dull passivity would be accompanied by mounting resentment at being excluded from the exercise of real power, and would finally be broken by a brief bout of self-assertion, after which the whole cycle would resume".

Mbandzeni's relationship with his *ndlovukazi* was particularly problematic. Even after his official ascension, Sisile remained the effective head of government. She continued to centralize power around the Royal Council and was instrumental in involving women in government affairs. More significantly, communications with the outside world were usually conducted in her name, and Mbandzeni came to resent her authority.

Matters came to a head when Mbandzeni started a liaison with Somdlalose, a pretty maiden who was about to be betrothed to Ludvonga before his sudden death. Despite Sisile's objections, the relationship continued and, around 1879, a child was born of the union. His name was Mdzabuko, and some proclaimed that he was the real heir to Ludvonga.

Sisile now started preparing Mdzabuko for kingship, shrewdly realising that he would require a long regency period during which she would remain in firm control of the kingdom. This was an untenable situation and, around February 1881, while everyone's attention was turned towards the Anglo-Boer War, Mbandzeni sent some poisoned milk to his son's nurse. Within hours, the young child was dead.

The death of Mdzabuko threw the royal kraal into turmoil. Accusations and counter-accusations flew about for a week before Mbandzeni removed himself, leaving Sisile and Somdlalose behind. Fearing the worst, the two women fled to the Transvaal with some loyal regiments. Mbandzeni's troops followed, but were turned back at Gobholo stream thanks to the heroic exploits of Mancibane Dlamini, which are still recalled to this day.

Sisile fled again, but was overtaken by Mbandzeni's men at Mpholonjeni where she was strangled. Back in Swaziland, Sisile's other supporters also fled, most notably a chief named Mtyce who left Hhohho with 2,000 followers. Then, Mbandzeni abruptly had a change of heart that demonstrated a sense of restraint that earned him a reputation for kindness and tolerance. Mancibane was subsequently allowed to return with honour, and Mtyce's men started trickling back home. A new queen mother, Tibati Nkambule, was installed and things got back to normal.

Once the Anglo-Boer War was over, the old border issue reared its ugly head yet again when a number of Boers flooded into Swaziland's disputed winter grazing land along the Komati River. Mbandzeni complained to the British, demanding that they be removed. But the British merely handed the complaint over to the Transvaal authorities, and Paul Kruger promised to remove the graziers.

As it turned out, J. S. Joubert was appointed to supervize the graziers, but he only investigated specific complaints and did nothing to remove the farmers from the land. Although previously, during the British annexation, the Swazis had granted grazing licences to white farmers in this part of the country, the new influx of graziers showed little sign of leaving, and the Royal Council became alarmed at the prospect that they would settle and gradually take over the valuable region. Around the same time, the council approached the British with a proposal to get a 16-kilometre corridor along the northern bank of the Phongolo returned, which had been given away several treaties back, but this appeal was refused.

The real problems started in 1883, when Mbandzeni gave permission for Thomas Wyld to prospect for gold in the northern Emjindini region, which was part of the disputed Komati winterveld. The king then sent representatives to the gold fields in the adjacent De Kaap valley and demanded that the prospectors working there pay for licences.

De Kaap was clearly beyond Swaziland's borders, and the ZAR State Secretary wrote to the British Agent in Pretoria. The Agent (G. Hudson) wrote back and told Mbandzeni to hold everything until he could come and investigate. This letter was then delivered to Mbandzeni by an ZAR messenger, which caused the king to doubt its authenticity.

He summoned a missionary named Joel Jackson to verify the letter. When the communication was indeed shown to be from Hudson, Jackson sat in on the ensuing discussion, during which Mbandzeni was forced admit that he had been wrong. The king subsequently withdrew the mineral concession to Wyld and henceforth refused to allow any third parties to observe his negotiations.

The issue of the northern border continued to be a bugbear for Mbandzeni; he tried to keep the boundaries as vague as possible, hoping to regain full control at a later stage. However, in 1884, the Boers waged a long and successful battle against Chief Mabhoko, which cost over £40,000. This 'Mapoch's War' proved that the formerly poor and disorganized republic was now capable of supporting an extended military campaign, without the help of the Swazi army, and the balance of power shifted away from Mbandzeni.

After the Mapoch War, rumours started spreading that the Boer graziers were planning an attack. There were also complaints that Vice President Joubert was stirring up trouble in his Wakkerstroom constituency to the south of Swaziland and promising imminent action against the kingdom. Although these stories may have been nothing more than idle gossip, they were cause for concern and Mbandzeni asked David Forbes (an early concessionaire) to inform the British Agent in Pretoria of his grievances.

As a result, Hudson sent his secretary, Rutherford, to investigate. Rutherford's findings were inconclusive, although he did note that Mbandzeni was unimpressive, saying the king had "very little influence … upon the counsels and conduct of the country's affairs … Listless in manner and trifling in business …; not seeming even to affect any great interest in what was going on; often almost childish in demeanour".

When Hudson received the report, he added a covering letter stating that there was mineral wealth in the kingdom which was attracting a steady stream of Europeans in search of potentially lucrative concessions. This, he concluded, might lead to turbulence along the border, and advised that something be done before things got out of control.

The documents were then sent to Sir Hercules Robinson (British High Commissioner at the Cape), who thought it might be prudent to appoint a British Resident in Swaziland to monitor the situation, as was allowed for in the London Convention. Following the tortuous route of Imperial bureaucracy, Robinson's report was sent to the Earl of Derby (Secretary of State in Britain), who replied that it wasn't a bad idea, but only if Mbandzeni would pay for the cost of the resident and a small police force.

Mbandzeni was not keen on the idea of having a British Resident in his kingdom, fearing that it would undermine his royal authority. He was also afraid that the resident would collude with his council or put British interests above the needs of Swaziland. In light of Rutherford's rather dismissive comments about the king, he was probably justified in his concerns. In short, Mbandzeni replied that he would rather stay as he was than have to deal with a stranger he didn't like.

Meanwhile, the appetite for mineral concessions in Swaziland had been growing steadily since alluvial gold was discovered in the eastern Transvaal, back in 1873. The first party of Australian prospectors entered Swaziland from Pilgrim's Rest in 1875, but found nothing. Then, around 1880, Tom McLachlan moved into the Pigg's Peak area and got a concession north of the Komati. Within a couple of years, David and James Forbes got the concession for Ngwenya Mountain, while Thomas Wyld bought the controversial concession in the far north, along the Crocodile River.

Subsequently, dozens of other speculators moved in to snap up the remaining mineral rights. Farming and grazing concessions were also secured, usually by ZAR farmers. Crucially, these white men often misinterpreted the concessions as deeds-of-sale while the Swazis saw them as temporary permits. This failure to communicate would prove to be a major problem in the future.

Nevertheless, dozens of white men (such as an ambitious journalist from Barberton called Allister Miller) started beating a path to Mbandzeni's door. The route they took led from the gold-rush village of Steynsdorp, around Ngwenya Mountain (where the current Oshoek border is today) and down to Grosvenor Darke's little store. From here (now a small settlement still called Darketon) they continued eastwards to Bombadier Mickey Wells' store on the banks of Mbabane stream. Then it was down Malangwane hill and through the valley of heaven to Mbekelweni, the royal kraal. This was located just a few kilometres away from Bob Rogers' store (which stood on the lands of Chief Manzini). Today, this route is still followed by the MR3 highway from the border to Mbabane and Manzini.

By the mid-1880s, the concession situation was getting out of hand and, despite Mbandzeni's reservations, it was decided that an impartial white man should be brought in to oversee the concessionaires and ensure that Swaziland got its fair share of the wealth. The question was—who?

After thinking about it for a while, it was decided that the eminent Sir Theophilus Shepstone had previously shown himself to be a friend of the Swazis. So a request was sent to the now-retired *Somtseu* (white father) to send one of his sons to take charge of concessionary affairs. Soon Arthur Shepstone was on his way to the royal kraal at Mbekelweni (the place of the appointed one).

He arrived in May 1884 and soon got down to business. Unfortunately, Arthur was keener on personal profit than he was on looking after Swazi interests, and he soon started making trouble. Nevertheless, within two weeks a *libandla* was convened and Shepstone was given the power to administer the concessionaries. He was also granted the right to prospect for gold on Forbes' Ngwenya concession.

This caused a rupture with the previously influential Forbes, and Mbandzeni soon revoked Shepstone's right at Ngwenya as well as his oversight of mineral concessions. Instead, Shepstone was given informal rights to prospect on McLachlan's Pigg's Peak concession. This trade-off suited no one and Shepstone threatened to leave. The Royal Council encouraged him to stay, however, and several months of negotiation followed as Mbandzeni grew increasingly suspicious of the whole setup.

Shepstone was soon fed up with the king's stalling and left in a huff. The Royal Council was dismayed but, even though the Swazi monarchy has its checks and balances, Mbandzeni's refusal to follow the wishes of the *libandla* could only be rectified by removing him from the throne, which they were reluctant to do.

With no one around to control them, the concession hunters continued to pour in and Mbandzeni continued to grant them concessions. This willingness to sign away valuable resources may be partly explained by the king's traditional understanding that the concessions were only temporary permits which could be revoked at any time. It has also been suggested that there was a general belief that every Boer who petitioned the king was either an official or had official connections with the ZAR government. As such, denial of a concession might offend someone in power and this perception was often played up by the concession hunters.

A good example of this kind of double-dealing took place in the middle of 1885 when Vice-President Joubert and landdrost Krogh of Wakkerstroom ordered a meeting with Mbandzeni. Acting as if they were on official business, they brusquely demanded that the king recognize a Boer protectorate over Swaziland. Mbandzeni stalled, saying that several councillors were unwell and no decision could be made without their input. The Boers then withdrew with instructions that they should be recalled when the council was available.

A short while later, Krogh returned in his private capacity and asked Mbandzeni for a grant over a huge tract of land in southern Swaziland. Since this sounded a lot less serious than giving up his nation's independence, the king duly awarded Krogh the grant. Now, it is unlikely that Joubert's protectorate threat had any kind of official backing, as the ZAR would have known that the British would not allow any form of annexation. So, the whole thing appears to have been a ruse cooked up by the two men whereby the king would be softened up by the first demand so that he would cave in on the second. Thus, Krogh and Joubert were able to gain a valuable concession that could be used to build up their political support in Wakkerstroom by providing land at a low rent for farmers in the area.

As a result of this and other sneaky gambits, Mbandzeni was gradually weakened and gave in to the increasingly onerous demands of the concession hunters. All the Royal Council could do was appeal to the British, who simply replied that unless Mbandzeni agreed to a resident commissioner, their hands were tied. With the king at loggerheads with his council and the concessionary vultures circling around the royal kraal, things were not looking good for Swaziland ...

'Offy' enters the picture

By the mid-1880s, the issue of the Komati winterveld came to a head. In 1884, Abel Erasmus, the ZAR border commissioner, started levying taxes from the Swazi living in the Komati area. There was an immediate uproar and the Royal Council appealed to the British to set up beacons along the disputed northern border, which was still unmarked north of Komati Gorge. This was probably a stalling tactic, as negotiations about the border would have taken a long time, but Erasmus kept on collecting taxes nonetheless.

In September 1885, Swazi opposition to this controversial practice turned violent when Matsafeni Mdluli (the Hhohho *indvuna*) told his people to stop paying taxes to Erasmus. The Boer commissioner responded by seizing cattle from non-compliant Swazis. This made things worse and, in March 1886, Hanyane Mkhatshwa (Mawewe's son) took up arms against Erasmus' police force. Mbandzeni was also angry about losing Hanyane's cattle which partially belonged to him (as they were originally a gift to Mawewe).

Then Hanyane got involved with a notorious 'border ruffian' named Charlie du Pont. Along with a bunch of other ne'er-do-wells such as Bob McNab, Du Pont had moved into Swaziland to get away from the law. Many of these hellraisers lived along the summit of the Lubombo, which gave them easy access into southern Mozambique. From this eyrie, this group of bandits spent their time raiding cattle, smuggling contraband, robbing returning mine workers, drinking and fighting amongst themselves. They were such a colourful bunch that the path which led from Tembe Drift (the nearest ship docking point to Swaziland) over the Lubombo, past Bob McNab's shack and along the Lusutfu Valley to Bill Fyfe's store on the western border became known as 'The Gin Road'.

It was on one of his 'trading trips' in Mozambique that Du Pont heard of the death of the Shangaan king, Mzila. Hanyane, as we've said, was the son of Mawewe, Mzila's brother and rival for the Shangaan throne. As such, Hanyane was a threat to Mzila's heir, and the Shangaan council conspired with Du Pont to lure Hanyane away from Swaziland and dispose of him.

Du Pont subsequently visited Hanyane and told him of Mzila's death. He then offered to accompany Hanyane to the Gaza Province of

Mozambique, where Du Pont promised to organize European support for a coup. Hanyane was thrilled and prepared to leave with Du Pont. However, Mbandzeni heard of these plans and detained Hanyane.

Du Pont was furious and demanded 750 head of cattle (to make up for the cattle Mzila's people had offered him). This was refused. Abel Erasmus also heard of the scheme and tried to levy a fine on Hanyane for participating in a political plot. Mbandzeni bristled at Erasmus' cheek and came to the conclusion that if he didn't get rid of the ZAR presence in the northern territory, his authority over the area would be over.

So, once again, Mbandzeni protested to the British, who once again wrote to the ZAR state secretary, who once again denied everything and, once again, the British wrote back to Mbandzeni that unless he allowed a British Resident into the country, her Majesty's government could do nothing to help.

Finally, in December 1885, David Forbes cajoled a response from Mbandzeni, which he presented to the British. It read: "[since the Swazi people had] not been in the habit of going out to work, they were very poor in cattle and money". Mbandzeni/Forbes then asked whether it would be possible for the British "to proclaim a Protectorate for the present to prevent any other power establishing a claim there, until they saw their way to paying for the expense of a resident". However, the clause in the London Convention that guaranteed Swazi independence specified that no one could annex Swaziland without the express approval of all sides, and this was something that the ZAR would never grant.

The stalemate continued in this manner until March 1886, when farmers on the vast Ferreira/Maritz grazing concession demanded autonomy and incorporation into ZAR. Despite Swazi protests, the settlers stubbornly insisted that the concession amounted to a deed of sale, and went ahead with their plans to create the 'Little Free State'. A few months later, the tag team of Joubert and Krogh again approached Mbandzeni with a demand that he accept ZAR dominion, only to return a short time later with a less imposing request for a hefty mineral concession.

Finally, Mbandzeni realized that he was being played and reconciled himself to the fact that he needed outside help to deal with these treacherous Europeans. And so it was, in November 1886, that Mbandzeni asked Theophilus 'Offy' Shepstone Junior to be his resident advisor.

It seemed like a good choice. 'Offy' Shepstone came from a good family, with strong ties to the British administration, and he appeared to be someone who would look after Swaziland's best interests. He also had two retainers in Swaziland at the time, and they helped present *uMfowethu* (our brother) a good light.

Unfortunately, Offy was a bit of a bad egg. He was low on scruples and on the verge of personal bankruptcy. He needed to make a lot of money fast and didn't really mind how. So he leapt at the Swazi opportunity and took up the post by February 1887. He was now in control of all concessions (including the collection of revenue) and white affairs in general. It was one helluva job description.

The British response was muted and it was clearly stated that Offy was working in his personal capacity, and not as a representative of Britain. The Boer graziers were outraged, of course, because they had been hoping to convert their grazing licences to freehold tenure. This was not going to happen on Offy's watch.

So talk of a Boer invasion started up yet again and the graziers visited Mbandzeni several times, under the leadership of Stoffel Tosen, to demand that grazing leases be extended to include mineral rights. Tosen was firmly rebuffed and he subsequently threatened an invasion, even nominating a date in April. Under pressure from the British, the ZAR clipped Tosen's wings and the invasion didn't take place.

But Offy's new role also made the British concession holders feel threatened. They didn't like being relegated to a secondary position under Shepstone, where they had previously enjoyed direct access to the king. Sensing rebellion, Offy quickly set up a 'White Committee' to oversee the unruly European population of the kingdom.

The whites were now split into two camps. Some, such as the powerful T. B. Rathbone, decided to hitch their wagons to Offy's rising star. Others, such as John Thorburn, remained vehemently opposed to the new advisor. Thorburn's tavern near Mbekelweni soon became a meeting place for white malcontents. The irrepressible Allister Miller later said that it was the availability of cold lager at Thorburn's that made most people turn against Shepstone.

Miller is once again making a joke at the expense of accuracy, but divisions within the white community were certainly hardening against Shepstone. While he did do some good work, such as assembling an official record of all concessions granted so far, Offy was incorrigibly corrupt. He soon started refusing concessions to certain people so that he could keep them for himself or award them to his friends. Forbes sums it up by saying, "We all knew that Shepstone was an adventurer—to a greater extent, I mean, than we were."

The ever-effervescent Miller has this to say on the subject: "There was something very exhilarating ... in the atmosphere at the Embekelweni in those days. Native and European alike were divided into three camps—Shepstonites, Thorburnites and spies. Suppose you were visiting the Embekelweni and you went first to Mr Shepstone, then you were a Shepstonite, but if you went to Mr Thorburn's you were a Thorburnite. If on the other hand you went to Mr Thorburn's and, after staying there [a] half-hour or so, went to say goodbye to Mr Shepstone ... then you were a spy".

Mbandzeni realized then that Offy was skimming money from the concession revenues which he was responsible for collecting. Under the original agreement Shepstone was entitled to half the revenues as a payment for his services, but this wasn't proving to be enough for the king's greedy advisor.

Offy's enemies also starting casting aspersions on Shepstone's loyalty after he granted a railway concession to the ZAR. Furthermore, Sheptsone had visited Pretoria and met Paul Kruger at the end of 1887 (although this may have been a diplomatic visit at the request of Mbandzeni).

The final nail in Offy's coffin came when a dispute broke out over Swaziland's eastern border with Mozambique. The Portuguese claimed that the border ran along the summit of the Lubombo, but the Swazis said it was the Tembe River, farther to the east. Nevertheless, in May 1887, the Portuguese offered farms for sale along the Lubombo. The Swazis protested and appealed for the formation of a Joint Commission, with representatives from Britain, Portugal and the ZAR, to settle the issue.

With Shepstone in charge of the Swazi delegation, the Royal Council felt confident about their case. But the commission found that the 1860

Swazi raids which had pushed the border to the Tembe did not qualify as a 'conquest' and that the Swazi settlements in the region were too recent for a meaningful claim. Furthermore, they declared that several treaties (some of which the Swazis hadn't been party to) defined the boundary as the top of the Lubombo.

The Swazi cause was lost, and the border was set in favour of the Portuguese. Mbandzeni was devastated and Offy was in the dogbox. Not only had Shepstone proved himself incapable of controlling the white population in the kingdom, he had stolen money from the king and failed to win over the border commission. He had to go. But Mbandzeni couldn't just fire Shepstone, because Offy now had powerful support in court and his family was still influential in Natal.

So, at the instigation of Offy's detractors, Mbandzeni demanded that Shepstone hand over his financial statements, detailing all revenues that had been collected. Offy refused and Mbandzeni sent him a letter that restricted his official powers.

Even though Offy was now no longer responsible for the revenues, he held onto his post as resident advisor and retained many of his political powers. He was even able to renegotiate his own remuneration—an annual salary of £600, as well as transfer duties on concessions that should have been payable to the crown. This prompted Shepstone to write in his diary, "Of course they are muffs, as the revenue from duties will be very considerable shortly".

Concession mania!

It has been said that the loss of Swaziland's eastern territories crushed Mbandzeni; his health started to suffer. Whatever happened, he certainly seemed to resign himself to his fate. As the dejected king said to Miller in November of that year, "I know the concessions are bad. But I have white men all around me. By force they have taken the countries of all my neighbours. If I do not give them rights here, they will take them. Therefore I give when they pay. Why should we not eat before we die?"

With control over the concessions now in the hands of the White Committee, with the opportunistic Allister Miller as its secretary, the rush for grants became a frenzy. Already, by 1886, most of the available winter pasturage had been signed away. By the end of 1887, most of the mineral rights had gone. But from 1888 the gloves came off, and concessionaires started applying for kingdom-wide monopolies over every commercial service or resource imaginable.

All in all, there were more than 500 concessions granted at prices that ranged from one goat to thousands of pounds. Apart from the grazing and mineral concessions, these included monopolies over pawnbroking, photography, auctioneering, advertising, banking, railways, railway refreshment bars, the generation and use of steam power (which was not part of the railways concession), insurance, lotteries, printing, the mint, patent medicines (awarded to the outlaw Bob McNab), all trading rights south of the Usuthu River, electro-chemical gold and silver processing, tanning and tanneries, the rights to deal spirits, import and manufacture of drill bits, tobacco, cement, milling, the right to build townships, gas manufacturing, oil extraction, orphanages, importation of machinery, manufacture of cotton and linen, dynamite, gun powder and wool washing. Towards the end, Mr R. Lessack even got the concession to grant concessions.

David Forbes describes the scene at Mbandzeni's kraal during the last feverish years of the king's reign: "There were dozens of men walking about the king's kraal with concession papers in their pocket, ready to be put before the king to be signed. We were keeping our eyes open for our respective agent, or special chief. He would at long last show himself and make a sign, as obscure as possible from the vision of the other white men. We strolled around as unconcerned as possible in the direction he had indicated, and there meet your chief who would tell you he had spoken to the king.

"When the interview was at last arranged with the king, your chief would take you by the hand along through the back passage of the kraal into the presence of the king, where he considered he had found a spot which was a haven of refuge from the white concession hunters. You would tell the king you wanted a piece of land as big as your hand, on which you wanted the mineral rights.

"If your luck was in, and the king was in a good mood, he would say 'let me see your money', and never in your life did you part with your money quicker and more willingly. The king would say 'where is the pen?' and it would come from your pocket; also a small bottle of ink. He would then make a cross where indicated, as his signature. Then there would be a scramble between the chiefs present to sign as witnesses, and the custom was to give each chief who signed one pound. A place was always reserved for Sandhlana and Tekhuba to sign."

The image of Mbandzeni hiding in his kraal, trying to avoid the ceaseless yammering of the concession hunters, is melancholic. The king clearly wasn't happy; his council was similarly distressed. Sandlane, a venerable elder statesman, was particularly opposed to the concessionaires' presence. However, many councillors in the court seemed to embrace this free-for-all and aligned themselves with certain concession hunters in exchange for kickbacks. So, even his most trusted advisors would hound Mbandzeni on behalf of their white 'colleagues'.

Mbandzeni's health worsened throughout 1888. By the end of the year, he was ailing and accusations of poisoning and witchcraft started to swirl around the court. Conflict also broke out between the younger regiments (who resented the pillage of their land) and the older councillors (such as such as Tikhuba, Kwabala, Bulana and Juako) who were said to be benefiting from the whole mess.

Then, in October, Sandlane was clubbed to death for allegedly plotting to replace the king with one of Mbandzeni's brothers. Several months of fighting followed, and the country was in a state of constant alarm. Tikhuba, it is said, took the opportunity to prey on the weak king and actively conspired with Thorburn and Miller to make the most of the political uncertainty.

And so it was, in early 1889 that Allister Miller replaced Offy Shepstone as the king's secretary. It was like giving your car keys to a crook. By now, it was increasingly obvious that Mbandzeni didn't have long to go, and the concessionaires embarked on a final scramble to get what else they could before he kicked the bucket. Now everything was fair game, and Swaziland was picked clean.

Unfortunately, the only help available to Swaziland came in the inopportune shape of Offy Shepstone. This dirty little pot now started calling the kettle black, and tried to stir up trouble against the Miller/Thorburn regime. Senior councillors such as Kwahlakwahla, Mhlonitwa, Maloyi, Mancibane and Tibati, the Queen Mother, supported Shepstone. There were even rumours that Natal was about to send in an army to reinstate Offy. However, Offy's diary shows that he was much more concerned about getting paid than he was about the fate of Swaziland.

By the middle of 1889, Mbandzeni was clearly on his last legs. Without Mbandzeni, there would be no more concessions, and there was a rush to the finish. The possibly delirious king thus ended his days in a flurry of last-minute concessions, one of which was signed just 36 hours before his death.

The extent of these final concessions was staggering. Bob McNab bought the right to all wood on the western side of the Lubombo (with the stipulation that the wood around caves is not to be cut). Farming, trading and wood rights over all mineral concessions were sold off to different people. N. H. Cohen got the right to collect and receive custom duties in exchange for a flat fee to the king.

It was a bunfight at the royal kraal. Syndicates were formed and a company was floated on the London Stock Exchange to purchase and exploit these ludicrous concessions in anticipation of the huge profits to come. In June 1889, the White Commission officially condemned some of the more outrageous concessions, but this seems to be because their members were negotiating in a personal capacity and cutting the commission out of the loop.

Then, towards the end, the king granted several concessions that would threaten Swaziland's ability to govern itself, and even its independence.

J. R. Harrington negotiated the 'power of attorney to collect the king's revenue', including licences and taxes, for a flat payment of £12,000 per year. This concession was sold to the ZAR a few months later.

Thorburn then cottoned onto the concept 'unallotted' and got the 'Unalloted Mineral Lands and Forfeited or Abandoned Concession' concession. This gave him mineral rights over all land not parcelled out by December 1888. He then went one step further and got the 'Unalloted Lands' concession which gave him farming rights over all land south of the Komati not accounted for by June 1889, including those lands that fell vacant once earlier leases had lapsed. By implication, Mbandzeni had given away the grazing rights around his own kraal.

Thorburn, for his part, soon sold all his interests to the Swaziland Corporation Ltd. and promptly left the country. He returned only once, to hire a party of Swazi dancers for a circus in Britain, but did pay homage to his generous benefactor by giving his son the unlikely name 'Lourenco Marques Mbandzeni Thorburn'. Meanwhile, Allister Miller married Thorburn's daughter and took over management of the Swaziland Corporation.

Finally, in October 1889, Mbandzeni died. He was still a young man of around 36. He was buried in a cave in the Mdzimba Mountains, close to his short-lived predecessor Ludvonga. As his secretary, Miller was responsible for opening the king's safe. It contained the grand total of £8,000—not much to show after selling off the nation.

The concession rush was finally over, but things were now in a colossal mess. Hundreds of unworkable concessions, representing almost the complete wealth of Swaziland, were in the hands of private individuals. The Swazis felt that the concessions were invalid and the concessionaires weren't about to back down from their claims. No one knew what was going to happen next.

Surprisingly, it was Offy who came to the rescue. The Royal Council now gave him sole control over European and concessionaire affairs and he tried to impose calm on the nation. Suddenly, *uMfowethu* seemed to grow a conscience. After the meeting that granted him his new powers, he wrote in his diary: "I shall never forget the scene. *Alone* with the whole nation represented. All looking to me, treating me as their king … Never in a savage country has the *whole* nation done as they did … I am in a fix with a tremendous burden on my shoulders to carry now. I only hope I shall carry it right and save the nation".

The end of Swaziland?

How could things have gotten so bad? Why didn't someone step in and stop the madness before it came to this?

Well, Mbandzeni must certainly accept some of the blame. Yes, he may have been broken by his territorial setbacks and his councillors were often unhelpful, but the king had the final say in these matters, and he said "yes".

Some recent chroniclers have therefore accused Mbandzeni of being overly acquisitive (with a penchant for fat women and greyhounds). Others have said he was an alcoholic who would sign anything for a swig of gin. But contemporary observers paint a much more even-handed picture of the king.

William Penfold, Shepstone's secretary, had this to say on the subject: "Umbandeni gave grants of land minerals freely—in most cases for very small amounts. The prevailing idea that the gin case was the medium is quite inaccurate. The notion that uMbandeni was a drunkard is an equally mistaken one. The writer saw uMbandeni continually from 1886 till his death, and never once did see him touch wine or spirits. Good strong kaffir beer he drank in large quantities, which accounted for his fat—but nothing stronger.

"He was an imposing personage and in all respects he looked a king. He walked with slow stately steps and carried himself with great dignity. To see him in front of his regiments with leopard skins on loins and shoulders and a single long white ostrich plume on his head, addressing some thousands of his men fully armed with their shields before them and bunches of black ostrich feathers on their heads was a sight not readily to be forgotten. It is a great pity that no photograph … was taken."

Mbandzeni's reluctance to be captured on film is reiterated in an 1887 report from the *Natal Witness* newspaper which states, "He will not allow his photograph to be taken on any consideration whatsoever … One artist said that Cetshwayo and Sekukune had allowed themselves to be photographed. The king's reply was, 'Yes, and where are they now?'"

Mbandzeni's pithy response shows that he was neither stupid nor naïve. Even the partisan Allister Miller wrote, "It is certain that Mbandnini was influenced by some logical consideration in the policy he adopted. He was a man of remarkable shrewdness, who relied more on tact than force to attain his ends. In 1881 the influence which was brought to bear on him by the British Government led him to accept the limitations of his western and northern boundaries".

So, clearly, the king was doing his best to keep his head above water in the face of strong cross-currents from the British, the Boers, the concessionaires, the farmers, the miners and his own council.

With regard to the external powers circling around Swaziland, we've seen that Britain had grown tired of the king's constant prevarication regarding the installation of a British Resident, and the British

A cluster of homesteads nestled among the boulders, high on the Mdzimba plateau

Above: Looking out over Maguga Dam from the MR1 road

Far left: The Hlope homestead, visited as part of a reciprocal cultural tour

Left: The Dlamini family patriarch takes his cows out to pasture

Top: A traditional dancing display at Mantenga Cultural Village
Above: Fascinating stone sculptures can be found in most of the craft markets, especially
those along the MR1
Right: A giant statue of the man himself at the King Sobhuza II Memorial Park and Museum

Above: Give him a hand – a woodwork artist busy sanding down his latest sculpture
Below: Weaving grass mats the traditional way, in the Ngwempisi Valley
Right: The beautiful Phophonyane Falls, near Pigg's Peak, said to have formed by the falling tears of a mournful maiden

FLYING-ANGELS

Top left: The enticing showroom at Swazi Candles is full of waxy delights, Malkerns

Far left: Celestial intervention at Rainbow Angel, Mantenga Craft Market

Above: A curio shop built around an old minivan, Mantenga Craft Market

Left: What do bald people want? Mohair. Richly coloured fabrics from Rosecraft Weavers

Top: The spectacular view from Shewula Mountain Camp over the Mbuluzi River valley
Left: The Mkhondvo River cuts an elegant course through Grand Valley, made hazy by the forested slopes
Above: No better way to cool down than swimming in the Mkhondvo, and you can do your washing too

Top: Bushman rock art at the Nsangwini shelter

Above: The Malolotja Nature Reserve is blooming marvellous

Left: Minerals have been mined from Ngwenya Mountain for more than 40,000 years, although this huge excavation is a bit more recent.

Above: The Mantenga Craft Market is full of things that are just begging to be bought

Far left: Wicker, woodwork and weaving at the Thandabantu craft market, Ezulwini Valley

Left: 'Do you think that giraffe will fit into our luggage?' Too many choices at the Buhle Besibeko Semaswati Handicraft market, next to the Ezulwini Sun

The perfect place to gather your thoughts, looking out into the Malolotja Nature Reserve.

treasury was also advising against any costly adventures in troublesome southern Africa. So, Britain resolved to toe a middle line that sought to stall British involvement while, at the same time, discouraging ZAR expansion. The ZAR, of course, was actively complicit in the concession rush and bought out many of the most important concessions in anticipation of future expansion.

But there is another, more insidious reason why the destruction of Swaziland was permitted: Rhodesia.

Many of the more sweeping concessions were backed by over £50 000 in loans from Hermann Eckstein and Company—a leading financial firm on the Witwatersrand goldfields, known as the Corner House. The first mention of such a venture in the company records comes when 'Messrs Kuranda and Marais' approached Eckstein with a proposal to buy several valuable concessions. Eckstein wrote that it might be worthwhile to "get hold of them with a view to [our] being able to dispose of these concessions to the government at a fair profit".

As it turned out, the asking price was too high and it fell to the colourful entrepreneur, Alois Nellmapius, to make the next proposal. He persuaded Eckstein to buy the Mint and Licences concession, which could be held in trust for the ZAR until it annexed the territory. The purchase price was £30,000, and the ZAR promised to pay £53,000, when Swaziland was theirs.

However, annexation was far from certain and the concession would be worthless without it, so Eckstein tried to secure some political guarantees that would support the ZAR's ambitions. But Eckstein's partner in Paris, Jules Porges, was against the project, as he didn't want to alienate the company's British interests. Eckstein argued that buying the concessions would make the ZAR feel obliged to the Corner House, which would stand them in good stead. As J. B. Taylor (another partner) candidly said: "there can be no sentiment at a moment when you have to choose between gaining and losing money and influence." Besides, with £30,000 already sunk into the project, there was no turning back.

Meanwhile, the ZAR was also busy buying up pivotal concessions, including railways, electricity and telegraphs. Allister Miller himself visited Pretoria to peddle concessions, although he later said that he had no political intentions and only did it for the money.

By now the monopoly concessions (which technically made Swaziland ungovernable) had largely fallen into the hands of the ZAR and the mining capitalists. The former wanted to annex, so that they could finally get their route to the sea, and the latter sought increased control over the subcontinent's economic and political life.

Then suddenly, on 3 May 1889, Paul Kruger made an offer to the British Government. He would relinquish any claims on the land north of the Limpopo, provided the ZAR was allowed to annex Swaziland, with the stated intention of building a road across the territory to Kosi Bay.

Now this may just have been Kruger chancing his luck, but it is unlikely that he was speaking unilaterally. At this time, Cecil John Rhodes was trying to get permission from Britain to start a Chartered Company that would take over Bechuanaland (Botswana) and Matabeleland (Rhodesia/Zimbabwe and Zambia). The ZAR had claims over the same territories, and Swaziland thus became a convenient bargaining chip.

Thus, by December 1889, the ZAR, Rhodes' Chartered Company, Jules Porges and Werner Beit (another powerful Randlord) were pressuring the British Government to agree to the annexation of Swaziland by the ZAR. And this was when Kruger made his offer. The timing seems a little bit too convenient to have been a coincidence.

Despite Kruger's overture and Rhodes' power, the British Colonial Office didn't want to make a decision just yet. Instead, they sent a joint commission to Swaziland under Sir Francis de Winton and General P. J. Joubert (of the ZAR). The British delegation also included Advocate Oliver Schreiner (nephew of the author Olive Schreiner) and Captain Baden-Powell (who would later found the Boy Scouts). The commission was instructed to observe and report but, prior to their arrival, the two leaders decided to establish a temporary administration for whites in the country and set-up a special tribunal to sort out the concessions mess.

By the time they arrived, however, Mbandzeni was dead. Furthermore, Tibati (the former *ndlovukazi* and now the queen regent) had removed Allister Miller from office and reinstated Shepstone as Resident Advisor. The joint commission, in accordance with Tibati and the Royal Council, then disbanded the White Commission and established a three-way Provisional Government Committee with Shepstone as the Swazi agent, Colonel Richard Martin as the British representative and D. J. Esselen acting on behalf of the ZAR.

President Kruger then asked for a meeting with the new British high commissioner, Sir Henry Loch, to sort out the Swaziland question. Rhodes also attended the meeting, which became known as the First Swaziland Convention of 1890. With Rhodes' plans for the land north of the Limpopo now firmly on the agenda, Loch and Kruger agreed that the 'Little Free State' concession along the north bank of the Phongolo River should be officially incorporated into the ZAR. This trade-off gave the Boers a potential route to the sea, and Rhodes got a free hand to embark on his great colonial adventure in the north. Paradoxically, the convention also confirmed Swaziland's independence and installed the 'triumvirate government' committee as the official government of Swaziland.

The new government then bought up Alfred Bremer's hotel and lands, close to Mbandzeni's old kraal, and 'Bremersdorp' became the new administrative capital of Swaziland. Outside the building a Swazi flag was flown, flanked by a British Union Jack and the ZAR Vierkleur (four colours). A civil administration was soon set up, which included five officials, an eight-man judicial committee, a jailer and five justices of the peace (at Pigg's Peak, Fyfe's Store, Forbes Reef, Mahamba and Lubombo). A police force was also established with twelve European and 36 African constables. The Government Committee remained in control of the country for the next five years.

Although the three-headed beast now in charge of state affairs quarrelled incessantly, it seemed certain that Swaziland would soon become part of the ZAR. All that remained was to work out the terms of the annexation. The conquest by the concessionaires was thus complete, and Swaziland would not regain its independence for another 70 years.

King Bhunu (1894–1899)

The next in line for the Swazi throne was a teenager named Bhunu (the Boer), and aged about 14. His mother, Labotsibeni Mdluli, became the new *ndlovukazi* and established her capital at kwaNobamba (the place of the catcher). In order to prevent several rivals to the throne from acting up, it was decided that the new king should be 'shown' to the nation earlier than usual, and so he was in June 1890—less than a year after Mbandzeni's death. William Penfold, Shepstone's secretary, wrote this account of the grand event:

"Whites were strictly prohibited from attending the ceremony. Nevertheless, after completion of the ceremony, Shepstone, [myself], Colonel Martin and Esselen were invited and shown the new young king who had curious old articles of regalia, which included an unornamented old iron rod which was struck in the ground in front of him. He sat on a tortoise shell and on his arm he had a particular large copper ring and in his hand he had a knife with burnt handle of Swazi manufacture and an assegai washed in gall of an ox".

Unfortunately, King Bhunu did not have an easy time of it. He had grown up during the concession rush and had formed an appropriately unflattering opinion of the white men who now effectively owned his country. Furthermore, the Triumvirate Government was firmly in control and Bhunu felt excluded from power. There was also growing tension in court between Tibati (the queen regent) and Labotsibeni (the *ndlovukazi*).

As a result of all this, Bhunu was bitter and frustrated. His feelings of impotence grew after he was officially installed as King Ngwane V in 1894, and he started exhibiting behaviour that won him an ugly reputation as 'headstrong, cruel and warlike'. Although some historians point out his moderation in the face of overwhelming odds, Bhunu was known to deal mercilessly with Swazi trouble-makers, and generally had them executed on the spot.

Meanwhile, the Government Committee was given the task of sorting out the concession debacle. With over 500 signed concessions ranging from the sublime to the ridiculous, it was decided that a Concessions Court be established to evaluate each claim. Three judges were chosen (although two would later leave) and they attempted to impose some kind of 'European' justice on the situation.

By the end of it, 364 concessions were found to be legally binding— including the outrageous Unallotted Lands concession that was granted just a few days before Mbandzeni's death, giving Thorburn and Watkins farming and grazing rights over one sixth of Swaziland for an annual rental of £50. The controversial 'taxation' concession was also upheld and quickly sold to the ZAR, who already had valuable monopolies on railways, electricity, telegraphs etc.

However, the rivalry between the Boers and the British had not been resolved and a Second Swaziland Convention was called between Kruger and Loch (no Swazi representatives were invited). This took place in 1893 and the 'Organic Proclamation' it generated essentially gave the ZAR all rights of protection and administration over Swaziland, stopping just short of outright annexation. On the plus side, the king would remain in control over Swazi affairs and the Swazi people were graciously promised that they would still be allowed to farm on the land.

The Second Convention document was presented to the queen regent for her signature, which was a prerequisite for the British government's acceptance of the convention. But Tibati refused to sign and decided to appeal to her counterpart, Queen Victoria, 'not because [they] loved her the more, but feared her the less'. Tibati also finally removed the ineffectual Offy Shepstone and replaced him with George Hulett, an advocate from Natal, in the new post of Chief Secretary to the Swazi nation.

With Hulett in tow, a delegation was sent to England towards the end of 1894. They pleaded their case to the Colonial Secretary, Lord Ripon, but received a very unhelpful response that basically said, "thank you for your allegiance in the past, but we think that it would be best if you pop along back to Swaziland and accept ZAR administration". It is thought that the reply was prepared before the Swazi delegation even arrived in Britain and, as soon as the response was delivered, the delegates were handed tickets for the first ship back to South Africa.

To drive the point home, Loch and Kruger met again at the third Swaziland Convention and made Swaziland a protectorate of the ZAR. The king would retain his position (as long as he didn't interfere with the white man's business), and the ZAR would continue to collect all private revenue in exchange for a monthly fee of £1,000. Furthermore, Swazi subjects would get a tax exemption for three years, thereafter getting taxed at the same rate as Africans living in the Transvaal. English and Dutch would be the official languages and the sale of liquor to Swazi people was prohibited.

Once again, the Royal Council refused to sign the document, but this time the convention made allowance for unilateral proclamations. And so it was, in December 1894, that the ZAR declared Swaziland would henceforth be its protectorate.

The Boer occupation

The new ZAR-run administration took over Swaziland in February 1895. They assumed control over the old triumvirate government offices at Bremersdorp/Manzini, and installed Johannes Krogh as the ZAR's Special Commissioner. The Swazi flag was taken down and a British consul was stationed in the territory to keep an eye on things. Louis Botha was as appointed Justice of the Peace and Native Commissioner, but only lasted about a year in the post before being called away on more important business.

It was a tough time both for King Bhunu and Swaziland. Apart from losing their self-determination, the Swazis also suffered greatly from the rinderpest epidemic which swept through the region. Within ten years, 90 per cent of all Swazi cattle had died and the nation was crippled by the loss. Furthermore, the king was reportedly fighting with his *ndlovukazi*, Labotsibeni, and there were constant threats of civil conflict.

The ZAR then suffered a major setback when the British pulled a sneaky move by incorporating the so-called Trans-Pongola territories into Zululand. This was a crucial chunk of land (later known as Ngwavuma) inhabited by Swazi-aligned tribes that lay southeast of Swaziland, between the Lubombo Mountains and the coast at Kosi Bay. The ZAR's long-deferred dream of establishing a free port was thus dashed once again and they found themselves the custodians of a uselessly landlocked territory.

The Swazis were similarly outraged by the British annexation of a district that they considered theirs (and still do). Things got even worse in 1898 when the ZAR began taxing the 'natives' with a poll tax of £2 per male and ten shillings per female, as well as with a road tax of 2/6d. Since the people of Swaziland had never worked on a cash currency basis, many men were forced to move to South African cities or the mines of the Witwatersrand to find jobs, and this greatly undermined the traditional social structures of the kingdom.

If that wasn't bad enough, Bhunu now started suffering from bouts of ill health. This resulted in a 'smelling out' of the witches who were trying to poison him, and a senior *induna* named Mbhabha was murdered as a result. Such goings-on were not going to be tolerated by the Boer Government, and Bhunu was summoned to court at Bremersdorp.

The king was outraged that he should be dragged before a court that had no authority over him, according to Swazi tradition, but the Boers were adamant. So, in May 1895, Bhunu marched into Bremersdorp, accompanied by 2,000 warriors in full regalia. According to some sources, Bhunu freely admitted to killing Mbhabha because he was a wizard, and Krogh replied that the matter would have to be referred to Pretoria.

Bhunu then reportedly told Krogh, "You say the matter will go further. You say that there are others who will inquire into this matter. Who are these others? I only recognize you. I was only shown you. I am very angry with you. I am so angry that if I could I would eat you up."

With that, a defiant Bhunu left the town. But the damage had been done. The spectacle of a singing, dancing, chanting Swazi horde was too much for the Boers and they responded by fortifying Bremersdorp. They also called for reinforcements from Pretoria. Soon there were around 2,000 white soldiers in Swaziland, armed and ready for battle.

Meanwhile, Bhunu moved with his regiments to a hideaway high on the slopes of Mdzimba Mountain. War talk swirled around the country and it seemed that a violent conflict was about to break out.

When Bhunu received a second summons to attend the court on a murder charge, it seemed that war was unavoidable. But the Swazi elders prevailed on Bhunu to retreat to Zululand, where he sought protection from the British.

The new British High Commissioner, Sir Alfred Milner, soon found himself caught up in the diplomatic furore. Kruger was now demanding that the Swazi monarchy be abolished and the country split into four chieftainships, following the model pioneered by the British in Zululand, with Kruger himself as the Paramount Chief. Milner refused to consider changing the terms of the 1894 convention, which guaranteed the authority of the Swazi king over 'native' affairs. Nevertheless, it was agreed that Bhunu be sent back to Swaziland on condition that his safety was assured.

Bhunu thus faced the court again in September, and the trial lasted two weeks. The indignant king was found guilty of permitting public violence and was fined £500. He was also told to pay an additional

£1,000 to the ZAR and £146 to the British Government to defray the costs of the trial and associated expenses. This was deducted from the king's annual salary of £12,000.

War had been averted, but the ructions caused by the case prompted the British and ZAR governments to add an amendment to the convention which made the king and his chiefs subject to the authority of the courts and laws of the ZAR. The king was now forbidden from passing judgement over serious crimes committed by his subjects and his traditional powers were subjugated in favour of the European court at Bremersdorp. It was a bitter pill to swallow.

The Anglo-Boer War

After all the excitement of Bhunu's trail, Swaziland settled down for a few months of peace and quiet. Queen Victoria's Diamond Jubilee and Paul Kruger's birthday were celebrated by Boer and Briton alike. Bhunu seemed to be playing ball, and was even invited to Pretoria for an audience with Paul Kruger himself.

This unlikely state visit took place in April 1899, when Bhunu rode into the ZAR capital with 1,000, warriors. Kruger apparently approved of the young king and tried to work his lugubrious charm on the Swazi monarch. Krogh was so encouraged by this meeting that he laid the cornerstone for a grand new government office in Bremersdorp.

But there were very dark storm clouds on the horizon. Conflict between the British and the ZAR had been mounting ever since the British defeat at Majuba in 1880. The lucrative Witwatersrand goldfields, discovered in 1886, had further raised the stakes. And Joseph Chamberlain's plans to establish a federation of southern African states under Britain were at a very advanced stage. War was becoming inevitable.

And so it was, in October 1899, that the Second Anglo-Boer War (also known as the South African War) broke out. It was to be a protracted 'war of attrition' that would change the face of southern Africa forever.

In the months leading up to the war, Swaziland's European population of around 1,400 was warned about the upcoming conflict, and many left the territory. Mines and ranches were shut down and even the British Consul eventually packed his bags. A few days before the war broke out, Krogh issued an official notice advising all Europeans to leave (except for those who might be called up for military service). Soon only a handful of Boer garrisons remained, and an administration centre was established at General Burgher's laager near Amsterdam on the western border.

A short time later, all the garrisons were withdrawn from the territory, as the men were needed elsewhere. The ZAR sent King Bhunu a letter by that said, "And now, Ubunu, the government places Swaziland under your care and trusts that you will act accordingly. Whereupon I want to advise you, purely as a friend, to rule Swaziland well and in peace".

According to some, Bhunu made the most of his long-awaited authority and began a reign of terror that drenched the country in the blood of his opponents. Others claim that he was not 'as cruel as a cat' and was merely flexing his political muscles for the first time.

Whatever the case, it was to be a short-lived victory. On 10 December 1899, just two months after war broke out, Bhunu collapsed during the *incwala* ceremony and died. He was in his early twenties.

The king's death was temporarily hidden from the people until the ceremony could be completed, whereupon he was buried close to his father on Mdzimba Mountain. The council now had to choose a new king, and quickly. But there were several wives with potential heirs, and the council could not reach a unanimous decision. Eventually, with Labotsibeni's guidance, the council settled on an infant named Nkhotfotjeni, the son of Lomawa—one of Bhunu's most recent wives. The new king's age meant that there would be a lengthy regency period; Labotsibeni rose to the challenge and ruled in conjunction with Malunge (a brother of Bhunu) until 1921.

Luckily, Labotsibeni was by all accounts a 'hale and hearty woman, alert and active, with an untiring zeal when it came to the government of the Swazi nation'. Another contemporary said that she was 'a woman of extraordinary diplomatic ability and strength of character, experienced and capable'.

Swaziland was also fortunate to be relatively untouched by the Boer War. Labotsibeni and her councillors determined that this was a white man's affair, and they resolved to remain neutral in the conflict. A couple of Swazis, of their own volition, acted as scouts for the British or the Boers and a couple of homesteads along the border were burnt down by passing commandos. But, on the whole, it was business as usual in the kingdom.

However, Swaziland was used as a convenient corridor through which the British from Natal could access the eastern Transvaal. This became important after the British decided to try and blow up the strategically important Boer railway line to Delagoa Bay, which ran across the Komati River north of Swaziland. David Forbes Jnr., an old Swazi hand, led one such expedition but failed to destroy the bridge.

Then a diminutive German adventurer named Ludwig Steinacker entered the picture. He was a former Prussian army officer who had been knocking around South Africa for a few years before being commissioned by the British General Buller to try his hand at some sabotage.

Steinacker and a handful of irregular soldiers thus rode off towards Swaziland. By the time they reached the Lubombo he had recruited a force of 40 men, and the group was nicknamed 'the 40 Thieves'. Steinacker then sent some Swazis to buy goods at Komatipoort, and they reported back that a Boer squadron of 100 men was guarding the bridge. Steinacker subsequently chose a smaller railway bridge between Malelane and Komatipoort, and successfully blew it to pieces.

It wasn't a major setback for the Boers, who quickly repaired the damage, but Steinacker was encouraged. Next, he managed to ambush a small group of Boers, capturing a general in the process. This delighted the British commanders, who promoted Steinacker to major and gave him permission to raise a troop of horsemen, who became known as 'Steinacker's Horse'. Their job was to patrol the Mozambique border and make a general nuisance of themselves—an obligation which they fulfilled with aplomb.

The base of Steinacker's Horse was on the Lubombo near the kraal of Chief Lomahasha, on the Mozambican border, and from this location he launched an attack on Bremersdorp in 1901. There were few people left to defend the small town and Steinacker captured eight men and their wagons. He also looted the little village and found £6,000 hidden under the floor of Gustav Schwab's store.

From their new headquarters at Bremersdorp, Steinacker's Horse proceeded to raid the Hhohho region where they captured Prince Mancibane, who was accused of helping the Boers. They also found another £3,500 buried under the floor of B. B. Stewart's shop at Oshoek, and they raided cattle with impunity.

Soon, the Boers were fed up with Steinacker's exploits and sent a commando of 150 men into Swaziland, under General Tobias Smuts. Naturally, Labotsibeni was aware of the Boer's presence in her kingdom, but maintained her neutrality. She did, however, keep a close watch on the movements of Smuts' men and had her scouts send regular reports sent to the royal kraal at Zombodze.

By the time Smuts had reached Mhlambanyatsi, Steinacker had been warned of the impending attack and removed himself to Lomahasha, leaving behind a small force of 30 men to guard the town. Then, under the cover of darkness, Smuts' men charged into Bremersdorp.

With over 3,000 passive Swazi warriors looking on from a hill on the other side of the river, Steinacker's garrison broke up and fled. The Boers killed four horsemen, wounded four others, and captured 17, along with ammunition, supplies and a Maxim gun. About 400 head of cattle and 50 horses were also recovered. Prince Mancibane was released and given a wagon as recompense for his troubles, and Smuts sent some cattle to Labotsibeni as a token of appreciation.

Engorged with victory and liquor, Smuts' men soon got out of hand and set fire to Bremersdorp. Fuelled by casks of gin and the stacks of concession papers housed in the government offices, the town was burnt to the ground. The next morning, only the stone-built jail and the schoolroom remained. Labotsibeni is said to have wept when she heard the news. Even though Smuts triumphantly returned to the Transvaal with horses, cattle, wagons and prisoners, he was reprimanded by his superior, General Louis Botha, and was eventually dismissed entirely.

Steinacker, meanwhile, lived to fight another day and his force grew to include up to 600 men. Steinacker's Horse proceeded to raise hell along the border, effectively cutting off communications between the Boers and Lourenço Marques until the end of the war (and for some time afterwards).

The British Protectorate

The Anglo-Boer war finally ended in 1902, and the nominally victorious British took over the administration of the Orange Free State, the ZAR (Transvaal) and, by implication, Swaziland. In September, F. Enraght-Moony was sent to Swaziland as the new Special Commissioner for the territory, along with a police force of around 150 men. Since Bremersdorp was destroyed, they established a new capital near Mickey Wells' store, on the banks of the Mbabane River.

Several new police posts and district courts were set up across the country. Moony's first act of law enforcement was to ban the carrying of spears. Many members of Moony's white police force went on to settle in Swaziland, where they became influential administrators and businessmen.

White Swazilanders soon began trickling back into the country, and Mbabane started to bustle. A postmaster was appointed, telegraph lines were erected and a 'passenger mule coach service' ran twice weekly between Mbabane and Breyten. The irrepressible Allister Miller, who still owned many valuable concessions, also returned and resurrected his *Times of Swaziland* newspaper. He soon became a leading figure in the town and the main street was named in his honour, until it was renamed Gwamile just a few years ago.

In June 1903, Britain issued the 'Swaziland order-in-council' and formally took over the administration of the territory. The kingdom was now under the authority of the governor of the Transvaal, who ruled on behalf of the British Crown. The governor (and later the high commissioner) was thus empowered to rule 'by proclamation'. However, the order-in-council did not specify the official status of Swaziland, and for the next 65 years it was legally neither a colony, a protectorate, a possession nor a protected state.

On the plus side, the British explicitly acknowledged that the governor was to 'respect any Native laws by which the civil relations of any Native Chiefs, tribes or populations are now regulated, except in so far as many be incompatible with the due exercise of His Majesty's power and jurisdiction or is clearly injurious to the welfare of the said Natives'.

Accordingly, in 1904, the governor of the Transvaal, Alfred Milner, issued a proclamation that stated the laws of the Transvaal would be applied to Swaziland. Sir Godfrey Lagden and Johannes Smuts (the former British Consul) were appointed to take charge of Swazi affairs from Pretoria. The Swazi Royal Council opposed this, as it implied that Swaziland was now a district of the Transvaal.

Following a delegation to Milner's successor, Lord Selborne, this arrangement was slightly changed by another proclamation in 1906 which shifted responsibility from the Transvaal governor to the British High Commissioner for South Africa. Then, in 1907, a resident commissioner and a several other British officials were sent to take up posts in Swaziland itself.

Meanwhile, a Concessions Commission had been established to sort out the exact boundaries of each mineral, land and grazing lease. After an extensive survey it was decided that all concessions should be partitioned into Swazi land, British crown lands and freehold titles. In other words, part of the leases that Mbandzeni had considered to be temporary thus became the concessionaires' private property in perpetuity.

Despite Swazi opposition to this scheme, Lord Selborne (known to the Swazis as *Lisolibovu*—red eye) issued the Land Partition Proclamation of 1907. A Special Commissioner named George Grey was appointed to implement this decree and when he finished, in 1909, 56 per cent of Swaziland was designated as 'Private European Land'. The rest was British Crown Lands, held in trust for the Swazi nation and, as such, the Swazi 'squatters' could be removed at any time.

With no title over their own land, the Swazis were justifiably aggrieved and sent a delegation under Prince Malunge to England to argue their case. The British seemed to be sympathetic and made a vague promise that they would hand over Crown Lands to meet the needs of Swaziland's growing population. This didn't happen, however, and instead some of the land was sold off to Europeans to defray the costs of administration. Furthermore, the Swaziland Crown Lands and Minerals proclamation of 1908 stated that all expired mineral concessions would revert to the British Crown, and not to the Swazi nation as was specified in the original concession documents.

Several delegations to the ever-changing High Commissioner (Selborne, then Gladstone, then Buxton) did manage to get promises of more land for Swazi settlement, but all the various lords-in-charge still refused to grant title deeds to the Swazi nation. Eventually it became clear that the only way to get the land back was to buy it from the new European owners, and Labotsibeni encouraged her people to go to the mines to find work. The money collected in this way was used to purchase 76 000 acres of land as 'national' property. This process continued throughout the decades that followed until more than 60 per cent of Swaziland was back in the hands of the nation (designated as Swazi Nation Land, and held in trust by the king).

Interestingly, in 1908, representatives of the Transvaal, Orange Free State, Natal and the Cape met up for a National Convention. The purpose was to draw up a constitution for the future Union of South Africa. During the convention, it was suggested that the three protectorates or High Commission territories, Basotholand, Swaziland and Bechuanaland (Botswana), be incorporated into the proposed Union.

For once, however, the British were reluctant to hand over the land without consulting the natives involved, and the initiative was dropped. Nevertheless, regular attempts to incorporate the protectorates into the Union were made over the years, but none were successful, especially after the draconian Land Act of 1913 was passed, which reserved over 80 per cent of the land in the Union for white people. One shudders to think what would have happened if these 'independent' states had been absorbed into a country that would soon be ravaged by apartheid.

King Sobhuza II (ruled 1921–1982)

After King Bhunu died in 1899, Labotsibeni reigned as queen regent until the new-born heir, Nkhotfotjeni, came of age. The name 'Nkhotfotjeni' translates as 'stone lizard', because the baby was conceived when Bhunu was living among stones like a lizard as a result of the war that was threatening to break out between the Boers and the Swazis.

As is the Swazi custom, Nkhotfotjeni was separated from his mother, Lomawa, for the duration of the mourning period. The infant was thus secluded in a special kraal called *umtsangala* and didn't see his mother for three years. During this time, Labotsibeni (his grandmother) supervised the 'orphan' child's development and ensured that he received good care from his nursemaids. Labotsibeni also gave Nkhotfotjeni the nickname, Mona (meaning jealousy)—a reflection of the turbulent relations that prevailed between Briton, Boer and Swazis at that time.

After the mourning period was over and a new homestead (called *lusala*) was built, Nkhotfotjeni was reunited with his mother. Labotsibeni now decided that the new king should go to a western-style school. Formerly, all Swazi kings had received a traditional education which was verbally communicated by experienced tutors who sought to transfer 'a totality of ideas, feelings, ways, habits and attitudes [that are] passed down from generation to generation'. However, Labotsibeni realized that the times they were a-changing, and wanted Nkhotfotjeni to be fully prepared to deal with these strange British people who were now 'protecting' the kingdom.

Although there were a number of missionary schools in the country, Labotsibeni didn't want the new king to get caught up in the competition that existed between the various denominations. Instead, she appealed to Lord Kitchener (governor of the Transvaal) to help build a new school near the royal residence. The result was Zombodze, the first national school to be built in Swaziland.

The British also went to find a suitable teacher for the school and sent a telegram to the magistrate in Willowvale in the eastern Cape, asking for an 'absolutely trustworthy native to educate a chief's son and others near Mbabane. A tactful man is needed whose presence would tend to combat the advice of certain half-enlightened natives whose influence is believed to be harmful'. Joseph Xaba was duly sent up, and proceeded to teach Nkhotfotjeni about the strange ways of the white man.

After he finished his primary education, Labotsibeni wanted Nkhotfotjeni to continue his studies. As there were no suitable institutions in Swaziland, this meant he would have to leave the country, and the council was firmly opposed to such an untraditional notion. Labotsibeni, however, was adamant because 'the white man's power lies in money and in books; we too will learn, we too will be rich'. Eventually the new king was sent to Lovedale in the Cape.

By 1918 the nation had decided that the king needed to return to Swaziland to complete his traditional education. Labotsibeni relented, but a tutor was found to continue Nkhotfotjeni's 'western' lessons. The future king thus grew up straddling a generic form of Christianity and traditional Swazi belief systems.

The following year the new king was shown to the nation at a special *sibhimbi* ceremony—an event that can be organized by any parent to celebrate a significant stage in their child's life. Lomawa sang and Labotsibeni started a chant that said "the whites want him to take over the reins of kingship". Around the same time, Nkhotfotjeni took his first wife.

Finally, by 1921, the young man of 22 was ready to be king. Labotsibeni (also known as Gwamile) stepped down after 32 years in power, and Nkhotfotjeni was crowned King Sobhuza II. Lomawa now became the *ndlovukazi*.

In her address to the assembled crowd, Labotsibeni read from a letter she had written to the Resident Commissioner, De Symon Honey: "This is the day I have always longed for. My life has been burdened by an awful responsibility and anxiety. It has been a life full of the deepest emotions that a woman has ever had. Sobhuza gets his name, title and position by the right of inheritance from his ancient house and the kings who have reigned over Swaziland from the immemorial. I and the nation have every confidence in him. I have brought him up as a Swazi prince should be brought up. His spirit is in entire accord with the traditions and feeling and aspirations of his countrymen, and I have given him the opportunity to obtain the very best training which any native youth can obtain here in South Africa. My duties towards him and the nation will never cease until death".

After his coronation, King Sobhuza II danced his first full *incwala* at Lobamba and his new royal kraal was built, called Masundvwini. And so began the longest reign of a monarch in the history of Swaziland.

Over the decades that followed, Sobhuza proved himself to be a peaceful man. He preferred discussion over violence. He believed in a non-racial society, and advocated unity among all Africans. He was also a proud Swazi, and worked tirelessly to regain his country's independence.

As such, his first target was to stop the controversial British 'rule by proclamation' of 1903, which the Swazis had nicknamed *madlangengwenya* (eats like a crocodile) because the British were seen to have grabbed the land and disappeared under the water.

This project started a year before his coronation, when Sobhuza led his first delegation to Cape Town to meet Prince Arthur of Connaught—the new British High Commissioner. It was a cordial affair. The prince thanked Swaziland for its contribution to the first world war (which included some funds and 67 men, black and white). In return, the king asked for the withdrawal of the 1903 order-in-council and requested that the Swazis be allowed to regain control of the national funds and for his authority to be restored.

The high commissioner refused all of the above, and furthermore politely requested that Sobhuza no longer refer to himself as 'King of Swaziland' and rather use the term 'paramount chief'.

Despite the rebuff, Arthur received a warm welcome when he visited Swaziland in 1922—although all audiences were strictly segregated along racial lines. On this occasion, Sobhuza asked for permission to send a delegation to England to argue the Swazi case in person. This request was granted, and the Swazi King arrived in London in January 1923. After meeting with the colonial secretary and King George V, the official reply was that there would be no change in the status quo and sorry for you!

Undeterred, Sobhuza then mounted a legal challenge against Allister Miller and his Swaziland Corporation Limited. More specifically, they challenged the 'Unallotted Lands' Concession which had been signed under some very dodgy circumstances. Unfortunately, the British had already expropriated the concession and the territory now belonged to the British Crown. Furthermore, in 1917, a portion of the land was granted to Miller as a freehold farm, and Miller proceeded to remove Swazi families from his private land despite an explicit clause in the contract forbidding him from doing so.

In any case, the British authorities were on Miller's side and the case was dismissed, with the British administration of Swaziland paying for Miller's legal fees. Sobhuza then applied for leave to appeal to the Privy Council in London, which was granted after a deposit of £500 was paid. A comprehensive case was put together in which the Swazis claimed that the British had no legal right to take over the land as the country had not been acquired by settlement, annexation, conquest or cession. But the Privy Council was unmoved and the appeal was denied.

And still the Swazis kept petitioning and complaining. Eventually several British officials became angry and issued veiled threats that, unless the Swazis started behaving themselves, the government would split Swaziland up into chiefdoms—just as they had done to Zululand. But it was to no avail. The Swazis continued to protest that they had been robbed of their territory by unscrupulous white men who had illegally manhandled the traditional Swazi concept of communal land ownership into the western concept of private tenure.

While all this was going on, the estimable Labotsibeni died in 1925. She had served her people well through two regencies, and had guided the nation for several challenging decades. Sobhuza lost a valuable ally and the Swazi nation lost a hero.

Towards independence

Opposition to the partition of Swaziland didn't subside in the years that followed. As the population grew and available land became scarce, the Swazis continued to complain and petition, but no one was listening.

Then, in 1940, Sobhuza appealed to King George VI—who would later visit Swaziland with his family—because the land shortage had now become acute. This time, the British decided to buy land from the white farmers for the Swazi nation. This became the first of three Swaziland Land Settlements.

Still, true to form, the British felt that the traditional Swazi way of farming was inefficient and repressive, and insisted that the land be organized into collective farms where everything was neatly organized and split equally among families. This was a totally alien concept to the Swazis, who refused to participate in the scheme. Eventually, in 1959, the land was given over to the Swazi authorities to disperse as they saw fit. Interestingly, some Swazi commentators have said that if the Swazis had been open to the collective farming suggestion, it would have revolutionized the food production of the kingdom and made it less reliant on imports from its neighbours. Ah well …

Sobhuza's other burning desire was to get the king reinstated as Swaziland's head of state. As things stood, the king was in charge of 'traditional' affairs and the high commissioner was in charge of the courts, police, finances, administration, foreign policy, etc. Additionally, in 1921, a European Advisory Committee (EAC) had been formed to look after white interests.

This division of power had never been popular, and opposition to the scheme became more strident after the Native Administration Proclamation of 1944 was issued, which gave the British commissioners power over Swaziland's traditional administration, such as the authority to appoint chiefs. The Swazis objected so vehemently to the proclamation that it was revoked by a second Native Administration Proclamation in 1950, which restored the *Ngwenyama's* portfolio over internal Swazi affairs (subject to British approval, of course). 'Native Courts' were also set up to settle less serious local disputes.

In the same year, 1950, the National Treasury Proclamation was issued. This provided for the establishment of a national fund that was administered by the high commissioner, who could allocate as much of the Native Tax to the fund as he saw fit. The king was then given permission to use the National Treasury; an important step forward in Swaziland's self-administration.

Meanwhile, during World War II, a regiment called the Swazi Pioneers served in the Middle East, Tripoli and with distinction at the Battle of Anzio under their commanding officer, Colonel Herbert Johnson. When the global conflict had ended, the king set up the Lifa Fund. Under Lifa, surplus cattle (herds of more than ten) were sold off and part of the proceeds were used to buy back more land for the Swazi Nation. Colonel Johnson also donated his estate to the people, with instructions that the proceeds should be used for the educational development of his troops' descendants.

Relations between the king and the commissioner seemed to improve after these developments and Sobhuza even attended the coronation of Queen Elizabeth in 1953. While he was away, the Royal Council was under the control of Nukwase, the *ndlovukazi* who had been appointed to succeed Lomawa after her death in 1938 (the first time in living memory that a Queen Mother had died before her son). Nukwase subsequently died in 1957 and was replaced by Zihlathi—Sobhuza's long reign certainly took its toll on *ndlovukazis*.

By 1954, the Union of South Africa was once again demanding that the three British Protectorates be incorporated into South Africa. However, the British had by now promised that no such action would take place without the express permission of the local authorities. This was not likely to be forthcoming, as South Africa was already firmly on the way to Grand Apartheid and no one (not even the European Advisory Council of Swaziland) wanted to be a part of that particular kettle of fish.

Nevertheless, the South African prime ministers J. G. Strijdom and H. F. Verwoerd continued to press the issue until, in 1960, it became clear that it was time to start talking about full independence for the protectorates. In Swaziland's case, the European Advisory Council made the first move by suggesting that a multi-racial legislative council be set up to administer Swaziland. Before the EAC got a reply from London, however, Sobhuza took up the initiative and held a number of meetings with prominent Europeans where he wholeheartedly gave his personal support for the creation of a new administration that would reconcile the needs of white and black Swazis.

The progressive king said, "We could come together on an equal basis, discussing matters of the territory of Swaziland as a whole. It would not lower our prestige and our dignity as people who have their own institutions and rights." In July 1960, these views were put before the annual meeting of the Swazi National Council (the *libandla*) where it met with unanimous approval. Britain also approved and, by November, official discussions had begun under the chairmanship of the Resident Commissioner.

A report was finally completed in November 1961. It recommended that all discrimination on grounds of race, creed and colour be removed from the laws of Swaziland. This was in stark contrast to developments in neighbouring South Africa which had recently withdrawn from the Commonwealth and declared itself a republic, determined to pursue its course of racial segregation.

Despite some opposition to the negotiation process from John Nquku, chairman of the Swaziland Progressive Party (formed in 1929), the official 'Proposals for the Swaziland Constitution' was released in March 1962. But the British still had reservations with regard to the framing of the new constitution.

Nascent Swazi politicians also had something to say about the matter; several new parties were established to propound their particular views. This all became a bit confusing. The Swaziland Progressive Party split into three factions (one of which became the Ngwane National Liberatory Congress). Two new parties were formed: The Mbandzeni Convention Party and the Swaziland Democratic Party. Leadership of these parties changed constantly and several arguments ensued. Additionally, many Swazis dismissed the whole concept of political parties entirely, claiming that they were irrelevant to the traditional system of royal government.

Discussions about the wording of the new constitution continued in London in early 1963, but no agreement was reached. Sobhuza was invited to attend the discussions, but he refused as he felt it would be inappropriate for the king to take sides in the 'sectional interests of his people'.

Eventually, in November 1963, the Swaziland Constitution was promulgated. There was still a lack of agreement on certain terms, however, and the document contained an ominous note that stated "the Secretary of State had been obliged to decide on his own responsibility what form the new constitution should take".

Despite this qualification, the constitution became law on 20 December 1963. Under the new dispensation, the Resident Commissioner became Her Majesty's Commissioner (HMC), with direct links to London. Provisions were also made for the formation of a legislative council and an executive council.

However, the complicated structure of the legislative council required the generation of white and black voters' rolls, and the HMC retained the power to nominate the majority of the executive council. The constitution also stipulated a popular vote on party-political lines. The king thus only got minor representation in the process.

Consequently there was much opposition to the new constitution. The Swazi National Council immediately sent a two-man delegation to Britain with a petition against several clauses in the document while, at the same time, two political parties sent telegraphs dissociating themselves from the petition. This reaction caused some confusion in London, and the Swazi delegation was brusquely told to go home and complain to the new HMC. The constitution was now law, and that was that.

But the Swazis weren't about to back down. Despite British opposition, a national referendum was held in May 1964 to determine support for the petition against the constitution. The results were overwhelming: 124,218 supported the petition, with only 162 opposed. But the referendum didn't change a thing, and the implementation of the constitution went ahead unaltered.

So the National Council decided to fight fire with fire and established its own party, the Imbokodvo National Movement, which was closely affiliated to the royal house. And, with that, the first democratic elections in Swaziland got under way in the middle of 1964.

The country was now reorganized into four districts: Hhohho, Manzini, Shiselweni and Lubombo (which remain in place today). The white vote took place in June and all four seats available on the legislative council were won by the United Swaziland Association, in which 85 per cent of eligible voters took part. The 'national' vote took place about a week later with nine seats going to the Imbokodvo ('Grinding Stone') and the two others going to the United Swaziland Association. Seventy-one per cent of eligible voters cast their ballots.

To qualify, voters had to be a British subject or a British 'protected person' over 21, who had lived in Swaziland for at least three years and paid direct tax. In the case of women, only one wife of a registered taxpayer could vote; a restriction that was problematic for a polygamous society. Votes were cast by punching a hole into a ballot paper with a six-inch nail.

With the successful completion of the voting process, the first meeting of the Legislative Council took place in September 1964. King Sobhuza was 'unable to attend', and *ndlovukazi* Zihlathi represented the *ngwenyama*. Unsurprisingly, given their overwhelming majority, Prince Makhosini of Imbokodvo immediately asked that a committee be established to review the constitution. The motion was carried and Britain approved the request.

The committee published its report in 1966. This was then passed by the legislative council and sent to London, where it was drawn up into a new constitution. This time Swaziland got a parliament comprising a House of Assembly and a Senate. The four districts were divided into eight regions, which would each return three members to the Assembly. Six other members were to be nominated directly by the king. Elected officials would sit for five years, unless the parliament was dissolved by the king.

The king thus finally got back his executive powers. He was also given the right to nominate the Chief Justice, judges and six members of the Senate (the other six were nominated by the Assembly). To advise the king, a cabinet of eight members was established, including a prime minister and a deputy prime minister. However, this cabinet was separate from *liqoqo*—the king's traditional inner council.

All in all, it was a great victory for Sobhuza and a surprising about-turn by the formerly intractable British Government. Clearly, this was all in preparation for Britain's imminent departure from the region. Bechuanaland/Botswana and Basotholand/Lesotho had become independent in 1966, and Swaziland wasn't far behind. In 1967 a general election was held under the new constitution, with a common voters' roll. Imbokodvo won all 24 seats, or 80 per cent of the popular vote. The Ngwane National Liberatory Congress won the rest of the vote, but failed to secure any seats.

All that remained was for Swaziland to win its full independence. The first step in this process took place in April 1967, when Sobhuza signed the Swaziland Protected State Agreement. This document gave Swaziland full control over its internal affairs and promised independence before the end of 1968. It also officially installed Sobhuza II as the King of Swaziland; 'paramount chief' no more.

At the official 'Protected State' ceremony, held on the old Lobamba parade ground (site of the current parliament building), a crowd of around 40,000 people gathered to watch as their vindicated king was sworn in for the first time since ascending to the throne in 1922. Sobhuza also announced Prince Makhosini as the first prime minister of Swaziland. The police band played the royal salute and a new Swazi flag was flown—the first time a Swazi flag of any sort had been hoisted since 1895.

The prescient address Sobhuza gave to the waiting nation is worth quoting: "I have emphasized time and again [the need for] co-operation and unity of the people, without which there can be no peace or progress. If the people are divided into camps to the extent of undermining one another, such a state is doomed to catastrophe, no matter how good and wise the leader may be.

"Demagogues of the world, too often under the cloak of liberty and democracy, have successfully undermined the spirit of unity and co-operation in a nation and have set one group against another only in the interest of gaining a brief day of power for themselves. When they succeed, they trample upon the very fundamental human rights which it is our duty to protect.

"I consider myself very fortunate that over the years I have been blessed with the full … support of my people. With this heritage, I have no doubt that Swaziland will grow from strength to strength to take its rightful place among the nations of the world."

With the king now firmly in control of the 'Protected State', Swaziland took the next step in September 1967, when both houses of parliament officially sent requests to Britain asking for the establishment of Swaziland as an independent kingdom. The date they nominated was 6 September 1968. This request was soon granted.

A delegation then went to Britain to iron out details at the Marlborough House Independence Conference. Two issues remained outstanding: minerals and land. The British acceded to the Swazis' request that all mineral rights should revert to the king, to be held in trust for the Swazi nation. The land issue, however, was deferred for further negotiations.

And so it was, at midnight on 5 September 1968, that Swaziland became an independent nation. A big shindig was held at the Somhlolo National Stadium, and 54 countries were invited to send representatives. King Moshoeshoe II of Lesotho attended, as did the presumably sceptical South African Minister of Foreign Affairs. Queen Elizabeth couldn't make it and her proxy, the Duke of Kent, was detained by the death of his mother. Still, Queen Elizabeth sent a gracious 'welcome to our Commonwealth of Nations' message through Sir Francis Lloyd, the former HMC.

In the weeks that followed, Swaziland quickly embraced its nationhood. It became the 125th member of the United Nations and joined the Organization of African Unity (now the African Union). It also joined the Non-Aligned Movement of States and established diplomatic missions in North America, Europe and Africa. It had been a long haul, but Swaziland was finally free once more.

Too many politicians

On the first anniversary of its independence, Swaziland finally got a visit from the British royal family in the personage of the Queen's cousin, Princess Alexandra, who officially opened the new parliament building. This exchange righted a feeling that the nation was handed its independence with 'the left hand', and Sobhuza was very pleased to welcome the princess to his kingdom.

Sobhuza also wasted no time in asking for a commission to sort out the land issue. At this time, 46 per cent of Swaziland was still in the hands of private individuals of the white persuasion. The British Crown held the rest, apart from the land which had been bought back by the Swazi people.

Following the commission's recommendations, the British Government agreed to purchase 960,000 acres of non-Swazi land with British funds and hand it back to the Swazi nation. It was a tacit acknowledgement of the injustice done to Swaziland through the various proclamations of the British administration.

Sobhuza also set up an autonomous committee to control the mineral rights and other revenues that Swaziland had regained during the independence discussions. This became known as Tibiyo Taka Ngwane (literally 'minerals of Swaziland') and, over the decades that followed, it became a national fund that was used to develop industry, education and infrastructure in Swaziland. Tibiyo also bought back more than 100,000 acres of land from the British Colonial Government at a cost of over £2 million.

Meanwhile, in 1972, new elections were under way. This time, however, the six active political parties fought a hard campaign and many Swazis were disconcerted by the rancorous process. As it turned out, the Ngwane National Liberatory Congress (NNLC) won all three seats in the Lubombo district. But information soon reached the deputy prime minister that one of the new NNLC MPs was not, in fact, a Swazi citizen, and he was served with a deportation order.

A legal challenge ensued, and the high court reversed the deportation order. Then the parliament passed an amendment to the immigration act which allowed for the establishment of a Special Tribunal which was beyond the reach of the courts. This tribunal revoked the offending MP's citizenship. But the Appeal Court declared the tribunal unconstitutional.

With the courts saying one thing and the tribunal saying another, a constitutional crisis erupted. So, in early 1973, the *libandla* met and resolved to ask the king to suspend the 'colonial' constitution in favour of a more 'Swazi-centric' dispensation. This proposal was supported by both houses of parliament, who declared that the current constitution was unworkable.

As such, in April 1973, Prime Minister Makhosini joined a meeting of the National Council and formally asked Sobhuza to suspend the constitution. While this whole affair may or may not have been orchestrated in conjunction with the Royal House, the king willingly complied with the wishes of his people and repealed the 1968 constitution. The attorney-general, David Cohen, then read a decree that disbanded parliament and made all political parties, trade unions and political meetings illegal. A 60-day detention-without-trial was also instituted, with the stipulation that this 'state of emergency' could be extended indefinitely if deemed necessary. The king now assumed full legislative, executive and judicial power.

It seems that the motivating factor behind this rather severe decree was Sobhuza's inability to reconcile the concept of a political opposition with the African experience. This was made clear by a reported exchange between the king and a visiting Canadian trade minister. When the king met with the minister, he was surprised to find that the Canadian delegation contained a member of the opposition party. The Canadians tactfully replied that "We work like a team when dealing with aid and international affairs. We may be political enemies, but we are not human enemies." The king replied, "Not in Africa. In Africa, the opposition is an enemy. Opposition parties always take an impossible stance and it becomes extremely difficult for the government to function effectively. Yours is a good example, and I hope that Africa learns from you."

Nevertheless, international reactions to the king's Proclamation to the Nation were generally negative. Sobhuza countered that Swaziland already had a traditional parliament; the *libandla* or National Council. Nevertheless, to placate his opponents, Sobhuza appointed a Royal Constitutional Commission to travel across Swaziland and gather opinions about what kind of constitution the people wanted.

In the meantime, the king was permitted to rule in conjunction with a council of ministers and passed laws as 'orders-in-council', much as the British had done under their controversial proclamation policy. But it was a difficult time, characterized by salary disputes, accusations of nepotism and concerns about mismanagement.

And the bad omens started stacking up. There was a disastrous *incwala* ceremony in 1974/5, in which several people were killed by a lightning storm. The *ndlovukazi*, Zihlathi, passed away a short time later and was replaced by a sister, Seneleleni Nxumalo. Prime Minister Makhosini also became gravely ill during 1975 and had to step down the following year. He was succeeded by Maphevu Dlamini, who was simultaneously the head of Swaziland's Umbutfo Defence Force.

Then, in 1977, the Royal Constitutional Commission announced its findings. Swaziland should remain a 'no-party' state, with the *libandla* as the only decision- making body. Swaziland was veering dangerously close to the totalitarian state that Sobhuza had warned against just a few years previously.

Undeterred by a series of protests and strikes, the king now pushed forward with his plans to incorporate the traditional *tinkhundla* system into the political system. *Tinkhundla* was originally devised by King Mswati II when he split the nation into a number of *inkhundla* (a grouping of local chiefs) for administrative and military purposes. Sobhuza had started resurrecting the system in the 1930s, and used it to recruit labour for the Swazi contribution to World War II.

By 1978 he was ready for a new election under the Establishment of the Parliament of Swaziland Order. Each *inkhundla* now became an electoral constituency which elected two members to the House of Assembly. Voting went as follows: on the appointed day every male and female over 18 years went to their nearest *inkhundla*. Here, the *indvuna* (head chief) and his inner council *(bucopho)* were responsible for determining the citizenship of each voter (there was no voters' roll). This hardened the distinction between Swaziland Swazis and South African Swazis, who were affiliated to chiefs outside the kingdom.

Once this was done, four candidates were announced by the *bucopho*. These candidates could be of any gender, race or social status, as long as they were not members of *bucopho*, who could not nominate themselves. Neither the voters nor the candidates knew who would be nominated before the official announcement.

The presumably surprised candidates were then asked to accept their nomination, whereupon they were ushered into a temporary enclosure that was split into four passages. Each candidate now sat on a stool in front of one of the passages and the voters had to walk through the passage headed by their favoured nominee. An electoral official counted each person who walked through the passage and the two candidates with the highest number of votes were sent forward to king for his approval.

In January 1979 the new parliament was officially reconvened by King Sobhuza. Regional councils were also established to replace the old district councils of the colonial era. The old constitution remained in abeyance, and political parties remained illegal.

To critics of the newly-enshrined *tinkhundla* system, the defiant Sobhuza had this to say, 'The world today is plagued by perpetual power struggles. You find innocent people, mainly children, suffering from starvation because of these struggles. If indeed you are unhappy in this country, go out in the world and see what is going on. Then come back and compare.'

The Diamond Jubilee

In mid-1980, *ndlovukazi* Seneleleni died. She was replaced by Dzeliwe. The resilient Sobhuza was now on his fifth Queen Mother. And he was still going strong.

In 1981, Sobhuza invited the heads of state of Lesotho, Botswana and Mozambique to the kingdom. Robert Mugabe of newly independent Zimbabwe was supposed to attend, but he had his hands full with the revolt in Matabeleland.

At this summit the king expressed his two defining beliefs: the importance of diplomacy over violence, and the need for African countries to find their own solutions based on indigenous systems. In this, he proved himself a true African Renaissance man, long before the term was popularized by Thabo Mbeki.

A few months later, the unflagging Sobhuza got involved in the ever-present border controversy with South Africa, which had been a hot-button topic for well over 100 years. By this time, several areas in the Eastern Transvaal had been put aside for Swazi settlement and, despite numerous attempts to have the territories reincorporated into Swaziland, they were instead unilaterally bundled into the semi-independent KaNgwane 'bantustan' (established by South Africa in 1977). The disputed Ngwavuma area (between Kosi Bay and the Lubombo, which had been excised from the kingdom by the British in the late 1800s) was similarly folded into the KwaZulu homeland in 1976.

Then a group of Swazi chiefs living in South Africa approached Sobhuza and asked to be reunited with their king. Sobhuza subsequently petitioned the South African Government who, uncharacteristically, felt that the borders were historically vague and supported the reintegration of all Swazi people into a common territory.

After South Africa announced that the disputed territories were going to be given back to Swaziland, the governments of KaNgwane and KwaZulu went to court to prevent re-integration. Several years of legal wrangling followed, until South Africa finally decided to drop the whole border adjustment issue, much to the disappointment of many Swazis.

Meanwhile, in 1981, the 82-year-old Sobhuza celebrated his 60th year as king. He was, at the time, the oldest living and longest reigning monarch in the world. In fact, throughout history, only two other kings have spent more than 60 years on the throne.

Although the elders had refused to commemorate Sobhuza's Silver and Golden jubilees, this Diamond Jubilee was hard to ignore. The country prepared for a right royal celebration to honour their beloved king. Invitations were duly sent around the world and a special village was built near Mbabane to house all the honoured guests who were expected to attend. The German Government even lent Swaziland 26 black Mercedes-Benz limousines to transport all the dignitaries to the various events.

And the guest list was indeed impressive. Princess Margaret represented her sister, Queen Elizabeth of Britain. Queen Mamahato of Lesotho and King Zwelethini of the Zulus were there. Presidents included Kenneth Kaunda (Zambia), Quett Masire (Botswana), Samora Machel (Mozambique) and Canaan Banana of Zimbabwe. Sixteen other countries and the United Nations also sent high-ranking envoys.

Festivities kicked off in the first week of September with the annual *Umhlanga* reed dance. Several days of speeches, royal receptions, garden parties and private meetings followed. The big event was a festive gathering at the Somhlolo National Stadium, where the large crowd was treated to a regimental display. After much singing and dancing, the king finally addressed the adoring throng.

He said: "I always feel that I have no enemy. He who regards himself as my enemy cannot succeed, because I will spare no effort in getting closer and closer to him until there is a conference. The alternative to talking is confrontation. Such attitudes among nations do not augur well for the future but [lead to] arms manufacture, arms stockpiling and eventually the destruction of the world human community. Our survival as nations of the world depends on inter-state and on international understanding." Nelson Mandela couldn't have said it better.

Queen Mamahato seemed to sum it up when she stated that "monarchy can be preserved and maintained only if the people are secured and satisfied". But all good things come to an end, and the enduring reign of King Sobhuza II finally terminated a year later, when he succumbed to pneumonia on 21 August 1982, aged 83 and one month.

The Swazi nation was deeply affected by the loss of their seemingly eternal monarch. After some controversy it was decided that Sobhuza should get a modernized funeral and, contrary to Swazi tradition, some of his belongings were buried within the royal kraal. This was later said to be a bad omen that presaged the troubles ahead.

King Mswati III (1986–present day)

After Sobhuza's death in 1982, the *ndlovukazi* Dzeliwe became queen regent and assumed control of the kingdom. The Royal Council then chose Prince Makhosetive as the new king.

Makhosetive was born in 1968 to Queen Ntombi, but his regency period wouldn't be without its difficulties. The problems started when Dzeliwe decided that the prince should be educated in England, and sent him off to Sherborne School without consulting the elders of the nation. This caused a great deal of bad feeling, which was compounded by a split between the queen regent and her *liqoqo*.

Conflict between Dzeliwe, the *liqoqo*, the prime minister and the parliament began to escalate. Traditionalists started arguing with reformists, mainly about the need for a new constitution that enshrined human rights and political freedom. Public statements about this issue were issued and then retracted. Diplomatic appointments were made and then reversed.

Things soon became a bit crazy. A leopard was spotted near the prime minister's home (the first such sighting in living memory) and was shot by guards. A few hours later, a duiker was seen in the same spot and was also shot. This was considered to be a very bad omen.

Then, in 1983, the situation got positively Byzantine. First, the Prime Minister, Prince Mabandla, advised the Queen Regent that the *liqoqo* was trying to undermine her position. After delivering this dire warning, Mabandla learnt that the *liqoqo* (dominated by Prince Mfanasibili, a cousin of the Crown Prince) was about to arrest him and fled the country. Mfanasibili and the *liqoqo* subsequently forced Dzeliwe to remove Mabandla from office and have him replaced with another cousin, Prince Bhekimpi Dlamini. Furthermore, the *liqoqo* presented the Queen Regent with two documents: one authorizing the next general election, due in October, and a second stressing that the queen be advised by *liqoqo* in all matters of state.

Dzeliwe refused to sign either and summarily dismissed the *liqoqo*. But the *liqoqo* wouldn't go quietly and responded by stripping Dzeliwe of her office. In her place, the Crown Prince's mother, Queen Ntombi laThwala, was prematurely installed as *ndlovukazi*—even though she was still in mourning for her late husband.

This wholly untraditional conduct threw the nation into a tizz. Junior princes started calling for a mass meeting at Lobamba, while senior royals urged people to stay at home. Several prominent figures, including the police commissioner, princes, princesses and commoners, were accused of causing trouble and arrested under the 60-day detention law. Mfanasibili even claimed that a number of royals loyal to Queen Dzeliwe were plotting to assassinate the future King of Swaziland who was still studying in England (where he was known as 'Mac' by his classmates). Meanwhile, ordinary Swazis were terrified of Mfanasibili because "his *muti* [traditional medicine] was powerful". In the midst of this 'traditional coup', the young heir-apparent was brought back from England. A few days later, the future king was officially 'shown' to the nation. He was wearing a traditional *emahiya* cloth, a *sizeze* (traditional battle axe) and the *ligwalagwala*—a crown of red feathers from a lourie bird, symbolizing intelligence and royalty.

With the nation somewhat settled by the appearance of their new monarch, the 15-year-old prince was able to continue with his studies, under the guidance of a private tutor from Britain. The second elections under *tinkhundla* went off peacefully and Ntombi released some of the political detainees. It seemed that things were returning to normal.

Then, in January 1984, Swaziland was hit by a freak hurricane, 'Demoina'. Known as *Zamcolo* by the Swazis, the torrential rain and gale-force winds caused widespread damage across the country. An emergency fund was set up and friendly nations from around the world sent donations to help Swaziland cope with the aftermath. Even apartheid South Africa sent helicopters and supplies. The Swazi people were also asked to contribute to relief efforts by donating money through the *tinkhundla*. But this process was badly mismanaged and several people were accused of corruption or incompetence.

The general state of chaos was enhanced by a new series of conflicts between Ntombi, her senior councillors and several cabinet ministers. It seemed that some people were trying to prevent Prince Makhosetive from assuming the throne. Consequently, the head of the police, the army chief and Prince Sozisa (the 'authorized person' of the *liqoqo)* were all removed from office. One princess even went to King Zwelethini of the Zulus to try and negotiate peace. She was subsequently arrested.

Things only started looking up when, in August 1984, the official mourning period came to an end—after only two years instead of three—and a *lusasa* was built for the future king. The new royal homestead was called Ludzidzini and the prince now started attending a number of important ceremonies, including the first reed dance to be held since Sobhuza's death.

To make matters worse, throughout this period, Swaziland was grappling with problems posed by her two neighbours. On the one side, South Africa had started cross-border raids to combat cells of the then-banned African National Congress who had set themselves up in Swaziland. This continued until the Swazi government withdrew its support for the ANC, fearing increased destabilization at the hands of the ruthless apartheid armed forces. On the other side, there was an influx of Mozambican refugees who were fleeing the civil war which racked that country from the mid-1970s until 1992.

Meanwhile, divisions within *liqoqo* continued to plague the royal house. Eventually, in 1986, Ntombi downgraded the *liqoqo* from the 'supreme council of state' (as it was designated by Sobhuza) to a 'council whose function is to advise the king and which shall consist of members appointed by the king to hold office at his pleasure'.

Finally, on 25 April 1986, Prince Makhosetive was crowned King Mswati III, to thunderous cries of "*Bayethe Nkosi!*" (Salute the King). He was, at the time, the youngest reigning monarch in the world. The usual host dignitaries attended the ceremony, including P. W. Botha of South Africa, Maureen Reagan (daughter of Ronald) and Prince Michael (on behalf of the elusive Queen Elizabeth).

But there was still one more thing to do before Mswati would officially assume the throne. He had to get married. According to Swazi custom, the king must marry a girl of the Matsebula clan before he can perform his first *Incwala*. This happy union took place in September 1986 and the king moved from his *lusasa* to his *sigodlo* (harem).

The modern monarchy

Once he had taken his first wife, Mswati settled into his throne and soon began to flex his political muscles. He disbanded the current *liqoqo* and chose new councillors who firmly supported the King's position as the absolute head of state. He reshuffled his cabinet to accomplish the same objective and installed Sotsha Dlamini as Prime Minister—the first person not of royal blood to hold the position. He also rehabilitated the disgraced Queen Dzeliwe and arrested those who were said to be responsible for her fall from grace, including the troublesome Mfanasibili—who was later released despite general advice to the contrary.

In response to this, one commentator complained that "under King Mswati, the traditionalist forces stamped their hegemony over the Swazi policy with more coercion, and less diplomacy [than] was associated with King Sobhuza". Others, however, have pointed out that the King showed great strength when he first came to power and this was necessary to fix a country paralyzed by four years of *liqoqo* misrule and corruption.

Unfortunately, in September 1987, there were more corruption scandals and Mswati dissolved parliament and called for new elections. This time, however, voter turnout was low and a small minority started voicing reservations about the *tinkhundla* system. Then, in 1990, the African

National Congress was unbanned in South Africa which encouraged the spread of multi-party democracy across the subcontinent, including Swaziland. The Swazi authorities responded by arresting members of the People's United Democratic Movement (PUDEMO), trade unionists, student leaders and leaders of civic organizations. Twelve people were subsequently charged with high treason but all were acquitted, except for six men who were found guilty of organizing or attending a political meeting and sentenced to short jail terms.

Things got worse in 1991 when there were a number of boycotts and student protests. Several new civic organizations were also formed and started agitating for change. Even though pro-democracy advocates made up only a small percentage of the population, Mswati decided to change tack and promised to revise the *tinkhundla* system. Accordingly, he established the Vusela (greeting) Commission which was sent to every *inkhundla* around the country to get input directly from the Swazi citizens. Vusela was tasked with discussing the electoral system and it concluded that several reforms were necessary. It also suggested that the Nation should be consulted on the issue of a multi-party democracy. The King accepted the findings of the commission and followed it up with Vusela II, which was to gather input on economic issues.

At the end of the Vusela process, a number of recommendations were made, including democratic changes: a universal suffrage, secret ballot elections, direct representation in Parliament and acknowledgement of the role of women in government. It also helped shape development plans and prioritized education, health, infrastructure, employment and investment. The King was fully supportive of these initiatives and continues to drive these policies forward.

While several critics rejected the entire Vusela process as a self-serving charade, most hold that it was the most democratic way to ascertain the people's views in accordance with Swaziland's culture and traditions. Be that as it may, the King approved the Vusela findings and ordered that elections should go ahead under the new system.

This ballot was held in 1993 but, by now, PUDEMO and the Swaziland Federation of Trade Unions had grown in confidence and embarked on a number of strikes and civil-disobedience programmes, which included border blockades. The King responded that "we cannot allow a tiny majority of the Kingdom to dictate what the rest of us should do, and, as your King, I will stand up to them".

Nevertheless, a Constitutional Review Commission was established in 1996 to determine whether the Swazi people wanted a change in the status quo (as was recommended by the first Vusela). After a lengthy consultation process, the CRC finally delivered its findings in 2002 and reported that the majority of Swazis, more than 90%, wanted the King's position as head of state to be maintained and even strengthened. Swazis had seen the problems caused by multi-party systems in neighbouring countries and wanted none of it. The various pro-democracy organizations were unimpressed with the commission's findings and continued to protest. Some even called for sanctions against Swaziland. But the King remained resolute, secure in the knowledge that the bulk of the population was behind him.

After the elections, the findings of the Constitutional Review Commission were adopted and the King ordered that a new constitution be drawn up to replace the suspended 1968 document. Under the new constitution, Mswati's position as an absolute monarch was entrenched but it did revoke his power to rule by decree and included a bill of rights. Nevertheless, political parties remained illegal and 'the Swazi King remains above the law, not subject to parliamentary legislation and with the power to dissolve parliament at any time'. The constitution was swiftly rejected by most opposition organizations, but their support base remained small—only around 10% of the Swazi population. Undeterred, proponents of a multi-party system continued to protest and several demonstrations turned violent. A couple of government institutions were even petrol-bombed. Consequently, in 2005 and 2006, some members of PUDEMO were arrested and charged with treason. In the last couple of years, this 'vocal minority' of pro-democracy organizations has continued to put pressure on the Swazi government. Border blockades, strikes, stayaways and demonstrations sporadically take place.

And so it is that today, 20 years after his ascension, King Mswati gets a lot of bad press which, because of protocol, he does not respond to. Some groups accuse him of being extravagant, while others lambast Mswati for being a polygamist. He was especially criticized in 2002 for "snatching" a young girl to be his bride. This story hit the headlines because the mother of the girl threatened to sue the King, but the case was dropped when it became clear that the girl had gone to the palace of her own free will and didn't wish to return home. In defence of Mswati, we have seen that Swazi custom states the King should try to marry one girl from each chiefdom in the country, so that everyone in the nation is 'represented at court'. It is also tricky to sire a suitable heir because of all the requirements that must be met, so it's the King's duty to have lots of kids. Therefore, polygamy is in the best Swazi tradition and criticism of Mswati's multiple wives is somewhat 'Western' in its perspective. Another criticism levelled at the King is his perceived mishandling of the HIV/AIDS crisis. However, supporters of the King say that the opposite is true and he has been progressive in his attitude to the pandemic. He was one of the first African heads of state to meet with and shake the hands of people living with HIV/AIDS, and he was the first leader in southern Africa to publicly acknowledge the crisis and give accurate statistics of the extent of the problem. He was also the first southern African leader to get tested for the disease and urged his people to do the same—with no dissident misinformation disputing the link between HIV and AIDS as was the case in South Africa.

But the King continued to court controversy when, in 2001, he re-instituted the ancient tradition of *umcwasho*, which encouraged all Swazi girls to abstain from sex for five years and banned any sexual relations with girls under eighteen. Any transgressors were given a substantial fine of one cow. It was a potentially noble initiative, supported by several health organizations, that was supposed to make boys think twice before having sex. Unfortunately, the *umcwasho* had several unintended consequences with reports of an increase in prostitution, a decline in marriage and an increase in abortions and infanticide. Mswati also broke his own rule by marrying a 17-year-old girl in 2005, but he did pay a hefty fine of 25 cows.

And then we come back to Mswati's continued refusal to allow multi-party democracy in the Kingdom. In 2008, the tension between autocrats and democrats reached boiling point. In this important year, Swaziland marked the 40th anniversary of its independence and Mswati celebrated his 40th birthday with plans for a big national 40/40 celebration. However, it was also an election year and several pro-democracy organizations launched an unprecedented series of protest actions that threatened to make the kingdom "ungovernable", which culminated in a mass march of around 20,000 people. The crowd sang seditious anti-Mswati songs and issued demands for better social grants for the elderly and improved health and education facilities. Order was eventually restored but the sight of thousands of Swazi protestors shouting previously unthinkable anti-Mswati slogans must have struck a chord and a mediation process is currently underway.

Interestingly, the pro-democracy organizations generally do *not* want the monarchy to be abolished. They just want a representational government of the people, as is the case in any democratic country, or as they put it, "reign, not rule". Only time will tell how King Mswati III will react to these demands. So, in conclusion, how can one sum up the Swazi monarchy under King Mswati III? Well, since the pro-democracy advocates get most of the press, let's look at it from the royalist point of view. Mswati remains extremely popular with his people. He has also used culturally appropriate methods to find out what the people want, both politically and economically, and has implemented the findings of these consultative commissions. And let's not forget that he still has to consult with his mother, the *ndlovukazi* Emakhosikati, as well as his various advisors before he can take any decisions. That kinda sounds like something akin to a democratic process. From this perspective, the various groups agitating for change—trade unions, 'intellectuals', the press and a few students—are swimming against the tide. They are marching along a path towards political pluralism, even though this is often against the wishes of the majority. Furthermore, Mswati has done some pretty impressive things in his time as head of state. He's ushered in a new constitution with a bill of rights and inaugurated a reformed electoral system. He has overseen a huge infrastructure development programme—including roads, communications and factory/office parks—and personally helped to secure major investments that have created new jobs. Additionally, he has taken a strong leadership role in respect of nature conservation, without which there would be no wild spaces or wildlife in the kingdom.

In the end, then, is the Swazi system really so archaic? Maybe it's just a case of different stokes for different folks. Most of the world's politicians act like they're kings anyway so what's wrong with a real one? And, to put the matter into its proper perspective: Swaziland remains peaceful and stable. Demonstrations are few and far between, the country isn't going up in flames and it isn't likely to.

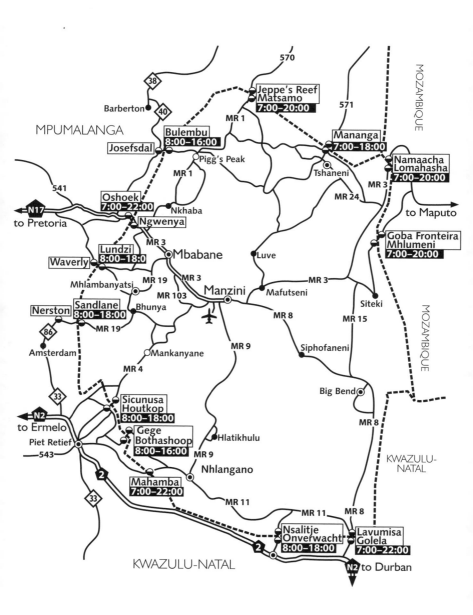

570

MOZAMBIQUE

38

Barberton

40

MPUMALANGA

Jeppe's Reef
Matsamo
7:00–20:00

MR 1

571

Bulembu
8:00–16:00

Josefsdal

Pigg's Peak

Mananga
7:00–18:00

Tshaneni

MR 1

541

Oshoek
7:00–22:00

Nkhaba

Namaacha
Lomahasha
7:00–20:00

N17

to Pretoria

Ngwenya

MR 3

Mbabane

Luve

MR 24

to Maputo

MR 3

Lundzi
8:00–18:0

Waverly

MR 3

Goba Fronteira
Mhlumeni
7:00–20:00

Mhlambanyatsi

MR 19

MR 3

Manzini

Mafutseni

MR 3

Siteki

MR 103

Sandlane
8:00–18:00

Bhunya

MR 8

MR 15

Nerston

MR 19

86

Amsterdam

Mankanyane

MR 4

MR 9

Siphofaneni

MOZAMBIQUE

33

Big Bend

Sicunusa
Houtkop
8:00–18:00

N2

to Ermelo

Gege
Bothashoop
8:00–16:00

Hlatikhulu

MR 8

Piet Retief

543

MR 9

Nhlangano

KWAZULU-
NATAL

2

Mahamba
7:00–22:00

33

MR 11

MR 11

MR 8

Nsalitje
Onverwacht
8:00–18:00

Lavumisa
Golela
7:00–22:00

2

KWAZULU-NATAL

N2 to Durban

Exploring Swaziland

Getting there

Driving

There are essentially only two ways to get to Swaziland: fly or drive. I would wholeheartedly recommend the latter. Mbabane is just four hours from Johannesburg (364km), six hours from Durban (635km) and a couple of hours from Maputo (224km). This is the perfect country for self-drive tourism as the roads are good, distances are short and the scenery is spectacular. So, load up the family wagon or rent a car in Jo'burg (or Durban) and hit the road. The 3,594km Swazi road network includes a well-maintained system of roads that link the major urban centres. The newly-built highway from the Oshoek border post to Mbabane and Manzini is impressive. Elsewhere in Swaziland, the tarred roads are quite suitable for any ordinary sedan car – apart from the occasional pothole.

If you have an SUV or a 4x4, so much the better. Swaziland has a fantastic matrix of gravel roads (in various states of repair) which will take the adventurous motorist deep into the mountains, past scattered villages and through the remote countryside.

Swaziland's also quite centrally located for incorporation into a longer southern Africa itinerary. The renowned Kruger National Park is relatively close by (Nelspruit is just 171km from Mbabane) and, if you have the time, you could tag on a trip to the eclectic wonders of Maputo, the pristine iSimangaliso Wetlands and/or the beaches of Durban.

If you're an international visitor and renting a car is not an option, there are several tour operators who offer a guided round trip from Jo'burg to Kruger and then down through Swaziland to the beaches of KwaZulu-Natal. It's a fantastic journey that offers a good alternative to the more mainstream delights of the Cape peninsula.

Backpackers can take the Baz Bus, a cross-country shuttle that has a stop in Mbabane (at All Ways Backpackers) and Malkerns (at Legends Backpackers). Transmagnific also operates a regular bus service between Jo'burg, Mbabane and the Kruger Park. Once inside Swaziland, public bus services, minibus taxis and hitch-hiking are all viable and reasonably safe options.

- Avis @ Matsapha Airport, Manzini: 268-518 6226; www.avis.co.za
- Affordable Car Hire, Mbabane: 268-404 9136
- Baz Bus: 27-21 439 2323; www.bazbus.com
- Comprehensive Car Rental: 268-404 6566
- First International Car Hire: 268-404 7991
- SiyeSwatini Transmagnific Shuttle Bus: 268-404 9977; www.goswaziland.co.sz

Flying

For those who simply have to fly, Matsapha airport is located near Manzini. It is serviced by Swazi Airlink, which offers several daily flights between Manzini and Johannesburg (departing from the international terminal, so bring your passport). Connecting flights to other South African and African cities are available through SA Airlink. Chartered flights can also be arranged, but the independently-run Swazi Express Airways has been in operation much longer. Car hire is available from the airport and in Mbabane. A new international airport is being built at Sikhupe, between Manzini and Mpaka. This project is part of the county's ambitious Millennium Project; the completion date is scheduled for 2010. It is hoped that the new airport, with a longer runway, will encourage other airlines to start flights into the country.

- Swaziland Airlink: 268-518 6155 / 27-11 961 1700; www.flyswaziland.com
- Matsapha Airport: 268-518 6115

Rail

If you really want to try something different, why not blow your budget on a luxurious train trip? The exclusive Rovos Rail offers a three-day tour that starts in Pretoria and takes in the southern Kruger Park, Mkhaya game reserve in Swaziland and the Hluhluwe game reserve before arriving in Durban. Fares range from R10,000 to R20,000 per person, all inclusive. It's pretty steep and you only stop for a few hours in Swaziland, but it'll be a trip to remember. Check out www.rovos.com

Driving from Jo'burg

If you are driving to Mbabane or southern Swaziland

The simplest way to drive from Jo'burg to Mbabane is via the N17 highway. Just get on the M3 heading south and drive straight through the Gillooly's Interchange (past the turnoff to the airport), following signs for the N3 to Durban. After a few kilometres you'll see a big cement factory on your right. A couple of hundred metres further on, there's a big interchange. Keep left and follow signs for Springs and the N17.

You will then drive through the Gosforth toll plaza (which only costs a couple of rand), past the gaudy Carnival City casino complex and through the mining town of Springs. Once you have cleared the various factories, suburbs and mine dumps around Springs, the sky seems to lift and the landscape opens out into a vista of rolling fields.

The N17 now undulates through the farmland for a couple of hundred kilometres as you drive past a number of small towns: Leandra, Kinross, Secunda, Bethal and Ermelo. This part of the country contains several large power stations that loom out of the fields and a network of enormous pylons criss-cross the highway. The smoke that belches out of these coal-burning behemoths may get in your eyes but, at dusk, the pollution catches the light to create beautiful sunsets that blaze with orange light.

A word of warning: the N17 is not in a good state of repair. Many heavy trucks use this road and the tarmac is often potholed. Overtaking should therefore be done cautiously, as the carriageway is narrow and there are many blind rises—not that this deters some kamikaze drivers. The signage also isn't great, especially as you come into a town, so keep your eyes open or you might lose the highway and find yourself driving through a residential suburb. The N17 is not tolled, but most people I've spoken to wouldn't mind paying a bit extra for a decent road.

In any case, at Ermelo the highway splits into the N2, the N11 and the N17. If you are specifically going to the southern part of Swaziland, follow the N2 to Piet Retief or Pongola. If you are heading for Mbabane, keep following the N17, which should be marked for Swaziland and the Oshoek border post (120km away). The N17 road now leads through an area that is famous for its wetlands, lakes and grasslands that harbour an amazing variety of birds.

According to the Swaziland Tourism Authority, an alternative route goes as follows: from the M3, take the airport road and continue straight towards Boksburg and Benoni, following signs for the N12 to Witbank. At Witbank, join the N4 east and continue for 65km until you reach the village of Wonderfontein, which is distinguished by the Total Service

Station, apparently. Turn right here and follow signs to Carolina and Mbabane. Pass through Carolina and 'turn right at the intersection just after the railway tracks' onto the R33. Keep on the R33 for about 40km until you join the N17. From this point it is about 62km to Oshoek. Do note that the N4 is heavily tolled.

At the Oshoek/Ngwenya border post, dispense with the necessary formalities and drive into the Kingdom of Swaziland on the brand new MR3 highway. The turnoff to the Ngwenya Glass Factory is found a short distance after the border post and is well marked. The turnoff to the MR1 that leads up to Malolotja and Pigg's Peak can be found a few kilometres farther along. If you continue on the MR3, Mbabane is about 23km from the border, the Ezulwini Valley is 34km and Manzini is 58km.

If you are driving to Northern Swaziland (Pigg's Peak or Mlawula)
If you are headed for northern Swaziland from Jo'burg, get on the M3 highway and take the airport turnoff. Then, follow signs for the N12 to Benoni and Witbank. At Witbank (about 125km from Jo'burg) the N12 joins with the N4. Keep heading east on the N4 past Belfast, Machadodorp and Waterval Boven as the road descends from the Highveld into the Lowveld. About 355km from Jo'burg, you'll arrive in the regional capital of Mpumalanga province, Nelspruit. The N4 is heavily tolled, so budget for about R100 each way.

From Nelspruit, keep driving on the N4 for another 62km until you see the turnoff for the R570. This road leads you down to the Jeppe's Reef/Matsamo border post (41km from the N4). This is the closest border to Pigg's Peak, which is about 40km south of the border.

If you are going to Hlane or Mlawula in the east of Swaziland, keep on the N4 for another 45km, until you see the turnoff for the R571. This will take you down to the Mananga border post, just above the town of Tshaneni (62km from the junction with the N4).

Alternatively, if you like to take the road less travelled, you might want to enter Swaziland via the stunning Saddleback Pass that leads from Barberton to Pigg's Peak via Bulembu village. To reach this road, take the R40 from Nelspruit to Barberton (46km) and then follow signs for the Josefdal/Bulembu border post (40km from Barberton). This amazing pass takes you right up over the mountains and offers breathtaking views into the green valleys of the Songimvelo Nature Reserve below.

Until recently, the Bulembu/Barberton route was a badly rutted gravel road that required a sturdy 4x4. Now, however, it is being tarred and widened and should be open to ordinary sedan cars in the near future. Either way, it's a spectacular drive and the tiny border post at Bulembu is always quiet. Do note, however, that the Bulembu border closes at 16:00, so make sure you get there on time or else you will have to take a long detour down a small gravel road that runs parallel to the South African border until you to reach the N17 near Oshoek.

Driving from Durban

If you are coming up to Swaziland from Durban, get on the N2 heading north and drive for 345km until you reach Pongola. From this small town, you can access the Golela/Lavumisa border post (about 10km away), which gives you access to the attractions of eastern Swaziland, including Nisela Safaris, Big Bend, Siteki, Hlane Game Reserve and Mlawula Nature Reserve.

If you are headed for Mbabane or Pigg's Peak, it is certainly possible to drive through Swaziland from Golela/Lavumisa, but you'll probably want to keep on the N2 until you reach the town of Piet Retief (127km from Pongola). From here, drive the 30-odd kilometres to either the Sicunusa or Mahamba border posts. Mbabane is about 90km from the former and 140km from the latter. The Grand Valley road from Mahamba to Mbabane is a particularly beautiful drive.

Crossing the border

Swaziland is an independent country and entry into the territory is only allowed through official border posts. Valid passports must be carried by all visitors, although visas are not required for citizens of SADC nations and many other countries. Check with your foreign office for details. A nominal road tax is payable on all foreign vehicles entering Swaziland (currently E50).

Please take note that the South African Police Service recently instituted a new requirement for people who are driving across the border. In an effort to curb cross-border vehicle crime, they are now asking that people bring their car licensing and/or registration papers with them—either the originals or a certified copy. People who are driving rental cars should ask for a letter of authorisation from their rental agency, which grants permission for the individual to take the car across the border. Apparently, if you do not have these papers, the police will use their discretion and they could turn you away if they think you look dodgy. So, it's not compulsory at this stage, but having the relevant papers at hand will make the process quicker.

While the main border post is at Oshoek/Ngwenya, there are other official entry points located at regular intervals around the circumference of Swaziland. These vary in size and organizational capacity, depending on the volume of people they have to process. The larger border posts are therefore the busiest, but they are also the most efficient.

Thankfully, the main border posts have now computerized their procedures and this makes a huge difference. In the past, I can remember the frustration of standing in long lines while searching for a pen to fill in little scraps of paper that had to get stamped by several different departments. Now, with barcoded passports, it's a simple matter of scan and go. What a pleasure!

They are also investigating plans to keep some of the larger borders open 24 hours a day but, for the moment, the opening and closing times for the border gates are as follows:

- Bulembu / Josefdal: 08:00-16:00
- Gege / Bothashoop: 08:00-16:00
- Lavumisa / Golela: 07:00-22:00
- Lomahasha / Namaacha: 07:00-20:00 (with Mozambique)
- Lundzi / Waverley: 08:00-16:00
- Mahamba: 07:00-22:00
- Mananga / Border Gate: 08:00-18:00
- Matsamo / Jeppe's Reef: 07:00-20:00
- Mhlumeni / Goba Frontiera: 07:00-20:00 (with Mozambique)
- Ngwenya / Oshoek: 07:00-22:00
- Nsalitje / Onverwacht: 08:00-18:00
- Sandlane / Nerston: 08:00-18:00
- Sicunusa / Houtkop: 08:00-18:00

The idiot's guide to Oshoek/Ngwenya border post

The road up to Oshoek is lovely. It leads along the top of a ridge with great views out over the distant mountains. You will also start getting a sense of the rural character of Swaziland as you drive through a number of small villages that culminate with a rather ramshackle conglomeration of houses around the border post itself. It appears as if they are building some kind of cultural village or accommodation facility in a cluster of beehive huts on the South African side of the border, but I could not find any additional information at time of writing.

Then, you must drive through the gates of the border post itself. Find a parking place (difficult at peak times) and go into the customs office. If you have nothing to declare (and who does?!) they will write down the make of your car, the registration number and number of passengers on a piece of paper. Take this paper and stand in the immigration queue, where you will get your passport scanned and stamped.

Once you have your customs slip and your stamped passports, get back in your car and drive up to the boomed gate that leads to Swaziland. Give the guards at the boom the customs slip and show them your passports. Then, depending on how shifty you look to them, your vehicle may be searched to a greater or lesser extent. Once you have satisfied the guard that you are not carrying contraband, you will be waved through into the tiny piece of no-man's land between South Africa and Swaziland.

After 100 metres or so, you will arrive at the Swazi side of the border post. Park your car again and go into the main building—hopefully the queue won't be too long! Once you get to the counter, your passport will be swiped and stamped. Then, you've got to go and get a little white slip of paper and take it to the road tax counter where you will pay R50 for foreign-registered light vehicles. Please note that credit cards and cheques are *not* accepted and there are no banks or ATMs at the border, so make sure you have enough cash. There is a tourism information bureau in the building where you can stock up on useful brochures and pamphlets, but this is not always open.

Once your road tax slip is stamped, you can go back to your car and drive up to the final boom gate, where you may or may not be subjected to a vehicle search. Depending on how busy the border post is, the whole process will take between 20 to 60 minutes to complete.

Oshoek/Ngwenya is open from 07:00 to 22:00, seven days a week.

- Oshoek border post: 27-17 882 0138
- Oshoek SAPS: 27-17 882 0001
- Ngwenya border post: 268-442 4138/4425

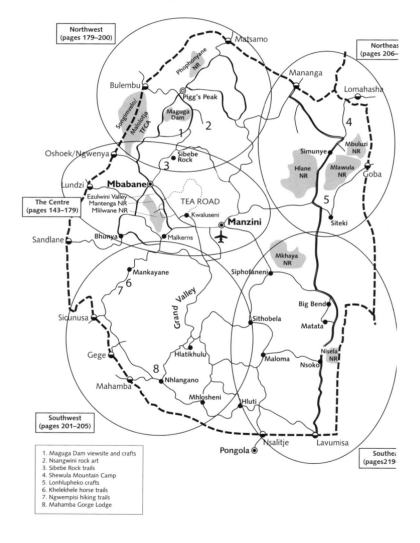

1. Maguga Dam viewsite and crafts
2. Nsangwini rock art
3. Sibebe Rock trails
4. Shewula Mountain Camp
5. Lonhlupheko crafts
6. Khelekhele horse trails
7. Ngwempisi hiking trails
8. Mahamba Gorge Lodge

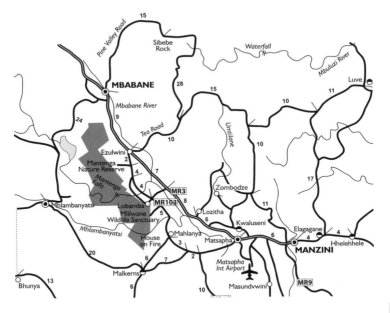

The Centre

Ngwenya

About 4km after the Oshoek/Ngwenya border post, you will see a
turnoff marked for the Ngwenya Glass Factory and Craft Village. This
road also leads to the Ngwenya Mine and Lion Cavern. Note that
Ngwenya is about 20km outside Mbabane and 30km from Ezulwini, so
you can either visit Ngwenya as a day trip, or plan to make a stop here
when you enter or leave Swaziland.

Ngwenya Glass Factory and Craft Village

Ngwenya Glass sells a wide range of hand-blown glassware, ranging
from beautiful vases to a bewildering variety of animal figurines in
various shades of kitsch. All the work is created from 100-percent-
recycled glass, and everything is done on site. An aerial walkway has
been constructed around the noisy factory, next to the main shop, and
this gives you an excellent overview (literally) of the glass-blowing
process. The heat from the glass-melting furnaces is unbelievable!

An attractive coffee shop is attached to the main building, where you can enjoy their selection of sweet and savoury pancakes while looking up at the peak of Ngwenya (Crocodile) Mountain. A craft village has been constructed next door to the factory, housing a number of intriguing stores that sell traditional Swazi crafts, homemade sweets and a toy shop that makes beautiful hand-carved rocking horses.

The story of Ngwenya Glass is inspiring. The factory was established in 1979 with the help of Swedish Aid, which brought master glass-blowers from Sweden to Swaziland to train the local people in this arcane art. The mentors stayed for two years, and the Ngwenya Glass Factory opened its shop to the public in 1981. Unfortunately, this community-run concern closed down in 1985 but it was re-opened two years later under new management.

Ngwenya Glass currently employs about 70 people, including three of the original glass blowers. The star blower is Sibusiso Mhlanga, who underwent advanced training in Sweden. His unique artworks are prominently displayed in the shop and sell for a high premium. Mhlanga also trains new apprentices in the factory. Apparently it takes about three months to learn the basics of glass gathering, which is a skill in itself, and one year to become a skilful part of the team. The glass comes mainly from bottles which are collected by communities from all over Swaziland. For many people, the money they get from the bottles is their main or even their only source of income.

According to the info boards stuck around the factory, Ngwenya Glass produces about 1,500 individual items every day. Eight people are needed to make a wine glass or an animal, such as an elephant or kudu, while three are needed for smaller objects like paperweights, fish or birds. All the blowers have to be right-handed, because the special chairs they sit in are designed for right-handed people. Ngwenya Glass exports its wares to South Africa and all over the world.

- Ngwenya Glass Factory shop, restaurant and craft village:
  268-442 4053; www.ngwenyaglass.co.sz

Handicraft
If glass isn't your cup of tea, there are a couple of other handicraft outlets in the vicinity. The old Ngwenya iron ore mine is the oldest mine

in the world (*see* below), next to which is the pretigious Endlotane Art Studio and Phumalanga Tapestries Workshop, specializing in large woven Bushman rock art and founder Christoph Reck's own contemporary designs.

Also try the Etulu Craft Village and Cultural High Grounds. Etulu is actually a multi-purpose venue that hosts weddings, parties and other cultural gatherings. Casual visitors are welcome, however, and there is a small but interesting Swazi Weavers shop that sells a range of woven mats, baskets and wall hangings made by local crafters. The shop contains several looms, and you could be lucky enough to catch a weaver at work. Refreshments may or may not be available and the courtyard is decorated with concrete chickens, which are good for a laugh.

- Endlotane Art Studio: 268-442 4940; www.endlotane.net
- Etulu Culutural High Grounds: 268-442 4037

Lion Cavern and Ngwenya Mine

Three kilometres away from Ngwenya Glass is Lion Cavern, reputedly the oldest mine in the world. The fascinating Ngwenya Mine Museum is adjacent to the cavern, and the whole complex is well worth a visit. To reach this excellent attraction, continue on the road that leads up the slopes of Ngwenya Mountain (said to look like the back of a crocodile) and follow signs to the Old Ngwenya Mine.

After a few kilometres you will reach an entrance gate. This is actually the southern-most part of the Malolotja Nature Reserve, administered by the Swaziland National Trust Commission (SNTC), and visitors have to pay a nominal fee to enter the reserve.

At the time of writing, non-residents will pay E25 per adult and E12 per child under twelve. Kids under four are free. This includes entry into the Mine Museum and an optional guided tour up to Lion's Cavern. When I was there, however, there was no one at the gate when I arrived, but it was open, so I just drove through. When I drove out, the guard was back in his hut—so I made sure to pay him before we left. Swaziland sometimes works on the honour system, so play fair!

As you drive higher up the mountain, the road narrows and winds through several cuttings in the mountainside. A short distance after the entrance gate, the tar switches to a rust-red gravel that will coat your tyres with a fine ochre-coloured powder. It's perfectly passable for most cars, however.

You will then come to a T-junction: the Visitors' Centre and mine museum is to the left, and Lion Cavern is to the right. Lion Cavern is only accessible as part of a guided tour, so go to the Visitors' Centre first. Note, however, that there is usually only one guide in attendance so, if the museum is locked, it means the guide is taking a group up to the cavern and you will have to wait. Alternatively, you can drive yourself to the cavern parking lot and wait for the guide there.

The diggings at Lion Cavern have been carbon-dated to 43,000 years ago, making the site the oldest known mine on earth. Perched high on an exposed promontory, these humble shafts were dug out of the rock by ancient Africans who extracted glittery specularite and blood-red haematite. It is thought that these minerals were crushed into a powder and used for body decoration and other ritualistic purposes. Haematite would later become a particularly important commodity as it was mixed with fat, grease and water to create the red paint that was used in many of the cave paintings which can be found around the region. Over time, haematite decomposes and rusts into a very stable compound, and this explains why these wonderful rock artworks have endured for so long.

The actual diggings at the cavern are not very extensive, only consisting of several shallow adits that have been hacked into the exposed rock face. The views from the cavern are spectacular, however, and visitors will enjoy looking across the Steynsdorp valley into the Songimvelo Nature Reserve on the South African side of the border. Incidentally, this mountain range is part of the Barberton granite-greenstone belt, which is one of the oldest identifiable rock-types on Earth. The granite-greenstone basement also contains fossilized evidence of cell division; one of the earliest forms of life found so far. There is even a theory that these 'cell fossils' belong to metal-processing bacteria, which would have found rich pickings in the ore deposits of Ngwenya.

The walk up to the cavern is pretty steep, but the path is well maintained and a stepped walkway gets you over the rocky parts so it's accessible for most people. Guided tours are available from 08:00 until 16:00. The return route should take about an hour to complete.

After the prehistoric miners moved on, nothing much happened at Lion Cavern for tens of thousands of years. Then, in the late 1800s, the mineral wealth of Ngwenya was noticed once again, this time by colonial prospectors. A short-lived gold mine was established on the lower slopes of the mountain in the 1890s, but this was soon forgotten. In 1946, however, vast iron ore deposits were discovered on the adjacent Bomvu ridge and, in the 1950s, the Anglo-American corporation secured the mining rights for the area.

The Ngwenya Mine duly started operations in 1964 and proceeded to extract 28,370,000 tons of high-grade iron ore before it was closed in 1977. Apparently, enough iron was recovered from this one site to manufacture every car that is currently driving around South Africa, Botswana, Lesotho and Swaziland.

In its day, the mine was a major source of revenue for Swaziland, accounting for about ten per cent of its annual Gross Domestic Product. Furthermore, in order to export the ore efficiently, a 210km railway line was built from the inaccessible mountain mine to the harbour at Maputo. There was so much ore, in fact, that the port at Maputo was too shallow for the three specially-designed ore tankers, built in Norway, and had to be dredged. When it was finally complete, this transport route gave other manufacturers in Swaziland a cheap and effective link to the global marketplace and helped kickstart the country's industrial growth.

But it wasn't all good news. You see, from Maputo, the ore was shipped to Japan, where a refinery was built to process the raw material. The finished product was then sold to Japanese companies and re-exported around the world, mainly as cars and trucks. Financing for the whole project was raised on the Johannesburg Stock Exchange and, as such, most of the profits from the mine went outside the country. So, although the mine provided employment and tax revenue, the people of Swaziland did not get the full benefit of their mineral wealth.

Apparently, this inequality infuriated King Sobhuza II to such an extent that he declared the mine should be closed down, even though there was plenty of ore left in the ground. Others say that a drop in world prices and declining yields made the mine unprofitable. Either way, the mine stopped digging in 1977 and by 1980, all the remaining stockpiles had been processed. The mine was then donated to SNTC for inclusion into the Malolotja Nature Reserve. Later, in 1995, the railway line west of Manzini, now long out of use, was taken up. Over the years several plans to re-open Ngwenya have been floated, but none have materialized.

Now, nearly 30 years later, there is another attempt to re-open the mine in order to capitalize on the high price of steel (although the recent financial crisis might scupper this latest scheme). We'll have to wait and see whether the noise of mining operations will shatter the tranquil mountain solitude once more.

In the meantime, visitors can explore the new mine museum, built on the lip of the vast terraced excavation pit, which opened in 2005. This installation has information about Lion Cavern, prehistoric cultures and the area's modern mining history. There are also a number of ancient artefacts on display and several unwieldy chunks of old-fashioned mining equipment to put it all into perspective.

- Malolotja Nature Reserve, Ngwenya Gate: 268-442 4241; www.sntc.org.sz

Ngwenya to Mbabane

After the turnoff for Ngwenya Glass and the Old Ngwenya Mine, the gracious double-lane carriageway of the MR3 continues through a basin of green fields dotted with homesteads. About 1km further along, you will see the turnoff to the MR1 highway that takes you to Hawane, Malolotja and Pigg's Peak. There is a large market at the foot of this off-ramp which can be trawled for a variety of traditional Swazi crafts.

As you continue to drive along the MR3, you will see turnoffs for several royal residences, such as Nkoyoyo and Maduna. These are not open to the public and visitors will probably be greeted by military guards. You will also see the sign for the Waterford-Kamhlaba International School. This is the most exclusive educational institution in Swaziland and, during the apartheid years, it was a favoured destination for the children of powerful black (and white) families from South Africa. Even a couple of Mandelas attended school here. Waterford-Kamhlaba is part of the United World Colleges movement which was founded in Britain, and the movement's patron is the Prince of Wales, who visited the school in 1987.

While some might say that the big, new MR3 highway is a waste of money in a poor country with bigger fish to fry, investment in infrastructure is a pretty safe bet. And it is certainly a big improvement over the old road, which was narrow and twisty. The improved MR3 is well lit; there are dozens of pedestrian bridges that offer safe access for people to cross from one side of the road to the other. This is a lesson that should be learnt by South African road builders, who force local residents to dice with death every time they want to get to the other side.

So, speeding right along, Exit 10 is marked for the Mbabane Country Club, which offers a golf course and a Sunday lunch with roast beef, no doubt. It is also marked for Sibebe Rock (*see* page 153). If you take this road, you will drive along a ridge on the top of Mbabane town before you come out on Somhlolo Road on the northern edge of the city centre. There are several B&Bs and guests houses along this stretch of road.

As you approach the outskirts of Mbabane, the impressive new highway falters. Construction on this part of the road is not yet finished, and you will be diverted onto the 'Bypass Road', a narrow detour that winds through the outlying suburbs of Mbabane. En route, you will pass an expanse of overgrown bush that is promisingly marked as the 'Mbabane Council Botanical Gardens site'. A few more twists and turns will bring you out onto the main road that leads into the middle of town. When the highway is complete, the MR3 will curve around Mbabane and lead directly onto the pass that takes you down into the Ezulwini Valley and Manzini.

- Stan's Lodge: 268-553 2041
- Ingwe Mabala Executive Hotel: 268-615 5226
- Nkoyoyo Guest House: 268-421 2422;
  www.thenkoyoyoguesthouse.com
- Kuthula Cottage: 268-404 6832

Mbabane

Mbabane (pronounced *m-Baba-neh* and not *Mba-baan*, as the whiteys say) is the administrative capital of Swaziland. All the major consulates and international organizations have their headquarters here and the bustling commercial hub of the city is always busy. Although it has an attractive setting, surrounded by the ancient rocks of the Dlangeni hills, it is a somewhat untidy town with a complicated city centre and scraggly residential suburbs spilling up the slopes.

The town has a population of some 100,000 people and you will find many restaurants, takeaway outlets, shops, guest houses, backpackers and B&Bs in the vicinity. There are also several small malls in the centre of town and, at night, you can get down at the town's bars and clubs. Someone recommended the Portuguese Club near the Spar—but enter at your own risk. After all, Swaziland isn't known for its nightlife.

In fact, to be honest, Mbabane doesn't have much to offer the visitor either by day or night. It is a fairly typical commercial centre where you can stock up on supplies, fix a puncture or grab a meal, but it isn't very pretty and you won't be encouraged to linger.

To make matters worse, the city centre is blighted by several incomplete buildings that further bring down the tone of the place. These half-built structures are the result of business disagreements, bankruptcies and/or shortages of funds and, even though they are located in prime positions, the offending concrete skeletons are unlikely to be fleshed out any time soon. After all, nothing happens very quickly in Swaziland.

However, since they are such distinctive landmarks, I took it upon myself to find out more. Apparently the big building on the hill was developed by SASSCO (the Swaziland Association of Savings and Credit Co-operatives). It was supposed to be an office block, but the whole scheme went bust and they're now looking for further investment to complete the project, so far without success. Sadly, in the meantime it stands forlorn and misshapen, looming over the city like an abandoned parking garage.

The other unfinished construction is in the middle of town, next to the Plaza Mall. The story is another sad tale of financial woe that involves two business partners who joined up to build a grand new shopping centre and office complex. Then the one guy went bankrupt and the other tried to buy up the building so that he could keep going. But the first guy refused to sell his share, claiming that he would soon have money again to complete the project. No agreement could be reached and the former partners went to court, where the judge ruled in favour of the bankrupt party. So, the building stands empty and the centre of Mbabane is scarred by an eternally dormant construction site.

The name of the settlement comes from Chief Mbabane Kunene, who was sent here by King Mbandzeni to look after some cattle kraals that were established to take advantage of the good grazing. 'Mbabane' is said to translate as a 'small and bitter Highveld plant', but it might also refer to the chief's allegedly dictatorial tendencies.

The current town of Mbabane dates back to 1887 when Bombardier Mickey Wells opened a little store and hotel in the area. This soon became part of a transport route from the Transvaal to Mozambique, which was so heavily trafficked that it became known as *Ndelakayomi* (path never empty).

A year later, Allister Miller arrived from Barberton. This notorious figure of the concessions era soon established himself as a figure of authority in the little village and went on to become secretary of the concession-holders' committee. As such, he had his fingers firmly embedded in many pies, and he kept them there for several decades.

Originally a journalist, Miller founded The *Times of Swaziland* newspaper in 1897 (which he ran almost single-handedly) and he also helped generate the first topographical map of Swaziland. He lived on the nearby Dalriach Farm (now a suburb of Mbabane), and the main road through town was formerly named after him. Recently, however, all the street names were changed to make them less Eurocentric. Miller Street has thus become Gwamile (Sobhuza II's grandmother, better known as Labotsibeni), and never the twain shall meet.

In 1902, after the Anglo-Boer War, the newly established British protectorate chose Mbabane as their headquarters as it was deemed to be higher, cooler and healthier than the old Transvaal Administration's capital at Bremersdorp (now Manzini). From this date, Mbabane began to grow apace.

According to the official visitors guide, other 'interesting' features in Mbabane include the old lamppost on the corner of Gwamile and Dr Shiahayi Road, which was once part of London's Waterloo Bridge. It also mentions the Old Secretariat, housed in a Cape Dutch-style building, which is directly opposite the City Inn, one of the oldest hotels in the country. I must confess that I have not spotted either of these landmarks, so can't attest to their tourism value.

At the end of Gwamile Street is the Mbabane Market. This was once housed in a series of old tin buildings, but these have been knocked down and replaced by a large concrete bunker. Venture inside and you'll find fresh fruit and veg, as well as the obligatory Swazi arts and crafts.

One place you really should check out is the Mountain Inn. It is poised on the very edge of town with an unrivalled view over the spectacular expanse of the Ezulwini Valley. Drink in the vista while you enjoy a cold beverage on the attractive terrace or enjoy a meal in their unintentionally retro-style dining room. To reach the Mountain Inn, follow signs to the left from the main road that leads towards Manzini.

Places to stay:

- Abacus Backpackers: 268-404 7854
- All-ways Backpackers Lodge (Baz Bus stop): 268-405 0741
- Brackenhill Lodge: 268-404 2887; www.brackenhillswazi.com
- Castle Hotel: 268-404 6439; www.swazi.com/hotels/castle
- Cathmar Cottages: 268-404 3387; www.visitswazi.com/cathmar
- City Inn: 268-404 2406; www.cityinn.sz
- Crisovik Guest House: 268-404 9883; www.crisovik.com
- Ekulindzeni Leisure Homes: 268-404 2575
- Ematjeni B&B: 268-404 3110; www.ematjeniswaziland.com
- Fair-Lady Mountain Cottages: 268-608 7613; www.fairlady.co.sz
- Green Valley Guest House: 268-404 4835
- Grifters Backpackers: 268-409 0056
- Jacana Lodge: 268-405 0671/2; www.jacanalodge.co.za
- Kapola Guest House: 268-404 0906; www.kapola_eden.co.sz
- Kent Rock B&B: 268-404 4826; www.visitswazi.com/kentrock
- Khula Golden Guest House: 268-404 5095
- Mountain Inn Hotel: 268-404 2781; www.mountaininn.sz
- Mountain View Cottages: 268-404 9085
- Nini's Guest House: 268-404 1879
- Penguin Guest House: 268-404 3045
- Red Berry B&B: 268-602 3160; www.redberrybb.co.sz
- The Rickden furnished flats: 268-604 7769; www.geocities.com/therickdenflats
- Thokoza Church Centre (for groups): 268-404 6681
- Tranquility Guest House: 268-404 2164
- Veki's Guest House: 268-404 8485; www.swazilodgings.com/vekis

Places to eat:

- Esangweni Restaurant (Pine Valley): 268-551 4436
- Finesse Restaurant: 268-404 5936
- Friar Tuck's @ Mountain Inn: 268-404 2781
- La Casserole Restaurant @ Omni Centre: 268-404 6462
- Pablos Restaurant / Caribbean Coffee House / King Pie / Green Room Bar @ City Inn: 268-404 8628
- Phoenix Steak House: 268-404 9103
- Plaza Tandoori Restaurant: 268-404 7599

To do:

- African Fantasy Curios: 268-404 0205; www.africanfantasy.de
- Indlinglizi Art Gallery and Coffee Shop: 268-404 6213
- Mbabane Golf Club: 268-404 9080
- Swanks Leather Goods: 268-404 3396
- Swazi Plaza shopping centre: 268-404 2531
- Serendipity Wellness Centre and Coffee Shop: 268-405 0452; www.serendipityhow.net
- The Mall shopping centre

Sibebe Rock

Located about 10km outside of Mbabane, Sibebe (Bald Rock) is the largest exposed granite pluton in the world. It is claimed to be the second largest freestanding rock in the world, after Uluru (Ayers Rock) in Australia. Although comparisons are understandable, the two sites are quite different. Uluru is a sandstone inselberg, literally an isolated 'mountain island' that was left behind after an old mountain range was eroded away. Sibebe, on the other hand, was formed when molten granite from the Earth's mantle pushed its way into a huge underground chamber, where it cooled and solidified into a dome before being exposed on the surface by erosion. Geologically speaking, the igneous Sibebe formation dates back about three billion years.

Today, this vast, bulbous formation of silver-grey stone remains a spectacular sight. The smooth flanks of the dome are streaked with dripping water that glistens in the bright sunlight, and the graceful slopes are partially cloaked with green vegetation. Unfortunately, the view from the road is limited by the mountainous topography that surrounds the rock, and the only way to truly appreciate the power of Sibebe is to walk up it.

There are a number of guided walking trails that will take you to the summit of Sibebe. These range from the gruelling 'steepest walk in the world' to more gentle ascents suitable for those who are not athletically inclined. Nevertheless, a walk to the top of the rock will take you from an altitude of 800 metres to 1,488 metres above sea level, so do your stretches! It takes about two-and-a-half hours to walk up and one-and-a-half hours to walk back down. Be aware that it can get very hot on the exposed rock face; guides advise that you start early to avoid the midday heat.

Those who are brave enough to tackle Sibebe won't be disappointed. The views are incredible and you will get to explore various caves, waterfalls and swimming holes en route. Birders may spot the rare blue swallow, the ground woodpecker and other avian delights. Plant spotters will also enjoy scanning the Sphagnum moss bogs for unusual specimens, such as orchids and the regionally threatened *Disa nervosa.*

Sibebe is located on Swazi Nation Land, which means it is held in trust by the king for the people of Swaziland. To further enhance this mandate, the guided walking tours are run by local community members as part of Swaziland's impressive Community Tourism programme.

Walking tours start from the visitors' centre at Mbuluzi Gate, which opens at 08:00. Prior bookings are recommended, but not essential. It costs about E25 per person. The small Sabie Coffee Shop offers refreshments, but it's probably a good idea to bring your own drinking water and hiking snacks.

If you are in the area during July, you also might want to try the Sibebe Survivor Challenge—an annual run/walk to the top of Sibebe. This fund-raising event is organized by the local Rotary Club, and attracts about 800 competitors. To reach the main Sibebe visitors' centre from Mbabane, follow Gwamile Street to the intersection with Somhlolo Street. Then follow signs to Pine Valley. A short distance out of town, you will see additional signs for Sibebe Walking Trails and Sibebe Community Trust. The narrow tarred road now winds through the beautiful Pine Valley, which boasts several unusual homes jutting out of the slopes, before turning to decent-quality gravel a short distance before the visitors centre itself. If you continue on this gravel road for about 30km, you will wind around the circumference of Sibebe before joining up with the Tea Road that leads down into the Ezulwini Valley.

- Sibebe Walking Trails and Sabie Coffee Shop: 268-404 6070
- Sibebe Survivor Walk/Run: www.sibebe.co.zs

Mhlambanyatsi and Bhunya

If you want to do a nice Sunday drive, take the MR19 from Mbabane to Mhlambanyatsi (Buffalo Crossing). This small town was originally established as a residential settlement for the workers of Usuthu Plantations. With 66,000 hectares under pine, this is ranked as one of the largest man-made forests in the world and Usuthu is a major player in the country's forestry industry, which collectively employs 8,000 people and contributes up to 15 per cent of Swaziland's GDP. The main paper mill at Bhunya produces about 100,000 tons of pulp a year.

The MR19 road therefore takes you through a series of vast pine plantations that sprawl over the granitic hills. Then, about 25km from Mbabane, you will arrive in Mhlambanyatsi. The evergreen Forester's Arms Hotel and Restaurant can be found nearby and is a popular place to stop over. Their Sunday lunches are legendary. The Meikles Mount Country Estate is also in the area, and they offer horse rides around Mhlane Mountain. There are several well-stocked fishing dams in the area, and the Usuthu Forests Country Club has a golf course.

From Mhlambanyatsi, you can either retrace your steps to Mbabane or continue on to Bhunya. From Bhunya, you can return to Mbabane via the Malkerns and Ezulwini Valley for an enjoyable round trip of about 100km—all on tar. Please note, however, that the MR19 between Mbabane and Mhlambanyatsi may be closed due to the continuing roadworks. If this is the case, you can still reach Mhlambanyatsi via the Malkerns Valley, although this route is much longer (70km each way).

- Forester's Arms: 268-467 4177; www.forestersarms.co.za
- Meikles Mount Country Estate: 268-467 4110
- Usuthu Forests Golf Club: 268-467 4021

Mbabane to Ezulwini

As you head out of Mbabane on the MR3 towards Manzini, the road dips over the crest of Malangwane hill and winds down to the floor of the expansive Ezulwini Valley—the Valley of Heaven, or Heavenly Place. This region is the tourism hub of the country, and visitors can spend several days happily exploring the dozens of hotels, restaurants, shops and attractions that are conveniently clustered in the compact Ezulwini area.

At the summit of the pass you will see the Old Barn Restaurant and Bar. This lively establishment offers good food, a wine cellar and a fully equipped children's room with a resident nanny.

As you descend the pass, there are excellent views of the wide Ezulwini Valley cradled between the Mdzimba and Malangwane hills, with the Mbabane River running along the floor. The pass is quite steep, however, so keep your eyes on the road. Before it was expanded into a four-lane highway, this was a narrow road with suicidal twists and bends. It's much better now, but you should still drive appropriately, especially in wet weather.

About halfway down, you may notice the semi-abandoned ruins of the old Swazi Inn Hotel on your left. This is another one of Swaziland's real estate orphans which, despite its excellent view site, has been standing empty for more than ten years. Apparently this establishment was owned by a Swazi tycoon who ruled over a considerable empire of coal mines, sugar plantations and other valuable assets. Unfortunately, he went bankrupt and his creditors started fighting over his remaining assets. With several financial institutions claiming ownership of the hotel, the situation became very complicated and the Swazi Inn fell into a legal limbo that has lasted for more than a decade.

A short distance further along, you will see a turnoff onto a gravel road marked for eDladleni Restaurant, the Mvubu Falls and Mvubu Falls Lodge all three are worth visiting.

eDladleni is an attractive restaurant that specializes in Swazi cuisine. Using only fresh, organic ingredients sourced from local farmers, the menu is tantalising and unusual. It's the perfect place to taste traditional Swazi dishes as served by a passionate cook, Dolores Goddefroy. They have even published a cookbook. When I was there, I commented that the free-range chicken legs I was munching looked big and strong. The chef agreed and said, "you can see they walked on the earth", which I found strangely comforting.

The Mvubu Falls Lodge is a simple establishment, offering accommodation in neat but rather ordinary rooms. However, there is an excellent bar and restaurant on the premises with an attractive wooden deck overlooking the Mvubu stream, and an ever-popular pool table.

The Mvubu Falls themselves are a series of lovely cascades and rock pools, set in a lush riverine environment. The falls can be reached via a pleasant walking trail that starts in the Lodge car park. The trail criss-crosses the Mvubu stream several times and is suitable for families. The route to the uppermost fall is about 3.5km (one way), and it should take between 90 minutes and two hours to complete the walk.

- Eden Guest House: 268-404 6317
- eDladleni Traditional Restaurant: 268-404 2106
- Mvubu Falls Lodge: 268-409 0078; www.mvubufalls.com
- Old Barn Restaurant and Bar: 268-404 2106

The Ezulwini Valley

At the foot of the Malangwane Pass, about 8km from Mbabane, there is an off-ramp from the MR3 that is marked with dozens of road signs for the Ezulwini Valley Hotels and Casinos, Malkerns Valley, Malandela's House on Fire, Gone Rural, the Calabash restaurant and many other attractions. This turnoff marks the start of the MR103, which used to be the old main road between Mbabane and Manzini before the new highway was built. The MR103 is now the most popular tourist route in the country.

With so much going on, you might fear that the Ezulwini Valley has become overdeveloped. Well, no. The buildings are unobtrusive and spaced far apart, and there are still lots of open fields, trees and little gravel roads leading off into the hills. Still, compared other parts of Swaziland, Ezulwini is like Las Vegas and some of my more earthy friends find it all too commercial for their tastes.

A short distance after the initial turnoff from the MR3, you will come to a little residential cluster. The small Thandabantu craft market is on the left and, to the right, you will find the famous Calabash restaurant and Timbali Lodge with its Boma restaurant.

The Calabash is worthy of special mention, as it has been the kingdom's home of fine dining for more than 20 years. The menu specializes in Austrian, German and Swiss cuisine, which betrays the nationality of the long-serving management team, and the restaurant also serves a variety of seafood dishes. An extensive wine list is available and the plush, air-conditioned interior offers diners a timeless slice of European sophistication, complete with the soothing sounds of light classical music, hushed conversations and the discrete tinkling of silverware on good plates.

If this is all bit too Olde Worlde for your tastes, the African-themed Boma restaurant at Timbali Lodge is right next door and its pizzas are highly regarded. Incidentally, Timbali used to be a caravan park but has now been transformed into a luxurious, if a trifle gaudy, hotel.

- The Calabash Restaurant: 268-416-1187;
  www.restaurant-calabash.com
- Timbali Lodge and the Boma Restaurant: 268-416 2632;
  www.timbalilodge.co.sz
- Thanda Bantu handicraft market: 268-416 2577

The Casino Resorts and the Cuddle Puddle
A couple of kilometres farther along, you come to the tourism epicentre of the Ezulwini Valley. This is centred around the three adjacent resort hotels operated by Sun International: the Ezulwini Sun, the Lugogo Sun and the flagship Royal Swazi Sun and Spa. Each resort is set in beautifully maintained grounds and offers a selection of bars, restaurants, swimming pools and activities, the details of which are too numerous to mention. A regular shuttle bus connects the three establishments. The Royal Swazi Sun also has a good golf course and a compact casino.

Just below the Royal Swazi Sun is the Cuddle Puddle, more correctly known as the SwaziSpa Health and Beauty Studio. This attractive complex is built on the site of a natural hot spring which has been channelled into a large outdoor swimming pool, and a variety of spa treatments and therapeutic massages are available. A small entrance fee is charged for admission, but many locals just strip off and splash about in the natural pool on the edge of the complex, which is reserved for the community. Interestingly, it's the hot springs that led to the development of the Ezulwini tourism hub in the first place. As David Johnson puts it, "decades ago, midnighters from the Swazi Inn and other diners-and-dancers were wont to drive down the hill and, evening dress or not (usually not) disport themselves in the spring". And that's how it came to be known as the Cuddle Puddle …

The development of tourism in Swaziland was slow, however. In 1907, there were five hotels in the country: one in Bremersdorp/Manzini, two in Mbabane, one near the Forbes Reef mine and one near the Pigg's Peak mine. In 1949, there were only four hotels in operation and, in 1960, there were still no tarred roads in the country. Then, in 1963, the government passed the Casino Act in an attempt to increase the number of visitors and to generate revenue.

The Southern Sun group quickly stepped in and built the Royal Swazi Spa Hotel with the first casino in southern Africa, which opened in 1965. The location for the hotel was right next to the Cuddle Puddle, which it bought the following year. Then, in 1969, a Swedish-trained beauty therapist named Jenny Thur set up a massage and beauty salon next to the spring, in partnership with the hotel.

This early version of a wellness centre was housed in an innovative complex of domed concrete structures, designed to resemble traditional Swazi beehive huts and, even though the spa has been expanded over the years, those original buildings are still standing. Naturally, the magnesium-rich water was used in many of the spa's treatments and therapies, and word of the facility soon spread. The spa subsequently passed through the hands of several managers until it was taken over by Horst Sayler, a masseur and physical fitness instructor with German training. He has now been running the Cuddle Puddle for more than 25 years, and is a consultant for the Swaziland Olympic Team.

Meanwhile, in the late 1960s, the Holiday Inn group came to southern Africa and built its first hotels at Ermelo, Hluhluwe and Ezulwini. This latter establishment opened to great fanfares in 1970, right next door to the Royal Swazi. A few years later, in 1974, the Ezulwini Holiday Inn opened across the road.

This cluster of sophisticated hotels began attracting scores of holidaymakers from South Africa, many of whom were keen to revel in the less repressed atmosphere of a country that allowed gambling

THE CENTRE

and interracial discourse—nudge, nudge. The soft-core porn movies screened in the Royal Swazi cinema were also very popular, as this kind of blue entertainment was forbidden in Calvinist SA.

In the years that followed, the Ezulwini Valley became the 'golden mile' of Swaziland's tourism industry, and many other hotels and attractions set up shop along the road. As for the original trailblazers, Holiday Inn and Southern Sun merged in 1983 to become Sun International, which now operates all three hotels in partnership with the Swazi Government.

With all the activity in the Ezulwini Valley as a spur, the tourism industry started to grow, from 90,000 visitors in 1972 to a peak of 130,000 in 1975. Then, political problems in South Africa grew worse and numbers dipped to a low of 76,000 in 1981. Things were helped by King Mswati III's coronation in 1986, which got lots of international publicity and helped reinforce the 'royal experience' of Swaziland. Then, during the 1990s, porn and gambling became legal in South Africa and, at the same time, competition among southern African nations for tourists became more fierce. So, to shore up visitor numbers, the tourism authorities switched emphasis and began to heavily promote the country's more compelling assets, such as cultural heritage, traditional ceremonies, natural beauty, adventure activities and the wonderfully peaceful atmosphere of the kingdom (especially when compared its crime-ridden neighbour).

This campaign delivered results—Swaziland now hosts over half a million visitors a year, who inject nearly E300 million into the economy annually. About 30 per cent of this is spent on curios and craft, and it is estimated that one in three households have at least one member involved in the handicraft industry. Most tourists still come from South Africa but German, Dutch and French guests are also common— especially as part of organized coach tours that incorporate Swaziland into a Jo'burg-Kruger-Durban itinerary. Backpackers and young people who do 'volunteer tourism' during their gap year are another significant sector of the industry. And to think that it all started with a bunch of randy revellers frolicking in the Cuddle Puddle.

- Ezulwini Sun Hotel: 268-416 6000
- Lugogo Sun: 268-416 4000

Left: All smiles after a successful family shopping trip to Manzini

Centre: Even unexpected visitors (i.e. lost) get a grin at the homestead above Khopho Hut, part of the Ngwempisi Hiking Trail

Below: In an apparently spontaneous gesture, the Dlamini children asked if they could get dressed up and do some traditional dancing, Mdzimba plateau

Above: Men in their traditional finery getting ready to enter the Royal Kraal on the last day of the Ncwala Ceremony

Below: Free-range cattle crossing the road on the way to Malolotja – drive carefully, there are no fences!

A stoned tribute
to Bob Marley and
the Rasta spirit,
Malolotja

Above: Finally, clocks designed for African conditions, from Rainbow Angel at the Mantenga Craft Market

Below: Light up your life with handmade candles from the Swazi Candles Factory in the Malkerns Valley

Handmade mats, rugs, baskets and other homewear is available at Gone Rural, Malkerns Valley

Top: Thousands of sprinklers irrigate the vast sugar cane fields around Simunye
Above: The low-level causeway over the Usuthu/Lusutfu River at Big Bend
Left: The gravel Tea Road undulates over the mountains above the Ezulwini Valley

Top left: An eager salesperson is just waiting to take your order at the Ngwenya Glass Factory Shop
Centre left: Ngwenya Glass produces a range of intricate and delicate glass figurines
Bottom left: Colourful curios cram craft markets across the country
Above: The blazing hot furnaces of Ngwenya Glass factory, where you can watch recycled glass being melted down and reformed into all kinds of wonderful objects

Above: A stony
countenance looking
out over the Mdzimba
plateau

Left: School kids pour
out of class in the
Ezulwini Valley

Top left: Mandla
Masuku, my excellent
tour guide, explains the
intricate etiquette of
Swazi traditional attire

Right: The colourful
workers' compound
at the old Bulembu
Asbestos Mine, now
turned into an unlikely
tourism destination

Above: The expansive view from the top of Bulembu, the pass of the Spider's Web

Right: Most homesteads cultivate their own plot of maize, to help keep the family going

A stunning sunset flares up and silhouettes the pine plantations
that surround the town of Pigg's Peak

A spectacular view from boulder-strewn summit of Mdzimba Mountain, down into the Ezulwini Valley

- Royal Swazi Sun and Spa: 268-416 5000;
  www.sun-international.com
- King's Cup Golf Tournament at Royal Swazi: 268-404 9693
- African Queen (shop): 268-516 4570
- Cuddle Puddle Hot Springs and Spa: 268-416 1164;
  www.swaziweb.net/cuddle.html

A few hundred metres south of the Ezulwini Sun is a large craft market, known as Buhle Besibuko Semaswati. This extended roadside complex consists of a long line of wooden stalls that collectively offer just about every type of Swazi craft imaginable. Whether you like weaving, baskets, wooden masks, animal figurines, printed fabric, stone carvings, baubles, bangles or beads, you will find something to buy here. There is a huge amount of stuff on sale but many of the stalls have similar products on offer, so take your time to look around before choosing the pieces you really want.

As is the case at most roadside craft markets, haggling over the price is part of the experience but don't be too ruthless—these traders have a meagre income, and the extra couple of bucks will mean a lot more to them than it does to you.

If you are looking for slightly more upmarket arts and crafts, visit the Swaziland Trading House, located in a large white building just behind the Buhle Besibuko market. This initiative is a joint venture between the Swazi Ministry of Enterprise and Employment and the W. K. Kellogg Foundation, which seeks to develop the international market for Swazi crafts by facilitating import and export activities. The casual shopper is also welcome, however, and the retail shop inside the Trading House offers specially selected handcrafts that are more unusual (and therefore more expensive) than the common or garden variety you'll find along the roadside. Locally produced clay pots, woven sisal baskets, tableware, accessories, clothing, jewellery and home décor are all available, and they will arrange for delivery just about anywhere in the world.

Across the road from the craft market is a petrol station that houses the First Horse Chinese Restaurant. This establishment is the last remnant of the old Yen Saan Hotel, a bizarre Chinese-styled building with scarlet trim that used to occupy the site many years ago.

Apparently, the food at the First Horse is good, but it looks decidedly dodgy ... my advice is to fill up your car, not your stomach. A better dining option is the lovely Woodlands Restaurant, located nearby, which serves good food on a large patio that overlooks the mountains. Alternatively, you could try the smart new Royal Villas complex which offers a 'pan-African' dining experience at the Lihawu Restaurant. Royal Villas also offers upmarket accommodation.

There are currently plans to develop a new five-star hotel, theme park and an international convention centre in this part of the valley. The hotel and ICC will rise up from the ashes of the Yen Saan Hotel, while the 'Africa in one location' theme park will be built on the site of the nearby greyhound stadium. This is all part of Swaziland's long-term 'Millennium Project'—a 25-year blueprint that seeks to invest hundreds of millions in the country's tourism and business infrastructure.

- Swaziland Trading House: 268-416 3286; www.swazimarket.com
- Woodlands Restaurant: 268-416 3466
- Royal Villas and Lihawu Restaurant: 268-416 7035; www.royalvillasswaziland.com

The Tea Road

At the northern end of Ezulwini, on the opposite side of the valley from the MR103, is the Tea Road—a gravel pass that twists up the side of Mdzimba Mountain. As the name suggests, in the 1970s there was an attempt to establish a tea plantation on the steep slopes, but it was unsuccessful. Today, this very scenic route is dotted with villages and makes for a good day trip, with grand views over the valley.

To reach the Tea Road, turn onto the little road next to the Thandabantu craft market, just before/after the turnoff to the Calabash and Timbali Lodge. There is a small sign marking it for the Tea Road and a bigger sign for Bethel Court Guest House. Dodge the chickens as you drive past Bethel Court and through a village with several co-ops and stores. You will soon cross a bridge over the main MR3 highway. Keep left at the fork in the road and engage a low gear, as the sandy path starts climbing up the mountain. This part of the road may be slippery in wet weather, when a 4x4 would be preferable.

Dozens of homesteads with small patches of maize now line the roadside. Near the top of the pass, you'll see a weird little house built on top of a large boulder. A little way on, you will see a large dome with a trig beacon on top. This is a good place to get out of the car and walk to the edge of the mountain for a view of the entire valley. Some distance further along, on the left hand side, you may spot a distinctive rock formation that is featured on Swaziland's paper currency.

From here, you can either return back down the Tea Road or continue over the mountains. If you keep going, the road now undulates over the green mountain-top plateau. This part of the range has several caves that were used to shelter the Swazi people during Zulu raids in the 19th century, but these are not open to the public.

At the next fork in the road, keep left (right takes you to a restricted army base). After this, there are a couple of other turnoffs along the way, but just keep tending right and you can't get too lost. If you do lose your sense of direction, there are several villages in the area, so don't be afraid to ask one of the passing locals for directions. The road will eventually bring you back to earth just outside Manzini, where you can get the highway back to Ezulwini. The distance from Ezulwini to Manzini is about 45km.

Mantenga Nature Reserve
A short distance further along the MR103, there is a turnoff marked for Mantenga Falls and Nature Reserve. This side road, which can also be reached from the Gables Shopping Centre, offers access to Legends Backpackers Lodge and the various attractions of the Mantenga Nature Reserve. The road rejoins the MR103 at Lobamba.

Mantenga is a great place to visit. This small reserve, measuring only 725 hectares, was established by the Swaziland National Trust Commission between 1979 and 1994. Its star attraction is the beautiful Mantenga waterfall—the largest in Swaziland in terms of water volume—which is part of the Little Usuthu River (Lusushwana). The falls can be reached via a short walking path and swimming in the large pool at the foot of the falls is permitted.

Although the reserve does not have any big game, you might spot vervet monkeys, baboons, serval, bushpigs, porcupines, rock dassies and bushbabies darting through the thick forest. Larger animals include kudu, nyala, klipspringer and grey and red duiker, and it is possible that elusive leopards live in the reserve. About half the reserve is covered by dense, indigenous forest. This lush canopy harbours a wealth of birdlife, including the endangered bald ibis. Tree-spotters should keep an eye out for waterberry (umncozi), kiaat (umvangati) and *Combretum molle* (imbondvo lomnyama). The remainder of the reserve, however, is part of an old gumtree plantation that has many alien species. This invasive vegetation is now being chopped down so that the natural ecosystem can resurrect itself.

Visitors to Mantenga should also take a tour through the Swazi Cultural Village, named 'Ligugu Lemaswati' (the pride of the Swazi people) by King Mswati III. This facility is designed as a living museum that showcases traditional Swazi lifestyles, circa 1850. The 'village' consists of 16 huts made from traditional building material, including wooden poles, grass, reeds, leather strips, earth and dried cow-dung. Each hut has a specific function and is furnished with period implements. A vigorous display of traditional Swazi dancing and singing is also part of the tour. You can even visit a genuine sangoma (diviner) who will throw the bones and foretell your future

Although some academics dismiss cultural villages as artificial and stilted, Mantenga is a pretty good example of its type. The village has been put together with passion and is often visited by Swazi school children as part of their cultural education. In any case, the guided tour is very informative, and guests will emerge with a much better idea of the principles and practices that underlie Swazi culture.

The reserve's gates are open from 07:00 to 18:30 daily; day visitors are welcome from 08:00 to 17:00. Tours leave at 09:00, 12:00, 14:00 and 16:00. Traditional dancing shows take place at 11:15 and 15:15. Entrance to the village costs E150 per person.

The on-site Swazi River Café serves breakfast, lunch and dinner buffets on an open-air wooden deck that overlooks the water. Traditional Swazi and western food is available; the restaurant is fully licensed. There are also regular braais held at the waterfalls every Sunday. Breakfast costs E95 per person, lunch is E120 and dinner is E180. Group rates are available.

There are several accommodation options available at Mantenga. The privately run Mantenga Lodge offers luxurious wooden chalets and hotel-style rooms in a beautiful setting. The SNTC also has 20 luxury tents available on a bed-and-breakfast basis (the first night is E585 for two people; additional nights are E535). And, if you want a more authentic experience, why not spend the night in one of the traditional beehive huts (only E80 per person, shared ablution facilities). If you have your own tent, you can camp in the reserve for E50 per night.

Finally, there is the Mantenga Craft Market. This fanciful collection of shops is housed in an old building just outside the entrance gate to the reserve. The market contains several above-average shops that offer a selection of unusual handicrafts, and is the perfect antidote for shoppers who are bored with all the repetitive roadside tat. My personal favourite is Rainbow Angel, which sells a range of unique and humorous wooden sculptures.

Rosecraft Weavers outlet is also nice, especially if you like Mohair blankets and shawls. If you like bling, check out the Guava Gallery— the only manufacturing jewellers in Swaziland. They also serve light lunches. Other shops that may be open (depending on when you visit) include Khaya Craft (sisal baskets), Shiba Rugs (woven mats), Benguni Craft (curios), African Fantasy (arts and crafts) and Hawu! Pots.

Mantenga Craft Market is also the home of Swazi Trails. This well-established tour operator offers full-day and half-day guided tours that can be mixed and matched to your requirements. These include History and Culture Trails, Art & Craft Trails, Wildlife Trails and Adventure Trails. They also offer white-water rafting in the Great Usuthu River, quad biking, guided hiking tours, abseiling, adventure caving, horse riding, mountain biking, paragliding, 4x4 excursions and rap-jumping. The nearby Legends Backpackers Lodge is affiliated to Swazi Trails and offers convenient overnight accommodation.

- Mantenga Nature Reserve and Cultural Village: 268-416 1151; www.sntc.org.sz
- Mantenga Lodge: 268-416 1049/21; www.mantengalodge.com
- Mantenga Craft Centre: 268-416 1136
- Swazi Trails: 268-416 2180; www.swazitrails.co.sz
- Legends Backpacker Lodge (Baz Bus stop): 268-416 1870
- Rosecraft Weavers: 268-416 1829; www.swazirosecraft.com
- Guava Gallery Manufacturing Jewellers and Bistro: 268-416 1343
- African Fantasy: 268-416 3117; www.africanfantasy.de

Lobamba

Back on the MR103, you will soon arrive at the Gables Shopping Centre. From the parking lot of this relatively new retail complex you will get an excellent view of two local landmarks: Sheba's Breasts and Nyonyane (Execution Rock). These two mountain peaks look across at each other from opposite sides of a wide valley and form a grand framing device for the entire scene. Execution Rock can be ascended as part of a guided tour that departs from Mlilwane (*see* page 168). Unfortunately, from the Gables, Sheba's Breasts are lined up one behind the other and you can only get a good view of the mountain's décolletage from the Malkerns side of the hills.

The Gables contains a small but well-stocked Pick 'n Pay supermarket, several useful shops and a number of restaurants, including Kanimambo (Portuguese), the Great Taipei (Chinese), Quartermain's (pub and steak house), the Bengal Tiger (Indian) and Linda's Coffee Shop.

Next door to the Gables is a clean and tidy craft market with a fairly typical selection of masks, sculptures and cloths. Across the road is the legendary Happy Valley Motel—home of the Sir Loin Steakhouse, Bella Vista pizzeria, a sports bar and the infamous Why Not Disco. At the back of the Why Not is the even more infamous If Not Go-Go Bar. This lurid establishment is dark and dingy, with deep red wall paper and a small stage for dancers to strut their stuff. The girls here are *very* friendly and if you aren't careful, you could pick up a lot more than you bargained for. Apparently, the Why Not and Happy Valley Motel are currently undergoing a facelift, which is probably for the best.

A short distance further along, situated about halfway between Ezulwini and Malkerns, is the royal centre of Lobamba. As we have seen, the Ezulwini Valley has played host to the kings and queens of Swaziland for over 200 years. Today there are still several important royal residences and venues in the area, including Ludzidzini, Lobamba, Lozitha State House and Embo State Palace. Many important cultural celebrations, such as the *umhlanga* and *incwala* festivals, take place in the area.

If you aren't lucky enough to be around during one of these national celebrations, you should still take some time to turn off the MR103 and visit two of Swaziland's important heritage sites. The first (and most revered) of these is the King Sobhuza II Memorial Park. Although it may be rather humble when you compare it to other international monuments, such as the Lincoln Memorial, this complex is a heartfelt tribute to the memory of Swaziland's beloved monarch, Sobhuza II—father of current incumbent Mswati III.

The park contains a huge statue of the king, surrounded by his optimistic motto 'I have no enemies'. There is also a sacred mausoleum that is guarded 24 hours a day (no photographs of the latter—they're very strict) and a museum that outlines the life of Sobhuza II and the role he played in the formation of the modern Swazi state. The complex was built with the help of the Taiwanese government.

Next door is the Swaziland National Museum and the headquarters of the Swaziland National Trust Commission, custodians of the nation's heritage and its national archives. Although there are some interesting exhibits in the museum, including a small replica of a traditional village, most of the installations are faded and in need of an upgrade. Nevertheless, you will be able to find out more about Swazi pre-history, ecology, social development and modern Swazi culture. And don't miss King Sobhuza's car collection, consisting of two mammoth old yank tanks which might have been impressive back in the 1950s, but are now just wryly retro.

Although the museum needs a major spruce-up, this institution plays an important role in the educational curriculum of the country. The SNTC tries to make sure that every school child in Swaziland gets to visit the museum at least once, and the museum also mounts roadshows that take the message of national pride and cultural continuity out into the local communities. Entrance to the museum or King Sobhuza Memorial Park is E20, but a double ticket that gets you into both is just E25, so go ahead and make a meal of it!

Across the road from the museum is the national parliament building. This hexagonal structure topped with a brass dome was a generous independence gift from Britain. It was officially opened in 1969 by Princess Alexandra, on behalf of Queen Elizabeth. The Somhlolo National Stadium, built in 1968, is also in the area and hosts sports matches, gatherings and the occasional music concert. It was particularly popular venue back in the 80s, when artists such as Percy Sledge and Peter Tosh performed in Swaziland and English soccer teams Spurs, Liverpool and Man United played exhibition matches.

- African Fantasy Craft Shop @ The Gables: 268-416 3469; www.africanfantasy.de
- Happy Valley Motel, Why Not Nightclub, Sir Lion Steakhouse: 268-416 1061; www.happyvalley.co.sz
- Kanimambo Restaurant @ The Gables: 268-416 3549
- King Sobhuza II Memorial Park: 268-416 2131; www.sntc.org.sz
- Quartermain's Pub & Restaurant @ The Gables: 268-416 3023
- Swaziland National Museum: 268-416 1516; www.sntc.org.sz

Mlilwane Wildlife Sanctuary

Mlilwane is Swaziland's oldest conservation area. It was established in 1961 when Ted Reilly turned the family farm into a game sanctuary to protect the dwindling stocks of wild animals in the Kingdom. The reserve opened to the public in 1964, and has since gone from strength to strength. Today, Mlilwane is the most visited park in Swaziland and offers visitors a wide range of activities. Day visitors will pay E25 per person for admission, as a once-off payment for an unbroken stay. Entrance is free with a valid Wild Card. Wild cards are available at the Big Game Parks' office in The Gables shopping centre.

Mlilwane covers 4,560 hectares and is split into two sections. The southern section is characterized by open grasslands and is dominated by the peak of Nyonyane Mountain, also known as Execution Rock. This lofty peak is historically significant as it was once home to ancient Bushmen, and several Swazi royal graves have been identified in the area. If you haven't already guessed, its gruesome name dates from previous centuries when convicted criminals were pushed off the precipitous summit to account for their sins (and feed the vultures).

The northern section of the reserve is more mountainous and is maintained as a wilderness area. As such, there are very few facilities and the only way to explore this pristine area is as part of a guided trail. Some remnants of the old tin mine that was located on Mlilwane can also be seen.

Game drives and horse rides are a major attraction at Mlilwane. These can be done as a self-drive excursion or as part of a guided tour in open Landrovers or on horseback. These safaris last about one-and-a-half hours and depart throughout the day, but the Sunrise and Sunset drives are the best bet (cost is about E150 per person).

There are a number of hiking and mountain bike trails through the reserve. Guides are available at a cost of E40 per person, and bikes can be rented by the hour. If you bring along your own bike, you may ride for no additional charge. Keen bikers might want to check out the annual Imvelo Classic mountain bike race, which is held in the reserve. Ambitious hikers can test their mettle by tackling the strenuous walk up to the top of Execution Rock. There is also a two-and-a-half-hour guided birding walk, which should appeal to twitchers (E75 pp).

If you like horse riding, Chubeka Trails offers a range of outrides that cater for all tastes. Kiddies' rides are available for only E15 a go; outrides are E100 per hour and the Rock of Execution Challenge, which takes you to the top of Nyonyane, costs E400 per person (including drinks and a snack). There are also a number of spectacular overnight trails, such as the one-night Cave Trail, the two-night Klipspringer Trail and the four-night Swazi Culture & Scenery Trail, which takes you deep into the isolated northern section of the park. All overnight trails are fully catered and cost between E1,000 and E5,500 per person.

In terms of dining options, the popular Hippo Haunt restaurant and bar overlooks the hippo pool and is a popular spot for a sundowner or an evening meal under the stars. There are also several communal picnic spots with braai facilities available.

Culture vultures might want to experience the traditional Sibhaca dancing display that takes place around the campfire every evening. And you can also take the Umphakatsi Visit, which drops in on the neighbouring chief in her homestead. This 'hands-on' cultural experience sounds like fun. Ladies are given traditional party cloths, *emahiya*, to wrap around their waists and female guests are encouraged to try their hand at grinding maize and plaiting mountain grass.

There are a number of accommodation facilities at Mlilwane. Lovers of luxury should try Reilly's Rock, which is redolent with colonial charm. This sumptuous hilltop lodge is the original home of Mickey Reilly, the founder of the Reilly dynasty, and the main building dates back 100 years. Rates vary between E575 and E725 per person sharing.

Moving down the scale, the main rest camp consists of six rustic wood-and-thatch huts and two comfortable beehive huts made of grass. Larger family groups may want to rent Shonalanga Cabin, which has self-catering facilities and a private braai area. The reserve also has three 'beehive villages', built in the traditional Swazi way. Rates hover around E225 pp sharing for the first two guests and E110 for each additional bed. Finally, there is a campsite with electricity points and a communal ablution block (E50 pp), and large groups can be accommodated in the Timberlog dormitory.

For the budget-conscious traveller, Sondzela Backpackers is a vibey spot which offers accommodation in dorms (E70 pp), double rooms (E100 pp) and twelve private rondavels (E110 pp). Sondzela also allows camping (E40 pp).

- Mlilwane Wildlife Sanctuary /Sondzela Backpackers/Reilly's Rock: 268-528 3943; www.biggameparks.org
- Imvelo MTB Classic: 268-416 3011; www.imvelo.co.sz
- Lizkar (Federation Equestrian International Africa Cup): 268-602 1275

Additional Ezulwini contacts

- Bethel Court: 268-416 1977; www.bethelcourt.co.sz
- Buhleni Farm Chalets: 268-416 3505; www.buhlenifarm.co.sz
- Ebuhleni Prestigious Guest House: 268-416 3466
- Ekuphumleni Guest House: 268-416 2313
- Elite Guest House: 268-416 1553
- Langa Restaurant: 268-416 4571
- Lidwala Backpackers Lodge: 268-550 4951; www.all-out.org
- Lisa's B&B: 268-605 3443
- Sleepwell Guest House: 268-416 1698
- Southern Cross Lodge and Backpacker: 268-622 7920
- Victory Guest House: 268-416 3309

The Malkerns Valley Meander
A short distance beyond the turnoff to the Mlilwane Wildlife Sanctuary is the village of Mahlanya, with a cluster of shops at the intersection with the MR27 to Malkerns, Bhunya and Mhlambanyatsi. There are several outstanding attractions along this Malkerns Valley road, so turn right and prepare to be amazed.

House on Fire and Malandela's

A few hundred metres after the intersection, you will see a sizeable collection of buildings that is marked as Malandela's and House on Fire. It may not look like much from the outside, but this is one of Swaziland's most remarkable structures and is a must-see.

Billed as an 'Afro-Shakespearian Globe Theatre', the House on Fire is an open-air performance venue that is used for music events and parties. It is built around an amphitheatre and is lavishly decorated with hundreds of sculptures, intricate mosaics and delicate metalwork. Everything has been executed with an amazing sense of detail and a generous sense of humour. A daytime stroll through the House on Fire is a delight for the senses and an evening performance in this unique space is an experience to be savoured.

The Malandela complex also contains a comfortable restaurant with a wooden deck, a cosy English-style pub and an excellent B&B with many hand-crafted touches. The shops include Ziggy's Internet Café, Baobab Batik, Zoggs Handicrafts and Gone Rural, a non-profit initiative which sells attractive homeware and jewellery made by members of the local community.

House on Fire/Malandela's started out life as a farm stall that was run by the Thorne family, who owned the surrounding farm. Then, since the patriarch of the clan liked to build things, a pub was constructed and a wine cellar was dug out. All the excavated soil was subsequently used to build the restaurant and shops. Next came the House on Fire and, finally, the B&B. In the future, Malandela's hopes to create an 'African piazza' with more shops and restaurants. I'm sure it will be spectacular.

House on Fire was the brainchild of Jiggs Thorne, who studied drama and other liberal arts in South Africa. During his time in SA, Jiggs made the acquaintance of several local craftsmen and artists, and when he returned to his homeland, he drew on these connections to create a collective of South African and Swazi artists who made House on Fire a new performance venue unlike anything else on Earth.

- House on Fire: 268-528 2110; www.house-on-fire.com
- Malandela's B&B: 268-528 3448; www.malandelas.com
- Malandela's Farmhouse Restaurant and Pub: 268-528 3115
- Gone Rural: 268-550 4936; www.goneruralswazi.com

- Ziggy's Internet Café and Tourism Information Centre: 268-528 3423
- Zoggs Handicrafts: 268-528 3466
- Baobab Batik: 268-528 3982; www.baobab-batik.com

Malkerns

A few kilometres down the road from Malandela's is the village of Malkerns, named after a turn of the century trader, Malcolm Kerns Stuart. This agricultural area is anchored by the large Swazican Cannery, established in 1954. It considers itself a world leader in pineapple- and citrus-segment products, and it grows most of its own fruit. The extensive pineapple farm is located adjacent to the cannery and is harvested from February to May, and again from August to November. The Swazican Citrus Farm in the Lowveld of the country produces 28,000 tons of citrus every year from its 2,200-hectare estate. The company is now run by the South African-based Rhodes Food Group—which is mildly ironic, given Rhodes' colonial background.

Malkerns village is a rather ramshackle place with a couple of restaurants, shops and a country club. It is very green, almost swallowed up by the dense vegetation, but it isn't particularly interesting. In the middle of the village there is an intersection with the MR18. Turn right if you are going to Mhlambanyatsi or the Ngwempisi Hiking Trail (see below). Turn left to visit the famous Swazi Candle factory and craft village. This latter road rejoins the MR103 a short distance down from the Malandela's turnoff.

Swazi Candles

Swazi Candles was started back in 1981 by several South Africans who wanted to escape from the repressive apartheid regime. So, they emigrated to rural Swaziland and began making hand-crafted candles in a cowshed. Over the years, they recruited and trained local people in this illuminating art, and Swazi Candles now employs over 200 people and exports its goods all over the world.

The Swazi Candle factory is an interesting place to visit. The workshop is open plan, so you can watch the candle-making process in detail. The shop has a vast selection of hundreds of candles in every shape, colour and pattern you can imagine.

The surrounding craft village has a large curio market, a Rosecraft Weavers outlet and a restaurant.

- Swazi Candles: 268-528 3219; www.swazicandles.com
- Rosecraft Weavers: 268-528-2039; www.swazirosecraft.com
- Sambane Restaurant: 268-604 2035

A little bit farther along the MR18 is Baobab Batik, a shop that sells locally produced prints, cushion covers, cloths and other homewares. It is located at the gate of the Nyanza Horse Riding School, which has self-catering cottages and offers horse rides through the countryside.

- Baobab Batik: 268- 528 3177; www.baobab-batik.com
- Nyanza Cottages and Horse Trails: 268-528 3090; www.nyanza.co.sz

Ngwempisi and Khelekhele trails

If you want to get away from it all and venture deep into the mountains of rural Swaziland, turn right at Malkerns village and follow the MR18 towards Mankayane (Little Steps).

After you pass the Luyengo Agricultural Campus of the University of Swaziland, the tranquil road rises and dips through the green hills before it starts climbing up into the Ntfungula Mountains. This is the location for two excellent community tourism projects that seek to help local communities uplift themselves by directly tapping into the valuable tourism industry.

First up is the Ngwempisi hiking trail. This beautiful route leads along the Ngwempisi River and offers walkers many opportunities to splash about in the cool water. There are several day trails available as well as a superlative three-night expedition. Groups of up to 16 people can be accommodated. The trail is self-catering, or you can arrange for the local community to supply home-cooked meals. The cost is E100 pppn. The nearby Horseshoe Estate has a cosy cottage called the Log House, where you can stay before or after you do the trail. The cottage is fully equipped and sleeps twelve; the cost is E110 pppn.

A little bit farther along the road is Khelekhele, which offers horse trails and a unique overnight camp, built on the banks of the river.

Note, however, that the road down to the river requires a 4x4 vehicle. It is self-catering and you must bring your own sleeping bag. They are apparently still training the horses, though, and the pipes carrying water to the overnight house have gone missing, so check before you go. Cost is E100 pppn.

Both Ngwempisi and Khelekhele were developed as part of the Swaziland Tourism Authority's Community Tourism initiative, and have received funding from international donors. As such, the stone-and-wood overnight camps are amazing, and have been designed to fit beautifully into the natural environment.

Unfortunately, both of these sites are let down by inadequate signage. The turnoffs from the main road are clearly marked, but once you leave the tar and hit the gravel, you're on your own. This can be very frustrating, and Khelekhele is particularly egregious in this regard. Still, getting lost is sometimes part of the fun, and the lonely gravel roads through the mountains are stunning.

- Ngwempisi Hiking Trails / Khelekhele Community Camp and Trails: 268-625 6004
- Horseshoe Estate Log House: 268-606 1512

Summerfield Botanical Gardens
Once you are back on the MR103, continue towards Manzini. After a few kilometres, you will see a large stone quarry (Nkwalini) and a road to the right marked for Summerfields Botanical Gardens. This is the first government-recognized botanical garden in Swaziland, and features both indigenous and exotic plants including cycads, succulents, palms and orchards, all set out on a beautifully maintained 96-hectare site.

The extensive Summerfield estate also offers accommodation in a number of upmarket suites or in the Dove's Nest guesthouse. Day visitors may want to try out the Grand Palm Cascades Restaurant, housed in a substantial thatched structure that is built on the edge of the 'lake' (more like a large pond).

If you continue on Summerfields road, you will eventually reach the Rosecraft Retreat and Sculpture Garden (about 30 minutes' drive; just follow the signs). This is the home of the Rosecraft community weaving project, nestled in the Makhungutsha mountains and surrounded by indigenous forest. It's a bit out of the way, but it's worth the effort. The sculpture trail is laid out along a bubbling stream with several small waterfalls, and there are several shady picnic areas, so it's well worth a wander. The Rosecraft workshop and factory shop are also on-site, so you can get in a bit of shopping at the same time.

- Summerfield Heritage Garden Villa Suites, The Dove's Nest Guesthouse and Grand Palm Cascades Restaurant: 268-550 3539; www.summerfieldresort.com
- Rosecraft Retreat and Sculpture Trail: 268-550 4385; www.swazirosecraft.com

If you continue on the MR103 past the turnoff to Summerfields, you will pass the substantial Taiwan Technical Mission. The relationship between the Republic of China and the Swazi Kingdom dates back to 1968, when the newly independent country of Swaziland embarked on a mission to establish diplomatic relations with other nations of the world.

At this time, the Taiwanese were struggling to maintain their international standing in the face of opposition from the much more powerful People's Republic of China on the mainland, which had never admitted the legitimacy of Taiwanese nationality. As such, the Taiwanese embraced Swaziland's overtures and the two plucky little countries became firm friends.

Over the years, Swaziland has stuck firmly at Taiwan's side, even as other governments capitulated to China's demands for Taiwanese isolation. In return, the Taiwanese have supported Swaziland with a number of investment grants that have been used to develop tourism, infrastructure, agriculture, vocational education and medical assistance. Taiwanese industries were also encouraged to set up shop in Swaziland and several important textile and garment plants have been established, creating thousands of much-needed jobs.

Today there are only a handful of African countries which acknowledge Taiwanese independence, and Swaziland is chief among them. King Mswati even visited Taiwan in 2006 and Taiwanese president Chen Shui-bian returned the compliment in 2007. However, not everyone supports the relationship. Apart from the economic implications of China's refusal to do business with anyone who acknowledges Taiwan, there are some Swazis who are complaining about the number of Taiwanese people who have come to live in the Kingdom. As usual, this latent xenophobia comes down to concerns about jobs and welfare or, as one rather angry local put it, "How can ten people work in one cellphone shop?" Anyhow, about 5km after the Nkwalini quarry, you will arrive at a large roundabout with a rather scruffy strip mall on one side. This is the intersection between the MR103 and the MR3. From here, you can nip back to Ezulwini or Mbabane on the MR3, or you can continue to Manzini.

Additional Malkerns contacts

- All Shades Green: 268-528 2125
- Brookside Lodge:268-528 3765; www.brookside-lodge.com
- Gugulethu Guest House: 268-606 7113
- Rainbird Chalets: 268-528 3452
- Sundowners Lodge: 268-528 3048; www.sundownerslodge.com
- Swaziland Backpackers: 268-528 2038
- Umdoni: 268-528 3009
- Willows Lodge: 268-602 1284; www.swaziwillows.com

Manzini

Manzini and the adjacent industrial area of Matsapha is the manufacturing centre of Swaziland. Accordingly, the region is mainly of interest to business travellers and there are several annual trade shows and fairs that cater to this market, such as the Swaziland International Trade Fair, which is held at the new Mavuso Exhibition Centre during the last week of August and the first week of September. The main airport is also located in Matsapha but, apart from that, there is little here to attract the casual visitor.

The town was established in 1885, when Bob Rogers opened a store housed in a tent close to King Mbandzeni's kraal at Mbekelweni. The following year, a concessionaire named Alfred Bremer bought the store and erected a hotel and trading station on the site. The town that grew up around the store became Bremersdorp and, later, Manzini (named after the local chief Manzini Motha).

Whatever its provenance, Manzini is undistinguished from a tourism point of view. The main roads through town are lined with shops and malls, and the pavements literally pulsate with people going about their business. There are also plenty of restaurants, bars and nightclubs (such as Y2K and Tiger City), but it's just not the kind of place that makes you want to hang around.

Despite this, the Manzini market, situated a block down from the local KFC, is quite interesting. This bustling open-air market is right next door to the large and chaotic taxi rank, and the whole area is pumping with energy and noise. Thursday is the big market day.

Unfortunately, it is not a friendly place and cameras are not welcome. While I was there, I was confronted by several angry vendors and taxi owners who insisted that I stop taking pictures. One guy even threatened to take my camera away. In general, the reactions I got were quite hostile, so I packed up my Canon and fled.

Interestingly, there is a general tendency for older Swazis to be suspicious of cameras and photographers. Several people told me that I mustn't take pictures of them because they didn't want to be on calendars in America. This attitude puzzled me, so I asked around for an explanation. According to one source, the whole thing dates back to 1984, when Swaziland was hit by the rogue cyclone Demoina.

Several countries and aid organizations subsequently donated money to help those stricken by the disaster, and a bunch of photographers came over to take pictures of the event. As it turns out, the affected people did not feel that they received any benefit from the interventions and came to resent the photographers as opportunistic parasites who profited from their misery. Over time, this attitude seems to have become entrenched in the minds of some Swazis, but rest assured that very few will be bold enough to confiscate your camera.

As part of the Swazi Government's impressive Millennium Project, a large complex is to be developed in Manzini that will include an adventure playground, sports complex and 30,000-seat stadium, as well as a number of factory 'shells'. The Mavuso exhibition centre is already complete. The rest of the facilities should be finished in the near future.

Golfers might want to check out the new Nkonyeni Golf Estate, located about 20km south of town on the MR9 towards Nhlangano. This vast development is spread over 500 hectares of bushveld, overlooking the Great Usuthu River. When it is complete, which it should be soon,

Nkoyeni will include a residential estate, a golf course designed by the world-renowned Phil Jacobs, a luxury hotel, a health spa and wellness centre and a game reserve.

Manzini contacts

- Emtini Lodge: 268-507 0025
- Esibayeni Lodge: 268-518 4848; www.esibayenilodge.co.sz
- Gardens Guest House: 268-505 9174
- Gibela Getaway: 268-505 3024; www.visitswazi.com/gibela
- Global Village Guest House: 268-505 2226; www.globalvillage.co.sz
- June Manor Guest House: 268-505 3865
- Kaikai Holiday Park: 268-505 6511
- Madonsa Guest House: 268-505 5725; www.madonsa.co.sz
- Manzini Golf Club: 268-505 2254
- Manzini Lodge: 268-505 5382
- Matsapha Inn: 268-518 6888
- Mozambique Hotel: 268-505 2489
- Myxos' Place Backpackers: 268-505 8363; www.earthfoot.org/sz.htm
- Nkonyeni Golf Estate, hotel and spa: 268-550 3527; www.nkonyeni.com
- Nokwane Guest House: 268-611 7791
- Our Dwelling Place: 268-505 3276
- Panata River Lodge and Cattle Ranch: 268-505 5762
- Park Hotel: 268-505 7423
- Rider's Ranch: 268-505 2881
- Rustic Tavern: 268-505 8437
- The Chef's Palace: 268-505 2005
- Tum's George Hotel: 268-505 2260; www.tgh.sz
- Umtfunti Guest House: 268-505 4684
- Ursel Guest House: 268-604 7525
- Winkler's Guest House: 268-505 7229

The Northwest

About 15km away from Mbabane, and a couple of kilometres from the Oshoek/Ngwenya border post, the MR3 meets the MR1. The latter road, also called the King Mswati II highway, heads north; winding through the mountainous highlands of northwestern Swaziland. It's an outstanding drive through green mountains, rural villages and

staggering river valleys. You can also find some of the country's finest tourism destinations along the way, including Hawane Nature Reserve, Malolotja Nature Reserve, Maguga Dam, Bulembu village and the town of Pigg's Peak (about 55km from the junction with the MR3). The wondrous Phophonyane Falls and the Pigg's Peak Hotel and Casino are about 10km farther along the road. So a journey from Mbabane to the Pigg's Peak hotel would be, let's see, around 80km one way.

If you want to go to the Kruger Park, keep going on the MR1 to the

NORTHWEST

Matsamo/Jeppe's Reef border post (40km from the town of Pigg's Peak). Another 40km of driving will deposit you on the N4 highway. The Malelane Gate into Kruger is now about 4km away, Nelspruit is 60km and Jo'burg is about 400km.

This part of Swaziland is known as the Hhohho region (which technically includes Mbabane). The name is said to be an onomatopoeic rendition of a baboon's staccato bark. Whatever its etymology, this is a fantastic alternative to the more mainstream attractions of Ezulwini. So, make it a day trip or, better still, try to spend a few nights in the area. Either way, you won't be disappointed.

The MR1 road is tarred throughout, but it is quite narrow in places and it tends to twist and turn as it traverses the steep valleys. So take a patience pill, because you'll probably find yourself stuck behind a slow-moving bus or truck for long stretches at a time, without any overtaking opportunities. My advice is to sit back, relax and enjoy the view.

By the way, you might have noticed all the curvaceous soapstone carvings on sale in the craft markets around Swaziland. Well, the soapstone comes from quarries in this part of the country and most of the carvers live in the vicinity. Now, the thing to note is that most of the carvings you've seen at the flea markets in Ezulwini and Mbabane are chosen for their transportability or their commercial appeal. So, if you want to see what the soapstone carvers can really do, you must check out the several 'specialist' roadside markets along the MR1.

There are some stunning pieces for sale at reasonable prices, many of which reflect the Rastafarian lifestyle of the carvers. I remember the first time I came to this part of the world I filled up my car with so many sculptures, the exhaust pipe scraped the ground all the way home. You will find at least three different markets on the road between Hawane and Malolotja.

Hawane Nature Reserve
About 8km from the intersection with the MR3, you will come to Hawane Dam and Nature Reserve. This small conservation area was established by the Swaziland National Trust Commission in 1978 to protect the marshes, wetlands and birdlife found along this part of the Mbuluzi River. The reserve also succours *Kniphofia umbrina*, an extremely rare species of Red Hot Poker that is endemic to Swaziland.

In 1988 a dam was constructed at the top of the Hawane Waterfall to provide Mbabane with drinking water. As a result, parts of the Hawane vlei were flooded and the nature reserve was extended upstream to ensure that the river remained unpolluted. The Hawane Reserve now includes Hawane dam, the dam wall and the marshy areas upstream. The reserve is administered by the rangers at Malolotja.

The northwestern end of the reserve, where the Mbuluzi River enters the dam, is a designated bird sanctuary that is home to hundreds of waterbirds such as flamingo, African spoonbill, purple heron, sacred ibis, bald ibis, greyheaded gull, whitewinged tern, Hottentot teal, redbilled teal, Cape shoveller, black duck, southern pochard, osprey and marsh owl. Water monitor lizards, Cape clawless otters, water mongooses and several species of frog can also been seen.

Canoeing, boating and boardsailing are permitted on the dam, but no power boats are allowed. Fishing is also permitted. Strangely, I remember there used to be a pretty little resort with picnic facilities and a restaurant overlooking the dam, but this seems to have disappeared completely.

Luckily, on the other side of the road, there is the highly-rated Hawane Resort. This well-established family-friendly complex offers accommodation in thatched chalets or in their backpackers' hostel. Guests and day visitors can also try out their Taste of Africa restaurant, which offers an extensive menu.

The resort is fully equipped and offers plenty of on-site activities, including archery, croquet, horse-riding, volleyball and bocce/petanque (whatever those are!). They also have Qolf, a form of off-course golf, which is apparently the new international rage.

If you are an outdoor type, there are several walking trails in the area, and the resort has a private gate into the marvellous Malolotja Nature Reserve. You can go kayaking on the nearby Hawane Dam, and fishermen will enjoy angling for carp, bream, bass, barbel and trout. Quad bikes are available for hire, or you can bring your own. Note, however, that motorbikes or quads can only be driven as part of a guided tour, as per an agreement with the local communities. For those who prefer pedal power, mountain bikes are available for hire at Malolotja Nature Reserve and Hawane can supply guides who will show you the best routes.

- Hawane Family Resort, Barnyard Backpackers and Taste of Africa restaurant: 268-442 4744; www.hawane.co.sz
- Lima Farm Cottage: 268-603 0154

Forbes Reef Gold Mine

About 7km from the Hawane Dam is a small building, identified as the Forbes Reef store. This area is associated with Swaziland's modest gold mining industry. Those days are long gone, however, and there is little reason to stop here any more. But you can still visit the old Forbes Reef diggings as part of a short walking trail that starts in the Malolotja Nature Reserve, just a couple of kilometres further down the road.

Although there is evidence that the Swazi people had been extracting the gold long before the Europeans arrived, the precious metal was first officially recorded in this area around 1872. A few year later, in 1880, David and James Forbes secured a mining concession for the Malolotja area, and the first systematic exploitation of the deposit began.

These early diggings were pretty experimental until, in 1884, the Forbes Main Reef was discovered by Alex Forbes, a relative of the concession-holders. Soon 30 other reefs were found within a 5km radius, but only ten were substantial enough to sustain viable mining operations. Unfortunately, during this first rush of activity, all signs of ancient Swazi mining excavations were destroyed.

Within a few years, Forbes Reef was producing 2,000 ounces of gold per month, and shares in the company were worth £5 sterling. Shafts were sunk to a depth of 115 metres and a dam was constructed to supply the mine with water. Workshops, a saw mill, an assay lab, a stone fort and other facilities were also constructed. Only the gold mine at Pigg's Peak was more productive.

So, things seemed to be going well—but there was a problem. The nearest railway line was several hundred kilometres away, at Biggarsberg in Natal, and the heavy ore had to be transported over the mountains in ox-wagons. This was a slow and expensive business, and the company struggled to maintain profitability.

Over the next 15 years, a number of additional gold mining operations were established in Malolotja, most notably at Avalanche Mine, but only those along Forbes Reef were able to maintain a consistent output. Then, in 1897, tensions between the British and the Boers reached boiling point. This culminated in the Anglo-Boer War of 1899–1902, and mining operations were severely affected.

From the outbreak of the Boer War until the end of the First World War in 1918, gold mining continued sporadically, and during the decades that followed, output continued to decline. Mining companies opened and closed regularly, concessions lapsed and ore grades became unpayable. By 1960, only the She, Waterfall and Lomati Extension mines remained operational. By 1967, all gold mining in the area had ceased.

But the lure of gold is enduring. In 1976 and 1977, the Red Reefs were mined with limited success and occasional attempts to find new deposits continue to this day. All in all, however, the total gold production of Swaziland is estimated at only around 250,000 ounces—a very small amount when compared to the huge output of neighbouring South Africa.

Incidentally, there are other minerals in the Malolotja area. We have already discussed the substantial iron ore deposit on Ngwenya Mountain and, in 1999, a Taiwanese company applied to mine blue chert within the Malolotja reserve. This decorative stone is popular in Asia, and the capacity of the mine was estimated at 300 tons per year for twelve years. Thankfully, there was strong resistance to the idea and an environmental impact assessment concluded that the operation would cause significant damage. It was subsequently decided that it would be better to develop tourism rather than mining, and all plans to start a chert quarry have been shelved, at least for now.

- www.sntc.org.sz/cultural/goldmines.asp

Malolotja Nature Reserve
This is my favourite place in Swaziland. I stayed here the first time I visited the country and immediately fell in love with the peace, the clean air and the endless mountains. In fact, when I think of Swaziland, this is the landscape that immediately springs to mind. I guess what I'm trying to say is that Malolotja is unforgettable.

The reserve was proclaimed in 1977, and was the first protected area established under the Swaziland National Trust Commission. At that time the land was being used for grazing sheep, but was of little agricultural value—so the former king, Sobhuza II, gave his blessing for the project to proceed. The land was soon bought (or donated) and the 63 families living in the area were relocated to better farming land. Subsequently, this breathtaking mountain wilderness quickly became one of the country's most magnificent conservation areas.

Today, Malolotja Nature Reserve covers an area of 18,000 hectares, making it the largest protected area in the Kingdom. It is adjacent to the 49,000-hectare Songimvelo Nature Reserve on the South African side of the border, and these two parks have been united in a Transfrontier Conservation Area (TFCA) that will eventually encompass the Bulembu, Makhonjwa, and Sondeza National Landscapes near Pigg's Peak. When it's all done, a protected area of 700 square kilometres will be created, with potential extensions of another 500 square kilometres. Bring it on!

The altitude in Malolotja ranges from a high of 1,829m at the summit of Ngwenya Mountain (second highest in Swaziland) to a low of 640m in the Nkomati Valley. As such, the reserve straddles the Highveld and the middleveld and supports a variety of habitats including short grassland, thick riverine scrub and Afro-montane forest.

There are also two main rivers which have carved deep valleys through the ancient mountains (some of which are made of rocks that date back three and a half billion years). The Malolotja River, meaning 'many rapids and cascades', originates in the east of the reserve and descends 900 metres before joining the Nkomati (river of cows) which flows from east to west through the reserve. In order to make this descent, the Malolotja River tumbles down several waterfalls. The largest of these, Malolotja Falls, is the highest waterfall in Swaziland, with a drop of 100 metres. These majestic falls are best viewed as part of a hiking trail.

Malolotja has 63 species of mammals. Most of these are pretty small critters, but there are several endangered or regionally-threatened species living in the reserve. Some animals, such as the Blesbok you'll see grazing near reception, have been re-introduced after years of local extinction. Nine species are found nowhere else in the country, including aardwolf, black wildebeest and red hartebeest. Other rare or vulnerable species include serval, white-tailed mongoose, antbear, grey rhebok, common reedbuck, oribi, klipspringer, red duiker, pangolin, honey badger, water rat, eland, common reedbuck, mountain reedbuck, leopard, striped weasel, African civet, Schreibers' long fingered bat, African wild cat and Meller's mongoose.

If you're lucky, you might even spot one of the two elephants who occasionally wander along the river valleys. Hippos are also occasionally seen in the Nkomati River. Finally, let's not forget the rock hyrax (dassies), if only because they are close relations to the elephant. Oh, and there are three species of grass-climbing mice and seven species of shrews.

With so many habitats on offer, there is a wealth of birdlife in Malolotja and over 280 species have been recorded. Furthermore, several endangered species come here to breed, so the reserve is a birder's paradise. Rare and threatened species include blue swallow, secretary bird, blackrumped buttonquail, striped flufftail, Stanley's bustard, grass owl, black stork, bald ibis, black eagle, crowned eagle, African marsh harrier, African finfoot, longcrested eagle, blackbreasted snake eagle, blackwinged plover, halfcollared kingfisher and ground woodpecker. More common are sunbirds, Gurney's sugarbirds, anteating chats, sentinel rock thrushes, buffstreaked chats, green pigeons, Knysna loeries, purplecrested loeries, bee-eaters, plumcoloured starlings, coucals and bushshrikes.

Malolotja has 91 species of herpetofauna (25 amphibians and 66 reptiles). These include 29 species of lizard, including the endemic Swazi thick-tailed rock gecko, the near-endemic Barberton girdled lizard, Delalande's Sandveld lizard, ornate Sandveld lizard, Transvaal crag lizard, montane burrowing skink, giant legless skink, ocellated dwarf gecko and all three of southern Africa's grass lizards (also known as snake lizards).

The 36 species of snakes found in the reserve include the near-endemic Swazi rock snake and a whole bunch of pretty toxic characters such as the puffadder, rinkhals, boomslang, black mamba, Mozambique spitting cobra, vine snake, short-snouted cobra and the South African rock python (not poisonous, but very big!).

Frogs include the rare Natal ghost frog, yellow-striped reed frog, plaintive rain frog, striped stream frog, grassland ridged frog, dwarf dainty frog, long-toed running frog and the rather common Mozambique rain frog, which can be heard croaking away during the summer months.

Although you are not allowed to fish in the reserve's rivers, anglers might be interested to know that 15 species of freshwater fish can be found within Malolotja's boundaries. These include the Incomati rock catlet, Pongolo rock catlet, pennant-tailed rock catlet, southern mouthbrooder, orange-fringed largemouth, shortfin barb, small-scale yellowfish, incomati chiselmouth and the stargazer mountain catfish—I know I'm going on a bit, but I just love the names! The reserve also contains several dams stocked with trout, which may be fished if you get a permit.

The wildflowers of Malolotja are justifiably famous; the reserve protects several threatened plant species. These include Barberton cycads, Kaapsehoop cycads and the unusual *streptocarpus* (which only grows a large, single leaf). There are also six species of proteas and four species of heaths. The reserve's vleis and bogs are particularly rich in plant life, such as amaryllids, orchids and lilies. Although the high-lying grasslands of the reserve do not have many trees, the middle and lower valley areas contain some impressive specimens of yellowwood, stinkwood and the forest fever tree.

Now that we know what kind of flora and fauna can be found in Malolotja, how do you get to see them? Well, basically, you have to walk. And that's a good thing, because Malolotja is one of the best hiking destinations in southern Africa. There are at least a dozen day walks within the reserve, of varying degrees of difficulty.

If you have bad knees, make sure you ask the ranger at reception to suggest an easy option as many of the trails have steep sections, especially when you have to walk into or out of a valley. The Malolotja Vlei walk (which has a bird hide) and the walk to the old Forbes Reef mine (bring a torch) are both suitable for the whole family.

More experienced hikers should definitely take advantage of Malolotja's extensive network of overnight wilderness trails that range from one to seven nights. All in all, there are over 200km of trails that criss-cross Malolotja and 17 overnight camps dotted around the reserve. Note, however, that while all the overnight camps are located near water, there are no other facilities available and hikers must be fully self-sufficient.

If you prefer wheeled transport, mountain bikes can be hired on a daily basis from reception and may be used to ride around the reserve. You can also use your car to drive around, but there is a limited road network and most of it is gravel of varying quality (particularly in the northern part of the reserve). Nevertheless, the roads will take you to some unforgettable viewsites and are well worth the effort. The Nkomati and Ngwenya viewpoints are particularly impressive. If you are not in a 4x4 or SUV, check with reception about the quality of the roads before you set off.

Accommodation at Malolotja consists of 13 fully furnished cabins, each sleeping a maximum of six (E230 per person for the first two, and E120 per additional guest). The cabins are nestled in a small hollow, surrounded by a forest of grey boulders set in a sea of tall grass. Each cabin has a fireplace, which is perfect for those nights when the mist rolls in and the wind blows up. If you are a Malolotja purist, make sure you stay in one of the five original log cabins (the others are newer and made of brick). These trusty stalwarts may be getting a bit long in the tooth, but you can't beat the smell of old wood and bitumen.

Alternatively, you can stay over in a rather basic A-frame hut that sleeps three. This is located the other side of the hill, facing the main road. There is also a campsite with 15 sites and a communal braai area (E60 pppn). Day visitors can take advantage of an attractive picnic site, built next to the cabins, with communal braai facilities (entrance to the reserve is E25 pp). The road to the cabins is suitable for all vehicles.

At this stage, Malolotja is entirely self-catering, and there is a small shop at reception that sells firewood and basic supplies. The small Boomerang Coffee Shop may or may not be operational when you visit, so it's best to stock up before you arrive.

- Malolotja Nature Reserve: 268-442 4241; www.sntc.org.sz
- www.peaceparks.org
- www.sntc.org.sz/programs/songimvelomalolotja.asp

Maguga Dam
About 6km after the Malolotja entrance gate, the MR1 crests a hill and the vast Komati River valley gapes before you. The floor of this valley is now filled with the placid water of Maguga Dam, and this is one of Swaziland's newest holiday destinations.

The dam is a joint venture between South Africa and Swaziland, and was officially opened by King Mswati III and the then-deputy president of South Africa, Jacob Zuma, in 2002. The dam holds 332 million cubic metres of water, and its wall is 115 metres high—one of the highest dam walls in southern Africa. The dam is mainly used for irrigation purposes; the local farmers have benefited enormously since the dam opened.

The main MR1 now continues straight ahead, snaking down the valley, across a new bridge (the old causeway is under water) and up the other side. It is a breathtaking road with great views, but there are no real tourist facilities (apart from a small craft market at the foot of the bridge). Instead, you should take the turnoff marked for Maguga Dam and Lodge at the crest of the pass. This tarred loop road crosses over the dam wall, about 8km downstream from the MR1, and there are several restaurants, lodges and attractions along the way. The Maguga detour rejoins the MR1 at a sawmill some distance beyond the Komati Valley, and it is only about 8km longer than the main highway from point to point.

The Maguga loop road leads through beautiful mountains studded with large granite domes and boulders. There are several rural homesteads along the roadside, each with their own mielie patch, and cattle can be seen grazing peacefully on the green slopes. All in all, it's most bucolic. If you want to spend some time in this rural wonderland, the Sobantu Guest House and Mthunzi's Paradise Village are both nearby and offer guests a real Swazi experience.

About 12km after you turn off the MR1, the road rounds a bend and a superb view of the dam is revealed, cradled between the soaring mountains. A short distance further on, you will come to Maguga Lodge. This recently completed complex is built right on the water's edge, and offers comfortable accommodation in 35 well-appointed chalets, as well as conference facilities. The spacious Lapa restaurant has a large wooden deck with an excellent view out over the water, so it's a good place to stop for a drink or a meal.

The lodge also offers fishing packages; keen anglers will be delighted to hear that the dam is well stocked with barbel, eel, carp, yellowtail, largemouth black bass, bream, Mozambican tilapia, blue kurper, vlei kurper, dwarf tiger fish and mosquito fish. Even more impressive are the dam's 'monster bass', which often weigh between two-and-a-half and five kilograms. The current Swaziland record catch of five-and-a-half kilograms was caught in the dam during 2007.

Ekuvinjelweni botanical gardens and tea room and the Swazi Ark arts and craft centre are in close proximity to the lodge. And if you are looking for a shot of adrenaline, pay a visit to Enkhaba Adventure Centre. This dynamic venue offers mountain-biking, hiking, rock-climbing, abseiling, quad-biking, horse-riding, boating, canoeing, caving, rafting, cultural tours, accommodation and camping.

Just below the lodge is a public picnic area and boat launching site. Permits are available from the information office on the other side of the dam. At this stage there don't seem to be any people renting out motorboats or jetskis, so you'll just have to bring your own! You can, however, rent a houseboat for the day or a couple of nights and spend some time cruising along the dam. Lightleys Houseboats and Hawane Resort both offer this innovative accommodation option.

The road now continues over the dam wall, which I must admit is a rather beautiful construction with a colossal spillway that runs down into the valley. Once across the water, the path starts climbing as you pass the dam information office (which may or may not have a restaurant next door) and the Komati Basin Water Authority (KOBWA) headquarters.

At the top of the hill, there is a large community-run craft market and coffee shop, with brilliant views out over the entire expanse of the dam. This facility is part of the Swaziland Tourism Authority's Community Tourism initiative, and it's definitely worth a stop.

- Mthunzi's Paradise Village: 268-608 0469; www.swaziplace.com/mthunzi
- Sobantu Guest House: 268-644 6620
- Maguga Lodge and Restaurant: 268-437 3970; www.magugalodge.com
- Enkhaba Adventure Centre: 268-602 0578; www.enkhabadventures.co.sz
- Maguga Dam Houseboats: 268-602 4054; www.houseboats.co.za/swaziland
- Hawane Resort Houseboat: 268-442 4744; www.hawane.co.sz
- Komati Basin Water Authority: www.kobwa.co.za

Nsangwini rock art

About 10km from the dam wall is a turnoff onto a gravel road marked for the Nsangwini Rock Art site. This is one of the best Bushman rock art sites in Swaziland, and it can be visited as part of a guided walking tour. Nsangwini is another feather in the cap of the Swaziland Tourism Authority's Community Tourism initiative, and the revenue it generates for the local people is invaluable.

The reception hut is about 7km from the main road on decent-quality gravel, and the route is well signposted. The drive up to Nsangwini takes you deep into the mountains and past several scattered villages. There are lots of pedestrians and cattle about, so drive slowly and take the opportunity to enjoy the lovely rural scenery. The people here are very friendly, and many will wave as you pass by. It is entirely appropriate to return the gesture.

When you arrive at the reception hut, you will be met by a guide from the local community. All the guides have had extensive training by experts in the field and they really know their stuff. You will pay your guide the nominal fee and, after a short introduction, it's time to hit the trail.

The walk down to the site is rather steep, so wear decent walking shoes (not flip-flops, like I did) and bring a hat, because it can get hot on the mountainside. The elderly or infirm may struggle a bit on the loose rocks; you should use your discretion before setting out. You should also bring your own snacks and drinking water with you, as the little kiosk at reception has a very limited range of goodies available. It should take about 20 minutes to walk down to the site and 30 minutes to walk back up, but the views down into the Komati Valley are ample reward for your effort and you can take it as slowly as you like.

The rock shelter itself is cool and shady, and the enigmatic paintings are a marvel. Our guide said that the earliest figures date back 4,000 years and that the newest ones are about 400 years old, so this shelter has been in use for several thousand years. It was first described by modern researchers in 1954.

Some of the more unusual images include several weird bird-like figures, which seem to be unique to Nsangwini, and two blue wildebeest (the only rock art depictions of this animal south of the Zambezi River). The most dominant image, however, is the large painting of an elephant.

This suggests that the site was associated with rain-making, as elephants are said to have the ability to smell out water.

The presence of the elephant may explain why this site remained in use for so long. As our guide explained, the Bantu migrants who settled in Swaziland didn't get on with the native Bushmen. However, they did appreciate the Bushmen's rain-making skills, and it is thought that Nsangwini was predominantly used for this purpose. There is even an image that shows a group of dark brown human figures (accompanied by fat-tailed sheep) approaching a group of light brown figures, and this has been interpreted as a depiction of the Bantu approaching the Bushmen for a rain-making ritual. It is the only known representation of non-Bushman people in Swaziland's rock art record.

Incidentally, the name 'Nsangwini' translates as 'cannabis'! According to the story, many years ago a Swazi nobleman was travelling through the area when he spotted some marijuana plants growing along the path. Naturally, he stopped to enjoy the herbal diversion, and the name stuck. Unfortunately, modern visitors are not encouraged to follow his example.

- Nsangwini Rock Art: 268-637 3767
  www.sntc.org.sz/cultural/rockart.asp

Pigg's Peak

The Maguga loop road rejoins the MR1 highway about 15km from Maguga Dam. There is a substantial sawmill at this junction, and from here it is about 4km to the small town of Pigg's Peak.

The settlement at Pigg's Peak began with the discovery of alluvial gold in the early 1880s. The discoverer, Tom McLachlan, quickly bought the mining concession for the area and proceeded to exploit the deposit with his partner, Walter Carter. Soon, prospectors from the nearby goldfields of Barberton, Pilgrim's Rest and Lydenburg (located on the South African side of the mountains) started straggling into the area and a little mining community began taking shape.

Then, in 1884, a man named William Pigg found the substantial Devil's Reef formation near the village. This quickly became the most important source of gold in the country, and the town that grew up in the shadow of the mine was named in Pigg's honour. In its heyday, the

NORTHWEST

Pigg's Peak mine employed 400 people and sunk shafts to a depth of 250 metres. There are no accurate records of how much gold was recovered, but it is known that 15,000 ounces were sold in 1911 alone. However, by 1957, the mine's output had dwindled to nothing and the entire operation was closed down.

Luckily, in the 1940s, Peak Timbers and Swaziland Plantations started establishing several enormous pine and eucalyptus plantations on the fertile mountain slopes around the town. These would eventually cover more than 35,000 hectares, and forestry is now the town's lifeblood. The huge asbestos mine at Bulembu was also a major contributor to the region's economy before it closed down in 2001.

Today, the town of Pigg's Peak is a sleepy little place. The main road is lined with tall eucalyptus trees, the homes have large gardens bursting with colour and the whole place is very lush and peaceful. You'll find all the usual stuff here (petrol stations, furniture shops, convenience stores, schools, churches, a country club etc.) but all the big attractions are several kilometres out of town so you'll probably want to keep going ...

- Highlands Inn: 268-437 1144
- Jabula Guest House: 268-437 1052; www.jabulabnb.com

Bulembu, Havelock Mine

At the top of the main road through Pigg's Peak, there is an intersection with a road that is marked for Bulembu. Turn left here if you want to visit the fascinating Bulembu village, or if you want to return to South Africa via the spectacular Saddleback Pass to Barberton.

The road to Bulembu winds through the plantations as it climbs ever higher into the mountains. The views get better and better as you ascend, but keep your eyes on the road, as this is an active forestry area and you will be sharing the narrow track with heavy-duty trucks hauling timber. The quality of the gravel roadway is also variable, so a sturdy car with good suspension is recommended. And keep the windows closed, because your tyres will kick up a fine red dust that gets everywhere.

But it's all worth it because, about 18km from Pigg's Peak, you will arrive at the remarkable village of Bulembu, and this place is something else. Perched high on a narrow ledge with jaw-dropping views on all sides, Bulembu has a breathtaking location just below the summit of Emlembe Mountain—the highest peak in Swaziland, at 1,863 metres.

The names Emlembe and Bulembu both derive from the term *esiKhalenisebuLembu*—the pass of the spider's web. This is the Swazi name for a narrow bridle path that eked its way through the steep gorges, around the girth of the mountain, over a natural stone causeway (the Devil's Bridge) and down into the Barberton valley. It's a precipitous route that was used by early gold prospectors as they straggled into Pigg's Peak to try their luck.

It was actually a group of prospectors who first started exploring the Bulembu area, back in 1886. These men had formed the Havelock Swaziland Prospecting Syndicate (named after the British governor of Natal, who had supported Boer annexation of the territory) and secured a mineral concession over the area. They did not report finding any valuable deposits, however, and the valley soon fell back into its lofty somnolence.

Then, around 1923, Gowran Fitzpatrick and some friends began scratching around in the nearby Dvudvusi Valley. Fitzpatrick was the caretaker of the Pigg's Peak gold mine, and he had some time on his hands because the mine was temporarily closed. Soon, several samples of asbestos fibre were found along the banks of the Tutusi stream, and Fitzpatrick quickly staked out 40 claims and formed a syndicate.

He then approached the British-Canadian mineral house, Turner & Newall, with an offer to exploit the find. But the pragmatic mining company felt that the area was too remote and the deposit too erratic to be profitable and nothing came of the venture.

Two years later, a prospector named Izaac Holtzhausen returned to the valley and proved the value of the deposit. He and his partner, Herbert Castle, once again approached Turner & Newall with their findings and the cautious Canadians sent some men to check things out. After eight months of investigation, they were satisfied. Finally, in 1930, the company bought 100 claims around the valley for £240,000. At the time, this was the largest amount ever paid for a 'base mineral prospect' in southern Africa.

However, the problem of transport remained. Bulembu was right in the middle of the 'spider's web', and there was simply no way that a practical road could be built into the region. So, in 1937, the company started building a mammoth aerial cableway that could carry the ore over the mountains to Barberton.

The cableway was an incredible feat of engineering. It had 224 cupolas that could each carry 170kg. These carriers were attached to a 25mm steel cable that was suspended from a series of 52 pylons, ranging in height from 4.5 to 5.4 metres, which spanned the deep valleys. The cableway was 20km long, and two small electric motors, one at either end, drove the whole system at 10.5km per hour. In places, the cableway was as high as 190 metres off the ground, and its longest span was 207 metres. At one time this was claimed as the longest cableway system in the world, outside of Europe.

Although the cableway is no longer operational, the pylons and cables are all still in place, and the whole structure is just crying out for someone to step in and convert it into a tourist attraction. I'm not sure if it's technically possible or financially viable, but it would be an awesome ride!

Finally, by 1939, the Havelock Mine commenced production, and the mining town of Bulembu was built to house the workers and management. This isolated settlement was perched on a narrow saddleback between two peaks, a short distance away from the noxious mine. As such, the village had to be largely self-sufficient and it grew to include a hospital, scientific testing facilities, jail, courthouse, police station, schools, stores, golf course, bowling green, cinema/theatre, club house, cricket pitch, squash court, polo field and a large swimming pool (with an incredible view).

Over the years, Havelock Mine flourished. It quickly became Swaziland's largest earner of foreign currency, and it retained this position until 1962, when it was overtaken by sugar. Production averaged a steady 30,000 to 40,000 metric tons a year, and it was one of the five largest asbestos mines in the world. This was at a time when asbestos was highly valued as the 'wonder mineral', thanks to its malleability and ability to withstand heat, and the village of Bulembu prospered. At its peak, it was home to a population of 10,000 people.

Then, things started to go bad for Bulembu. You see, unfortunately asbestos is toxic, and the inhalation of asbestos fibres can cause serious lung disease. This condition had been observed in asbestos workers for many years but, starting in the 1980s, several countries banned asbestos-based consumer products, and world demand began to fall. The resulting decrease in prices coincided with declining yields at Havelock, and the mine started to become unviable. By 2000, production at the mine had dropped to 12,690 tons, and the mine was closed the following year.

The village of Bulembu became a ghost town virtually overnight, with only about 150 residents. The old tin-roofed homes stood empty and the hospital was abandoned with all its equipment intact. It was a place frozen in time and space.

In 2003, however, the Bulembu Development Corporation bought the 1,700-hectare property, including the entire village. This was then transferred to a non-profit organization called Bulembu Ministries, who had a vision to resurrect the community. They have already set up more than eight homes, where children orphaned by AIDS are raised in a nurturing environment and a school has been established. The timber industry is also involved in the town's affairs.

So, amazingly, there are now big plans for Bulembu. The town's owners want to expand their humanitarian mandate, and fund-raising branches have been established in several countries. The potential is certainly there. The existing infrastructure includes around 1,200 residential homes, an 80-bed hospital, an industrial complex with warehouses, and three schools with a total capacity of 1,800 students.

The tourism possibilities of Bulembu are also endless. With an outstanding location and a fascinating history, this is a unique destination. Already, visitors can stay at the Bulembu Country Lodge, housed in the old mine manager's house and director's cottage. This facility has twelve en-suite bedrooms and three home-cooked meals are served every day. At night, braais are held under the stars and, occasionally, local villagers will come over for some traditional dancing. Stand-alone houses in the village can also be hired on a self-catering or full-board basis.

Guests at the lodge have a number of activities available to them. You can walk into town and look at the old buildings along Winston Churchill Street; splash around in the cool swimming pool that looks out over a breathtaking valley; or creep into the dark, eerie 280-seat cinema that is completely intact, right down to an old tree that is marooned on the stage—a relic of some long-forgotten Christmas pageant.

NORTHWEST

Hikers will absolutely love Bulembu. There are many walks through the mountains and a great hike up to the summit of Emlembe. Walkers will enjoy the numerous waterfalls, rock pools and clear streams; the bird-watching is pretty good, too. Mountain bikes are welcome but, at this stage, you have to bring your own.

- Bulembu Country Lodge: 268-437 1998; www.bulembu.org

The Saddleback Pass to Barberton
If you like mountain passes and you have a sturdy vehicle, you really should try to work the Saddleback Pass into your Swaziland itinerary. This gravel road is an equivalent of the old bridle path from Barberton to Bulembu, and it's a glorious drive.

From Bulembu village, follow signs to the Josefdal border. The road now climbs steeply up through the trees for a short distance and then emerges starkly on the mountain face, with a sheer drop down into the valley on your left. After a few kilometres, you will reach the Bulembu border post. There are no computers here, so you'll have to fill out the forms manually but the post is usually quiet and there shouldn't be much of a queue.

The road now continues up towards the Josefdal border post, on the South African side. The views out over the lush Songimvelo Nature Reserve are unforgettable, but people with a fear of heights (like my mother) might feel a bit exposed.

A couple of kilometres beyond the Josefdal border post, there is a gravel road heading off to the left. This will take you past the abandoned asbestos mine at Msauli/Diepgezet; a South African equivalent of Havelock, complete with a ghost town village, golf course and a colossal semi-vertical shaft. After 50km this road eventually joins the N17, a short distance away from the Oshoek border.

Back on the Saddleback Pass road (now marked as the R40) the views go on forever as you ride high along the mountainside. Above you, the Havelock ore cableway is your constant companion as it swoops from ridge to ridge. Finally, about 40km after the border, you will eventually descend into the picturesque town of Barberton, dusty but happy. The journey should take an hour or two, depending on the roadworks.

Yes, that's right. Roadworks. For some reason best understood by the authorities, this remote and twisty route is now being tarred and widened. It's a big project involving dozens of trucks, hundreds of workers and heavy earth-moving machinery, all toiling away on the heights. Apparently, the purpose of this is to create a new tarred-link between Barberton and Pigg's Peak. I really can't understand why they are going to all this trouble and expense to join two relatively isolated settlements, but I was told that the old gravel road was in really bad shape and perhaps the needs of the timber industry have something to do with it. In any case, when it's all done, the new road will be accessible for any car, and the delights of the Saddleback Pass will be available to all.

- Barberton Tourism: 27-13 712 2880; www.barberton.co.za

Phophonyane Falls Ecolodge and Nature Reserve
About 7km from the town of Pigg's Peak, you'll see several turnoffs marked for Phophonyane Falls Ecolodge and Nature Reserve. Hidden deep in the pine plantations, this privately owned conservation area is a gem of a spot and highly recommended for a day visit or an overnight stay.

The gravel road leading into the reserve is about 4km, depending on which turnoff you take. You can also get into the reserve from the Pigg's Peak Casino road. Either way, it's passable. When you're through the pine plantation you soon cross a little river and then turn off down a shady lane that leads through thick, sub-tropical forest.

At reception, you'll notice a hand-crafted feel and an attention to detail that makes Phophonyane (meaning 'little waterfalls') something special. The sprawling lawns and gardens are impeccable. The accommodation is both comfortable and classy. Everything is well kept and appealing.

The falls themselves are thrilling. Cascading over an outcrop of dark stone, the Phophonyane River tumbles 80 metres before flowing through a series of cascades and rock pools that stretch for nearly 2km. The ancient rocks clearly exposed along the river's course are part of the 3.5-billion-year-old Ngwane gneiss formation, which ranks among the oldest in the world.

The walk down to the foot of the falls is short and steep, but it's well worth the effort. The trail starts out with a lovely meander through the indigenous forest, followed by a strenuous trek back up via a series of steps—or you can do the trail in reverse if your knees prefer. You can swim in the pools at the bottom of the falls and there's a semi-natural rockpool built halfway up the slope in which to cool down.

There are a number of other walks in the 700-hectare reserve, and birders will be kept happy with 230 species, such as narina trogon, purple-crested loerie and wood owl. Small game can also be spotted, including red duiker and bushbuck.

Other activities include a 4x4 drive up into the Gobolondlo and Makhonjwa mountains that form a dramatic backdrop to the reserve. Makhonjwa, incidentally, translates as 'that which is pointed at' referring to a traditional belief that pointing at an exposed peak will induce rain.

And while we're on the subject, Swazi legend has a romantic tale to account for the creation of the falls. It happened many years ago, as these things do, when a beautiful maiden and a handsome warrior fell in love. To win her hand, however, the warrior had to hunt down a leopard, so he quickly set off up the slopes of the fearsome Gobolondlo on his quest.

Alone and lost on the mountainside, the warrior strayed into the territory of several witches who were angry at his trespass. As a punishment, the witches turned him into a white flower, forever stranded in the mountain fields. When the warrior didn't return, his beloved was devastated. She sat on the river bank and wept. And it is her endless tears that flowed together to become the gushing Phophonyane waterfall.

In more modern times, the upper reaches of the falls were home to the first gold prospectors in the area. Several small mines were established in the hills around the reserve, and a little railway was built to transport the ore down the falls. A water-powered stamping mill was also erected at the foot of the falls to crush the rocks. The overgrown remains of this operation can still be seen.

The reserve was established by Rod de Vletter whose father bought the property in 1975 when it was a rundown farm. After many years of hard work, it opened to the public in 1986. Rod and his wife Lungile remain very much hands-on managers. Everything is meticulously maintained with all construction and decoration done by members of the community. Local materials are used wherever possible, including making their own earthen paint; the ecolodge prides itself on its commitment to recycling and environmental management.

Phophonyane is about to be gazetted as a national reserve and Rod and Lungile are currently working with their neighbours to establish a regional conservancy—a worthy initiative that will see the area enlarged to 3,000 hectares.

The clientele is mostly international and, while they want to expand their customer base, Rod and Lungile are careful not to attract the wrong sort of crowd. This is a very peaceful and private reserve and certainly doesn't need hordes of noisy yobos.

Accommodation (self-catering included) at Phophonyane comes in several shapes and sizes. There are three cottages that sleep between two and five; two luxurious beehive huts that each sleep two or three; and five tented camps built on the river's edge, built for two. The lodge has a capacity of 24 beds. Costs vary between E420 and E630pppn. The welcoming Driftwood restaurant serves meals, if you don't want to self-cater. Day visitors are welcome and are charged a reasonable entry fee of E40pp. The lodge has a stunning pool, Internet, a TV room and a library.

All in all it's a wonderful place to be. The sound of falling water fills your senses and the views are enchanting. Apparently many of the neighbours have lived to be 90 or older—so there must be something in the air at Phophonyane. Check it out for yourself.

- Phophonyane Falls Ecolodge and Nature Reserve: 268-437 1429; www.phophonyane.co.sz

Orion Pigg's Peak Hotel and Casino

About 10km north of Pigg's Peak town is the Orion hotel and casino—famous as the home of the All-Africa Poker tournament. The large hotel is surrounded by green hills and tall pine trees, and it has all the facilities you would expect from a casino resort.

There's tennis, bowls, squash, mini-golf, hiking, horse riding, table tennis, a pool table, mountain biking, volleyball, a gym, a sauna and a kids' playground with a jumping castle. You can eat at one of the two restaurants, or have a snack in the poolside courtyard. The hotel also has five conference venues, a curio shop and the ever-popular casino with tables and slots. All 102 rooms have a balcony with a view out over the valley. To be honest, the whole place is a little bit 70s for my taste, but it's homely.

A few hundred metres further along the road is a well-established craft market. This is home to the Coral Stephens handweaving studio and school, which was started in the 1940s by the wife of one of the first forestry officers in the region. Over the years, Stephens and a colleague named Sylvia Mantanga—a Xhosa weaver from the Transkei—trained hundreds of women in the fine art of spinning, drying and weaving mohair. Today, the studio is still an important source of income for the local community and currently employs 40 people, who produce distinctively colourful curtains, carpets and blankets.

The complex also contains Tintsaba Crafts, who have been weaving sisal into beautiful baskets and other decorative items since 1985. In 1999, a silver studio was incorporated into the workshop and they now produce an interesting range of jewellery that combines metal and natural fibres.

Incidentally, the Stephens' family home, Boshimela (house of many chimneys), was the location for Swaziland's first, and so far only, feature film, *Wah-Wah*, based on actor and director Richard E. Grant's experiences about growing up in colonial Swaziland.

The Matsamo/Jeppe's Reef border post is about 30km from the hotel, and this offers access to the Kruger Park. It is also an alternative route back to Jo'burg, via Nelspruit on the N4 highway. If there's time, you can make a final stop at the Matsamo Cultural Village, located just on the South African side of the border. It has two traditional Swazi villages, and knowledgeable guides will show you around. Accommodation is in 14 'en suite guest hives', and they can host up to 60 in traditional beehive huts with a central ablution facility. The African Theatre restaurant has a natural stage where folk songs are performed, while Ekaya offers a more intimate dining experience.

- Orion Pigg's Peak Hotel and Casino: 268-437 1104;
  www.piggspeakhotel.com
- Coral Stephens Handweaving: 268-437 1140;
  www.coralstephens.com
- Tintsaba Crafts: 268-437 1260; www.tintsaba.com
- Matsamo Cultural Village: 27-13 781 0578; www.matsamo.co.za

The Southwest

Below Manzini, the landscape softens out a bit. The mountains settle down into more manageable hills, and the honest soul of rural Swaziland starts to reveal itself. This region straddles the administrative provinces of Manzini and Shiselweni—not that you'd notice—and it's somewhat off the tourist map, but close enough for a day trip, and there are a couple of choice destinations hidden away in the hills.

From Manzini, it is 105km to Mahamba via the Grand Valley Road (MR9). If you're like me and you don't like driving back the way you came, you can do a round trip back to Manzini via Sicunusa and the Malkerns Valley for about 220km (including 38km on gravel).

Sidvokodvo

The MR9 road from Manzini to the fiendishly difficult-to-say village of Sidvokodvo provides 22km of pleasant but un-memorable driving. The Nkonyeni Golf Estate is nearby (*see* Manzini on page 176) and so is a biker's haven known as Rider's Ranch, clearly identifiable by a big motorbike mounted on their gate. This place is so 'in', I couldn't find any contact details—not even on Google! I'm guessing they operate through word of mouth. The Ranch hosts regular rallies for those in the know.

The actual village of Sidvokodvo is nicely situated on a small hill close to the wide Lusutfu (or Usuthu) River. If you feel like an adventure, take a detour to see the Bulunga Falls on the Lusutfu. Just cross over the river and head left onto the gravel road that runs parallel to the water. Drive for about 15km, and then ask for directions. The falls are a short walk from the road.

Grand Valley

After crossing the Lusutfu, the MR9 heads into the Grand Valley; a stunning declivity carved out by the Mkhondvo River. The road rises and falls along the lush eastern flank of the valley, offering great views over the mountains and into the forestry plantations beyond.

At one point the road runs right along the banks of the river, and many locals use this stretch of river for swimming or washing their clothes. It's a lovely spot, filled with the sounds of happy, splashing children and the gentle lowing of cows as they cross through the waist-high water.

Hlathikhulu

About 62km from Manzini, you will come to a turnoff for Hlathikhulu, a village with a couple of shops, houses, a hotel and a church dotted along a tidy main street. It is situated high on a ridge, overlooking the Grand Valley, and was founded as an administrative centre for the area. The name means 'large forest' or 'big bushes', depending on the translator's sense of hyperbole. The Hlathikhulu road loops back to rejoin the MR9 after 10km (going straight on, the MR9 covers the same ground in about 6km). Both these routes are tarred and offer good views. The faded Assegai Inn is the only accommodation in Hlatikhulu town, but Kubuta Farm offers guests a rural retreat, tucked away in the hills to the east.

- Kubuta Farm: 268-344 1626; www.visitswazi.com/kubuta
- Assegai Inn Hotel: 268-615 8283

Nhlangano

About 25km south of Hlathikhulu is the small town of Nhlangano. It is a centre for the timber and agricultural industries that flourish in the area. The government is trying to further develop Nhlangano's potential by building a number of factory 'shells' as part of its Millennium development project. Several Taiwanese companies have already set up operations here.

From a tourism point of view, the main attraction is the attractive Nhlangano Hotel and Casino, located 2km out of town, in the Makosini Valley. It was originally built in 1978 as a joint venture between Holiday Inn and the Swazi government, and I can't resist quoting from an old advert from 1983 which says 'There's excitement and gaiety in Nhlangano's friendly casino, in the swinging 777s Club and disco, and a theatre showing films that would have the censors blushing.' The hotel is now independently run, and caters for the whole family.

The Nhlangano area is rich in history. This is where the first Swazi clans established themselves after moving over from Mozambique several hundred years ago, and its close proximity to the neighbouring Zulu kingdom meant that it was at the frontline of the many conflicts that broke out between the two groups. The district name, Shiselweni (place of burning) refers to the burning of King Ngwane II's kraal during these turbulent early years.

During the concessions era, the land around Nhlangano was bought by Transvaal farmers who named it Goedgegun ('well favoured'). These settlers went so far as to elect their own 'president' and, for a while, the area was known as the Little Free State.

The town was officially established in 1921 and was renamed Nlhangano (the meeting place) in honour a meeting between King Sobhuza II and the British King George VI and his wife, which took place here during the latter's Royal Tour of 1947. Swazi leaders also met British Prime Minister Harold McMillan in Nhlangano as part of his month-long tour of the African colonies.

It was this tour that prompted McMillan to make his prescient 'Winds of Change' speech to the South African Parliament in 1960. As he said,

"The wind of change is blowing through this continent. Whether we like it or not, this growth of national consciousness is a political fact." It was a pertinent observation and, over the decade that followed, Britain negotiated independence for most of its African possessions. South Africa, on the other hand, ignored the message and plunged further into the depths of apartheid.

- Nhlangano Hotel & Casino Royale: 268-207 8211; www.nhlanganoroyale.com
- Phumula Farm: 268-207 9099; www.phumulaguestfarm.co.za
- Nhlangano Golf Club: 268-207 8887

Mahamba Gorge

The Mahamba border post is about 15km south of Nhlangano on the MR9. Just before the border, there's a gravel road to the right, marked for Mahamba Gorge.

This area is where, in 1844, Christian missionaries first set up shop in Swaziland. For a couple of years, things went well. The congregation grew quickly, and a school was established. Then the Wesleyan missionaries inadvertently got caught up in a royal row between the king and a rebellious relation who was hiding nearby. This squabble soon degenerated into a violent skirmish that erupted in the mission yard. None of the missionaries were hurt, but it was a scary experience, and they decided to leave the country immediately. Many converts followed the departing preachers, and the place became known as Mahamba (the runaways).

The gravel road to Mahamba runs along the foot of a low ridge with open farmland and villages to the right. After about 2km you'll see a small sandstone church, designed in the Gothic style. It was built in 1912 by the Methodists, and is the oldest intact European place of worship in Swaziland.

About 3km farther on is Mahamba Gorge, a steep defile cut through Mahamba Mountain by the Mkhondvo River. It's an eye-filling destination that offers good walks and birding. An easy stroll along the river takes about 90 minutes and provides the best views of the gorge.

The Mahamba Gorge Lodge has recently been built on the edge of the river, overlooking the main face of the gorge. This is another one of Swaziland's Community Tourism programmes, and the attractive stonewalled cottages were built with the assistance of the European Union. Members of local Methodist church help the community run the lodge.

This rustic lodge offers comfortable accommodation in six self-catering units, each with its own balcony. There is no electricity, but there is solar power for lights and gas for heating. The interior décor is simple but functional, and the whole atmosphere is very peaceful. Units (sleeping two) cost around E300 per night.

Apart from the river walk into the gorge, you can also tackle the hike to the top of the gorge, where you will find green mountain-top meadows and grand views across the border. Birders will want to take the pleasant walk through the forest and along the river's flood plain, where there are plenty of species to spot. This is one of only two places in Swaziland where the bald ibis nests. Mountain bikes are welcome, and guides are available on request. Fishing is also allowed, and there is a short trail to a nice river beach where you can go swimming.

Curios, made by a lady in a nearby village, are sold in the reception area. Food and snacks are sometimes available, but it depends on supplies. Probably better to bring your own picnic lunch and eat it on the banks of the river. A small entry fee is charged for day guests.

- Mahamba Gorge Lodge: 268-617 9880

Nhlangano to Manzini via Sicunusa
From Nhlangano, you can return to Manzini via the rural centre of Sicunusa and the Malkerns Valley. Just head west on the MR13 (gravel road) for 38km; a relaxing drive through the plantations of the Shiselweni Forests. At Sicunusa, turn right onto the tarred MR4. This attractive road leads to the village of Mankayane and the Malkerns Valley before reaching Manzini (76km from Sicunusa). For more information about this route, read the 'Malkerns Meander' section.

If you head east from Nhlangano, the tarred MR11 trundles through the hills and past several small villages such as Dwaleni, Mhlosheni and Hluti (the Lame One) until it reaches the border town of Lavumisa, 90km away. From here, you can visit the attractions of the southeast, including Nisela Safaris and Big Bend (*see* page 176).

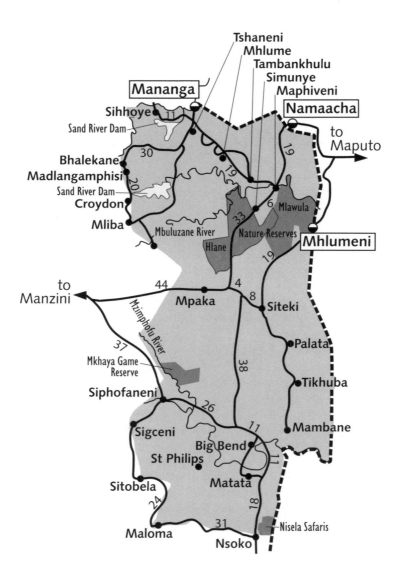

Tshaneni
Mhlume
Tambankhulu
Simunye
Maphiveni

Mananga

Namaacha

Sihhoye   11

Sand River Dam

to
Maputo

30

Bhalekane
Madlangamphisi

19

Sand River Dam

20

Croydon

6   Mlawula

Mliba

33

Mbuluzane River

Nature Reserves

Hlane

Mhlumeni

19

to
Manzini

44

4

Mpaka

8

Siteki

Mzimphofu River

Palata

37

38

Mkhaya Game
Reserve

Tikhuba

Siphofaneni

26

Sigceni

11

Mambane

St Philips

Big Bend

11

Sitobela

Matata

24

8

Maloma

31

Nisela Safaris

Nsoko

The Northeast

As you head east from Manzini, the tarred MR3 leads down to the low-lying bushveld of Swaziland. Due to the lower altitude, this part of the country is hotter and more humid than the mountainous west, and malaria is endemic. As the old saying goes, 'Only fools and impala live in the Lowveld', and nowadays there are no impala left. But don't let that put you off. The Lowveld has some great destinations to explore. The great bushveld plains of eastern Swaziland stretch unbroken to the 500-metre-high Lubombo Mountains (meaning 'the ridge' or 'bridge of the nose') which run from north to south and act as a physical border between Swaziland and Mozambique. You can see the ridge, hazy in the distance, looming over the Lowveld plains, and most of the tourist attractions in the region are clustered towards the northern part of the range, so that's where we're going next.

From Manzini follow the MR3 for about 8km to the little town of Hhelehhele where there is a junction with the MR8 that leads down to Siphofaneni and the southeast (see below). Keep going on the MR3 for another 36km to the scattered railway town of Mpaka. During the concessions era, this was known as the 'Gin Road', and it was well-travelled by a variety of rascally rustlers, smugglers and other nogoodniks—such as an infamous horse thief with the wonderfully appropriate name of Bob McNab.

Mpaka is the location of the now-defunct Mpaka coal mine, which still has considerable reserves left in the ground and may be re-opened in the future. It is also home to the Swazi Secrets cosmetics factory, a community-owned enterprise set up to empower rural women. Their skin-care products are based on Marula oil, which is rich in natural antioxidants, and they produce hand-made soap, lotion, lip balm, shampoo, facial scrub and shower gel to the 'highest standards of Fair Trade, environmental sustainability and ethical biotrade'. Swazi Secrets products can be bought directly from the factory shop at Mpaka, or from one of their various stockists across the country. Swazi Secrets: 268-333 3281/2; www.swazisecrets.com

There is a dusty roadhouse in the area that specializes in Mozambican dishes. Sikhuphe International Airport is being constructed nearby as part of Swaziland's Millennium Project. It is scheduled to open in 2010.

Siteki

About 8km east of Mpaka is an intersection with the MR7 to Siteki (12km away). Just after this junction you will find the Lonhlupheko Craft Market, another one of Swaziland's Community Tourism projects. Local crafters sell a variety of wares at the market, and there are toilet facilities.

Siteki (formerly called Stegi) is located on top of the Lubombo ridge, and the road up to the town has magnificent views over the Swaziland Lowveld. It is an otherwise humble place. The busy main street is filled with shops, the houses have lush gardens overflowing with trees, and there is a hotel (that was recently put up for auction). There is also a small cultural village and craft centre in the middle of town and a couple of guest houses in the surrounding countryside.

The settlement was initially established because its lofty altitude offered a respite from the humid Lowveld plains. It was also an important patrol post on the frontier between Swaziland and Mozambique. In fact, Siteki's name means 'marrying place', because King Mbandzeni granted permission for one of his regiments stationed along this part of the frontier to take wives. Despite this rather romantic moniker, Siteki became somewhat notorious as a refuge for the various smugglers and highwaymen who took advantage of the porous border during the early years of the last century.

Perhaps the most interesting thing about Siteki is that it is home to a government-supported Inyanga and Sangoma School, which trains traditional healers and diviners in their ancient art. Herbs and plants required by students are collected from the nearby Muti Muti Nature Reserve (*muthi* means traditional medicine). Apparently, tours of the school can be arranged.

From Siteki, you have several choices. You can return to the MR3 and continue towards Hlane; you can drive 16km eastwards on the MR7 to the southern gate of the Mlawula Nature Reserve and then head north on gravel through the reserve towards Simunye; you can continue for another 12km past the Mlawula Gate to reach the Mhlumeni border post with Mozambique; or you can head south on the tarred MR16, through the cattle ranches, to Big Bend. For the sake of continuity, we are now going to return to the MR3 to visit Hlane.

- Mabuda Farm B&B: 268-343 4124; www.mabuda.co.za
- Siteki Hotel: 268-343 6573
- Lituba Lodge: 268-628 3942; www.litubalodge.com

Hlane Royal National Park
If you continue on the MR3, about 10km after the turnoff to Siteki you will rumble across a cattle grid and enter the grounds of Hlane National Park. The highway cuts right through the middle of this important conservation area and there are no fences so, as the warning signs say, 'pedestrians and cyclists beware of lions and leopards' and 'motorists beware of big game crossing'. The main entrance gate is about 6km further down the road.

Hlane (Wilderness) is Swaziland's biggest protected area, measuring 30,000 hectares. Traditionally, this was the location of *Butimba*, the royal hunt, which took place every year at the king's invitation. By the 1960s, however, the catch had been reduced to a motley collection of cane rats and scrub hares. Ted Reilly then approached King Sobhuza II with a plan to restore Hlane to its former glory through a conservation programme. The idea appealed to the king, and the land was put aside as a refuge for the kingdom's rapidly diminishing game stocks in 1966. The reserve is now held in trust in for the nation by the king and managed by Big Game Parks.

After its establishment, Reilly and his rangers had their hands full. Even with the king's blessing, it took several years to get the poaching under control. Once the sanctity of the park was secured, game was brought back from Mlilwane to restock Hlane, while other animals were brought in from South Africa to supplement the breeding populations.

Within ten years Hlane was once again home to large herds of zebra, wildebeest and other game. Then, in 1986, two orphaned elephant bull calves were purchased by Big Game Parks from the Kruger Park. These were joined by another group of 18 pachyderms in 1987, which were split between Hlane and Mkhaya. Finally, at the behest of King Mswati III, three young lions were donated by South African National Parks in 1994 and released into a special enclosure.

Since the lion represents the king *(ngwenyama)* and the elephant cow represents the Queen Mother *(ndlovukhati)*, this was a particularly significant moment for conservation, as it was the first time in decades that the two symbols of Swaziland's royal house could be seen in the kingdom. Leopard and cheetah joined the lions in 1995. The symbolic importance of the lion and the elephant is one of the reasons why Hlane has endured over the years, even in the face of pressure from the powerful sugar industry, which has extensive plantations adjacent to the reserve.

Today, Hlane supports four of the Big Five: lion, leopard, elephant and rhino. There are also small populations of giraffe, hippo, crocodile and hyena. Large numbers of zebra, wildebeest, impala, kudu, waterbuck, warthog and duiker can be seen as well as baboons, vervet monkeys, ostrich, steenbok, nyala, bushbuck, waterbuck and jackals.

As you would expect, there is a wealth of bird life in the park. Red-billed quelea nesting colonies can be seen during the season, and Hlane has the most southerly nesting colony of marabou stork in Africa. The birds of prey are particularly impressive and the reserve is well populated with bateleur, martial eagle and five vulture species, including the highest density of nesting white-backed vultures in Africa.

The ecology of Hlane is diverse and ancient, consisting of Swazi bushveld and knobthorn parkland savannah (said to one of the finest examples of its kind in Africa). There are also extensive thickets and dry riverine forests that boast some ancient hardwood trees that date back 1,000 years. Giant leadwood, tamboti, marula and knobthorn trees can be seen growing out of the thick grass mantle (predominately red tiger grass and buffalo grass).

Visitors to Hlane can enjoy a network of self-guided game viewing routes or take a guided game drive on an open Land Rover. Other activities include guided walking safaris, a self-guided walking trail along the Umbuluzana River and guided mountain-bike trails through the reserve. Bikes can be hired at the gate, or you can bring your own. You can also go on a self-drive cultural tour to a local chief's village. The visit is facilitated by one of Hlane's rangers, and this is a great way to experience life in a real Swazi homestead.

There are two rest camps at Hlane. Ndlovu is located a short distance away from the main gate, overlooking a waterhole. It is a rustic place, surrounded by tall trees, with an open-air restaurant and a game-viewing deck. Accommodation is in thatched rondawels with self-catering facilities that sleep between two and eight. A recent development is the Wisteria group of 14 rondawels, which are self contained with hot and cold watered basins and showers. There are also two large 4x2 bedded cottages which are complete with kitchen and cooking utensils. Camping sites with a recently upgraded ablution block are also available. There is no electricity at the camp, and this adds to the tranquil atmosphere. At night, fires are lit in the *lapa* and guests can gather round to enjoy the rustling darkness.

Bhubesi Camp, in the northwestern corner of the park, overlooks the Umbuluzana River. It is a private camp with six modern stone cottages that sleep four people each. There is electricity, but no restaurant, so it's very much a self-catering affair. All in all, Hlane is both simple and delightful. It's said to be reminiscent of the old Kruger Park rest camps, before they became too 'commercial'. The reserve is only about 100km from the Ezulwini Valley, so it's do-able as a day trip; but you won't regret spending a night or two in one of their chalets. Accommodation will cost between E210 and E250 pp sharing for the first two guests and E130 for each additional bed. Bedding and towels are supplied. Entrance to the reserve is E25 per person, or free to holders of a valid Wild Card. Game drives will set you back about E150 pp, and guided activities cost between E75 and E120.

- Hlane Royal National Park: 268-528 3943; www.biggameparks.org

Simunye
Seven kilometres east of the Hlane Gate is the neat little company town of Simunye (we are one). Surrounded by vast sugar cane fields, this estate was built to house the employees of the Royal Swaziland Sugar Corporation, one of the biggest companies in Swaziland.

Since its inception in 1973, Simunye and the nearby Mhlume estate have grown to house about 23,000 people. The complex includes two clinics, two country clubs, a private English-medium primary school and the prestigious Mananga College high school. There are also seven government-owned schools on the estates.

All in all, the RSSC controls approximately 15,600 hectares of irrigated sugar cane on land leased from the Swazi nation, and manages another 5,000 hectares on behalf of third parties. They harvest 2.3

million tons of cane per season, which is delivered to the group's two sugar mills, where it is crushed a combined rate of 700 tons per hour to produce 430,000 tons of sugar a year (two thirds of the country's sugar). There is also a sugar refinery, which produces 150,000 tons of refined sugar, and a large ethanol plant. Furthermore, they support 2,500 small-scale rural farmers across Swaziland, who collectively supply the company with 1.2 million tons of sugar cane.

For the visitor, Simunye offers a petrol station and a convenient shopping plaza, with about a dozen shops selling food, supplies and clothes. The Simunye Country Club has a restaurant with an extensive menu, and offers overnight accommodation in self-contained cottages. The club is somewhat colonial but the green lawns, blue swimming pool, kids' playground and many sporting facilities are all well-maintained. If only they didn't play Chris de Burgh music on the terrace!

- Simunye Country Club and Guest House: 268-313 4000; www.visitswazi.com/simunyeclub
- Royal Swaziland Sugar Corporation: www.rssc.co.sz

The Lubombo Conservancy and TFCA
About 8km from Simunye, there is an intersection with the MR28. This road leads along the foot of the Lubombo, where a number of conservation areas are clustered. This is part of the 60,000-hectare Lubombo Conservancy, which will eventually include Hlane, Mbuluzi, Mlawula, Shewula, Inyoni Yami Irrigation Scheme and Nkhalashane Ranch. A management committee has already been established, infrastructure is being upgraded and malaria control programmes are in place.

Recently, the Lubombo Route was launched. This tourism corridor runs along the Lubombo Mountains, from the Kruger Park in the north, down the eastern spine of Swaziland and back into South Africa to connect with the iSimangaliso Wetlands (formerly St Lucia) and the Hluhluwe Game Reserve. Sounds like a great itinerary to me.

Furthermore, the conservancy is part of a larger scheme to establish the Lubombo-Goba Transfrontier Conservation Area (TFCA) that will unite national, private and community-owned land in a single reserve through which animals can freely roam. When the conservancy is finally linked to the Goba communal lands on the Mozambique side of the border, it is estimated that the total area under protection will be around 4,195 square kilometres.

- www.lubomboconservancy.org
- www.peaceparks.org
- www.noboundaries.co.za
- www.sntc.org.sz/programs/lubombo.asp
- www.isimangaliso.com

Mbuluzi Game Reserve
A few hundred metres down the MR28, you will find the entrance to the beautiful Mbuluzi Game Reserve. This privately owned reserve was established in 1980, and is a conservation share-block scheme. As such, it has a maximum of 49 shareholders who are each allowed to construct a lodge on the banks of the Mbuluzi River.

The landscape in Mbuluzi is diverse. The reserve covers 3,000 hectares and is part of the regional Lubombo Conservancy. Two perennial rivers run through the park: the Mbuluzi and the Mlawula—but swimming is not recommended because of the threat of bilharzia (and the crocodiles).

With an altitude that varies from 150 to 460 metres, Mbuluzi offers dense riverine forests, knobthorn savannah, acacia bushveld and open grasslands. Distinctive vegetation includes sycamore figs, wild date palms and cycad forests.

The reserve has a good network of gravel game-viewing roads (self-guided) on which you can spot giraffe, kudu, wildebeest, waterbuck, zebra, impala, bushbuck, nyala, duiker, warthog, jackal, hyena, crocodile and hippo. On a night drive, you might see leopard, hyena, civet, genet, jackal, honey badger, serval, antbear and pangolin. High-clearance vehicles are recommended, as there are several low-level river crossings in the reserve.

There are a variety of choices for accommodation in Mbuluzi. The lodges and tented camp are private and discreet, tucked among the riverine vegetation. The accommodation is extremely comfortable, ranging from large thatched cottages surrounded by green lawns to luxury tents overlooking the Mlawula River; some of the sites include swimming pools. A rustic campsite is also available on the banks of the Mbuluzi River, within easy walking distance of rapids and lovely rock formations. Firewood and lanterns are provided in the campsite, and there are hot showers—make sure a fire has been lit under the boiler at least in hour in advance.

There are a number of walking trails in Mbuluzi and this is a great way for birders to get up-close and personal with the 300 recorded bird species, including whitebacked night heron, yellow wagtail, grey-hooded kingfisher, Pels fishing owl, dwarf bittern, narina trogon, African finfoot, crested guinea fowl, scops owl and fiery-necked nightjar. Overnight guests are allowed to fish in the rivers, which have a good population of largescale yellowfish, barbel and bream ... but if you hook a crocodile, you have to throw it back.

- Mbuluzi Game Reserve: 268-383 8861;
  www.mbulizigamereserve.co.sz

Mlawula Nature Reserve
A couple of kilometres beyond the Mbuluzi Reserve Gate is the entrance to Mlawula Nature Reserve. Measuring 16,500 hectares, this reserve straddles a transitional zone between dry thorn savannas in the west and moister coastal thickets in the east. The reserve consists of three distinct ecological zones: the Ndzindza plateau, the 500m-high rhyolite ridges of the Lumbombo and the basaltic Siphiso Valley (where most of the game is found).

As such, the reserve has over 60 species of small and large mammals, including large herds of zebra, wildebeest and impala. Endangered or rare species include pangolin, samango monkey, oribi, spotted hyena, honey badger, water rat, red duiker, klipspringer, common reedbuck, mountain reedbuck, common waterbuck, aardwolf, leopard, cheetah, serval, striped weasel, black-backed jackal, African civet, Schreibers' long fingered bat, African wild cat and Meller's mongoose.

Mlawula is particularly rich in bird species, with about 350 of the 500 recorded species in the whole of Swaziland. Some of the rarer ticks include Rudd's apalis, pinkthroated twinspot, saddlebilled stork, secretary bird, lappet-faced vulture, white-headed vulture, tawny eagle, African hawk eagle, bateleur, white-backed night heron, black stork, marabou stork, black eagle, martial eagle, crowned eagle, African finfoot, barred owl, African broadbill, woolly-necked stork, yellow-billed stork, white-backed vulture, long-crested eagle, black-breasted snake eagle, giant eagle owl, half-collared kingfisher and red-billed oxpecker.

Other fauna statistics include an estimated 20,000 species of insects, 10,000 species of spiders, about 40 different kinds of fish (permits for fishing are available) and plenty of amphibians and reptiles, including the Southern African python, crocodile and the Natal hinged tortoise.

The flora of Mlawula is very rich, with 1,035 recorded plant species, including 55 aliens. The deep rocky ravines are particularly important, as they succour the unique Lubombo Ironwood and a cycad *(Encephalartos umbuluziensis)* found nowhere else on earth. Many uncommon succulents and climbers can also be found.

With such a diverse landscape and so many forms of life, Mlawula was considered as a conservation-worthy area for many years. It was even proclaimed as a reserve in the early part of the 20th century, but was subsequently deproclaimed and subdivided into cattle ranches.

Then, in the 1970s, the Niven family donated their 485-hectare Blue Jay Ranch to the Swaziland National Trust Commission, and this became the Ndzindza Nature Reserve in 1978. Cecily Niven, incidentally, was the daughter of Percy Fitzpatrick, author of *Jock of the Bushveld.*

Soon afterwards, the surrounding Mlawula Estates land was purchased, funded in part by Havelock Mine, and the government donated the adjacent Nyala Ranch. Mlawula (Gift) Nature Reserve was officially proclaimed in 1980.

Visitors to Mlawula can enjoy a 54km of game drives through the reserve, leading to enticingly named spots such as the Python Pool, Hippo Pool and Baboon's Cave. The roads are gravel but in good condition, and the views are superb. Mountain bikes are permitted. You can also rent a quad bike from reception for E150 for two hours (but you must stay on the demarcated roads).

If you really want to get to know the reserve, however, you should tackle one of the excellent walking trails, ranging from one-and-a-half hours to two days. A walk to the top of the Lubombo is highly recommended, and there are many shady caves and overhangs in which to chill out. Trails are self-guided, or a ranger can accompany you. You must carry all your own water, however, as the river water may contain bilharzia. And use a good insect repellent, because there are plenty of ticks in the long grass.

Snakes aren't too much of a problem in the reserve, but I did get a fright on one hike when I suddenly heard a hissing sound coming out of a bush just by my foot. Instinctively, I froze. Then an enormous water monitor lizard burst out of the bush and sped down the rocks into a nearby pool. I screamed like a little girl!

Accommodation at Mlawula is unusual and totally in keeping with the idiosyncratic nature of the reserve. The Sara tented camp is located on top of a ridge close to the main gate and offers four furnished safari tents, sleeping two or three. Each tent is private and has a wooden deck with a great view over the reserve. The unique open-air shower perched on the cliff edge is quite memorable. In the centre of the camp there is a well-equipped kitchen, lounge area and communal toilets under a large thatched boma. The camp is self-catering and has no electricity, but gas stoves, gas fridges and paraffin lanterns are provided. Cost is about E150 pppn.

A short distance away from the camp is Mapelepele Cottage. This used to be the rangers' house, but has now been upgraded into a self-catering family unit that sleeps eight. It is built on two levels and has a full bathroom (indoors), lounge, fireplace, braai area and baboon-proofed porches if you want to sleep outside on hot summer nights. There is no electricity, but a gas geyser, stove, oven and fridge will provide you with the basic mod-cons. Kitchen utensils, bedding and towels are supplied. Cost is E500 for the first four people per night, and E150 for each additional.

Campers can stay at Siphiso campsite, which has a thatched ablution building and a welcoming lawn area with tall trees and braai facilities. Cost is E60 pppn. Mlawula also has an environmental education centre with a dormitory. There are picnic sites for day trippers, who will be charged an entry fee of about E25 pp.

The main gravel road through the Mlawula Reserve runs for 20km from the northern entrance gate to join the MR7 highway 16km outside Siteki. From Siteki, you can return to the MR3 at Mpaka, and this route is a great alternative to retracing your steps through Hlane.

However, we still have one more stop to make before leaving Mlawula because, just before you reach the southern gate of the reserve, you will come to the large and impressive Magadzavane Lodge.

Built on a ridge with stunning views, Magadzavane is brand, spanking new—so new, in fact, that it's incomplete. When it's finished, however, it will offer luxury accommodation in several dozen en suite units, a restaurant, conference centre, bar and swimming pool. It looks like it will be a great place to stay and a lot of money has been put into the place (including some international donor funds from Taiwan). Unfortunately, there was an oversight in the planning stages, and they are having trouble running water up the mountains to supply the complex. The newly built entrance gate is also slightly too small to admit coaches and buses. Hopefully, however, all this will be resolved and the Lodge will open in the near future.

- Mlawula Nature Reserve: 268-383 8885; www.sntc.org.sz

Shewula Mountain Camp
If you keep north on the MR3 beyond the turnoff to Mbuluzi and Mlawula, you will soon come to an intersection with the MR24. Turn left here to go to Tshaneni and the border gate with South Africa (37km). Go straight if you want to reach the Lomahasha border post with Mozambique (20km). From the border, the cosmopolitan delights of Maputo are only 80km away, all on tar.

Keeping straight, about 11km after the intersection you will see a small sign for the Shewula Mountain Camp to your right. This small gravel road climbs the Lubombo and takes you deep into a network of rural villages that nestle on the mountain-top plateau. Just follow the signs and, after about 15km, you will come to a beautifully rustic little place located right on the lip of the Mbuluzi River valley.

With an incredible view that is said to stretch over for 100km, Shewula is a community-run camp that offers accommodation in four comfy rondavels that sleep six each.

There is also a campsite and a communal kitchen and dining area. The camp is self-catering, but all catering utensils are provided. Traditional meals can also be prepared by the camp's staff on request. There is no electricity on this high mountainside, but paraffin and gas are on hand to provide light, heat and hot water.

The main reason to come here, apart from the awesome view, is the walking and cultural trails. Local community members will be happy to take you around the area where you can visit homesteads, traditional healers and schools. There are also some excellent nature walks that take you down into Mbuluzi Gorge and through the Shewula Nature Reserve.

- Shewula Mountain Camp: 268-605 1160; www.shewulacamp.com

Tshaneni

If you go left at the intersection of the MR3 and the MR24, you will drive through attractive boulder-strewn hills and the sugar plantations of Tambankulu and Mhlume.

Tambankulu, on the right-hand side, was established by the Hersov family back in 1951 as a cattle ranch. In 1955, the Mhlume canal and irrigation works were constructed, which transported water 60km from the Komati River, and the land was converted to sugar farming. Then, in 1978, some of the land was sold to the Royal Swaziland Sugar Corporation based at Simunye. The South African Tongaat-Hulett group purchased Tambankulu in 1998 and, today, the estate produces 62,000 tons of sucrose from its 3,816 hectares. The Tambankulu Country Club has a golf course, restaurant, bar, two swimming pools, a tennis court, conference venues and 16 air-conditioned chalets for overnight guests.

About 30km from the intersection, you will arrive at the town of Tshaneni. This is home to yet another country club with a golf course— those sugar barons sure liked their golf! Mananga Country Club also has overnight accommodation. The nearby Sand River Dam has boating facilities available—ask at the country club for information.

South of Tshaneni is the Mnjoli Dam. This used to be the location of the Dvokolwako diamond mine, jointly owned by Tibiyo Taka Ngwane (the government's development agency) and Trans Hex. At its peak in 1988, the mine was recovering 72,676 carats of industrial grade diamonds a year, but declining yields and a falling diamond price forced the mine to close in 1996, with the resultant loss of 250 jobs.

From Tshaneni, the Mananga border post with South Africa is about 7km away. On the other side of the border, the R571 road heads north for 60km before it joins the N4 highway, close to the Komatipoort border post with Mozambique. From this point, the Crocodile Bridge Gate into the Kruger Park is 13km away and Nelspruit is about 100km. Incidentally, the former Mozambican president, Samora Machel, died in plane crash in this area in 1986, and the site is now marked by a memorial. Some say the South African government of the time had a hand in the crash and, periodically, further investigations, allegations and counter-allegations crop up, but it's all still shrouded in murk.

Alternatively, from Tshaneni, you can take the road less travelled and head west (following the MR5, the MR6 and the MR2) to join up with the MR1 road at the town of Pigg's Peak. This section of road is apparently tarred (it wasn't a few years ago), and it leads through some lovely rural scenery.

- Mananga Country Club and Guest House: 268-607 7769
- Mananga Golf Club: 268-323 2404
- Tambankulu Club and Guest House: 268-373 7111

The Southeast

From Manzini, the MR3 heads east into the humid plains of the Lowveld. At the town of Hhelehhele, 8km from Manzini, there is a junction with the tarred MR8 that leads southeast to Siphofaneni, Big Bend and Lavumisa. This is the least developed region in Swaziland in terms of tourism and anything else, but there are still a couple of choice destinations to check out.

Mkhaya Game Reserve
About 44km from the intersection with the MR3, the MR8 passes through the small towns of Siphofaneni and Phuzamoya. At the latter, you will see a parking area for Mkhaya Game Reserve. This secretive conservation area is home to some of Swaziland's most endangered species. It is only accessible as part of a guided day tour or if you stay overnight, so advance booking is essential.

Mkhaya was established by Ted Reilly's Big Game Parks organization as a secure holding 'pen', where depleted game stocks could re-establish themselves in peace. The land was purchased in 1978 and opened to the public in 1987. Around the same time, a number of elephants from the Kruger Park were re-settled in the reserve. In 1995, six highly-endangered black rhino were brought in from South Africa in a project funded by the Taiwanese Government. In 1997, two baby elephants were calved—the first to be born in Swaziland for over 100 years.

Today, with the help of several generous donors, the reserve boasts four of the Big Five: leopard, buffalo, elephant and rhino. Giraffe, hippo, crocodile, roan, sable, tsessebe, eland, kudu, waterbuck, nyala, zebra, wildebeest, impala, warthog, grey duiker, steenbok, ostrich, bushbaby and vervet monkey are also present, as are lesser-seen species such as red duiker, suni, genet, lynx, baboon, serval, mongoose, jackal, leopard, hyena, honey badger and pangolin. As such, it is one of the best game viewing destinations in the kingdom.

Mkhaya is also home to a 'thoroughbred' herd of Nguni cattle. This ancient bovine bloodline dates back several thousand years, to the days of the original Bantu diaspora that brought the Nguni people (including the Swazi) into southern Africa. Thanks to their ancient heritage, Nguni cattle have developed a natural resistance to disease and became a vital component of traditional faming societies in the sub-continent.

Unfortunately, during the last couple of hundred years, the breed was diluted by less resilient modern cattle strains and, by the middle of the 20th century, the noble Nguni herds were in danger of disappearing. This prompted Ted Reilly to initiate the Southern African Nguni Breed Society, and Mkhaya was originally purchased to give Swaziland's remaining Nguni stock a safe haven.

Day trips through Mkhaya begin at the Phuzamoya pick-up point at 10:00 and return at 16:00. The cost is E440 pp; this includes game drives on an open Land Rover and a good lunch. Guests must make their own way to the pick-up point, which is about 85km from the Ezulwini Valley.

If you've got the budget, the overnight accommodation at Mkhaya is outstanding. Stone Camp, laid out along the banks of a dry riverbed, consists of twelve semi-open thatched cottages built with rough-hewn dolerite rocks. The emphasis here is on understated luxury, and each nicely-appointed cottage is integrated into the surrounding bush. There is no electricity in the camp and, at night, the pathways between the units and the central lapa are lined with glowing paraffin lanterns. Stone Camp costs E1,000 pppn/s and this includes all meals, game drives and walking safaris.

- Mkhaya Game Reserve: 268-528 3943; www.biggameparks.org

Big Bend

Twenty-four kilometres east of Mkhaya is the town of Big Bend, so named because it is located in the crook of a sweeping curve in the Great Usuthu River (also called the Lusutfu). The town is surrounded by large cattle ranches and the enormous plantations of the Ubombo Sugar Estate. The town got its start with Allister Miller, the incorrigible colonialist, who wrote a booklet entitled *Swaziland—the California of South Africa* in 1907. In this little gem, Miller predicted that the malarial Lowveld, then only inhabited during the winter months, had good soil and would one day be a prosperous farming area.

Despite his exhortations, British settlers were more interested in healthier places such as Hlambanyatsi and Malkerns, and the seemingly worthless land south of the Usuthu River was declared part of the 2,500-square-kilometre Hlatikhulu Nature Reserve.

Undeterred, in 1912, Miller and a wealthy stud-farmer named E. W. Evans bought a mammoth farm north of the river, which they named the Bar R Ranch. It was more than 380 square kilometres in extent— the biggest ranch in South Africa. Within two years, they had amassed over 2,000 head of cattle.

Unfortunately, stock numbers fell as a result of disease, drought and attacks by wild animals. Packs of African wild gogs and crocodiles were a particular problem, and were exterminated as vermin. Nevertheless, by 1923, the ranch had over 18,000 head of cattle. Vegetables, maize, cotton and citrus were also grown on an experimental basis, thanks to the erection of a gas suction pump that drew water out of the Usuthu River.

Then there was a slump in world beef prices, and the ranch was forced into voluntary liquidation in 1927. The cattle were sold off, and the land was effectively abandoned. It wasn't until 1942 that a group of investors headed by Carl Todd stepped forward to buy the ranch. The land was subsequently split up and sold off into a number of smaller ranches, Bar J, Bar Circle, Bar R, Diamond C, Pendora, Majombie, Crookes Plantation, etcetera. Todd kept the prime Big Bend estate, Miller's old base, for himself.

Gradually, under the aegis of Hendrik van Eck, several farms were re-merged to create Ubombo Ranches. Ubombo soon began to move away from cattle ranching and started developing the land's crop-growing potential. But despite the proximity of the Great Usuthu River, water continued to be a problem and in the early 1950s, construction began on a 32km irrigation canal.

This was opened in 1954 and, as a result, Ubombo boomed. The system was later supplemented by the Van Eck Dam in 1970 and the canal was further enlarged in the 1980s, when a hydro-electric plan was also added. The canal now delivers 130 million gallons of water a day to the fields of its shareholders through a network of furrows that collectively measure over 100km.

After trying their hand at a variety of crops, including rice, Ubombo Ranches switched to sugar in the 1950s. An old sugar mill was bought from a farmer in Mtubatuba and transported up to Big Bend on trucks. It started operating in 1958, and was so successful that it was replaced by a bigger mill in 1960. Around the same time, the 'town' of Big Bend was established to service the area.

Finally, in 1996, Todd's Big Bend Sugar Company and Ubombo Ranches merged to create Ubombo Sugar Estates. This new entity was bought by the South African Illovo Sugar Group the following year. Ubombo Sugar now has 1,193 hectares of land under cultivation. The mill crushes 400 tons of cane per hour and processes over 200,000 tons of sugar a year (85,000 of which is refined). Ubombo Sugar also manages 2,360 hectares of irrigated sugar cane on behalf of Tibiyo Take Ngwane (the government fund which manages development in the kingdom) and supports many small independent growers.

In terms of tourism, however, Big Bend is somewhat lacking. The town is small and straggling, with a couple of shops, guest houses, a post office and the obligatory country club with a golf course. The Bend Inn, situated on a hill at the top of town, offers sundowners on their patio with a view over the river. When it opened in 1960, the Bend Inn was described as 'the last word in luxury and service'. Sadly those days are no more.

If you drive through the town, the gravel road heads past the sugar fields, over the irrigation canals and down the banks of the river itself (8km away). The road now crosses a low causeway over the river and, on the other side, you'll find the Matata shopping centre, established in 1886 and once the biggest supermarket in Swaziland.

The main MR8 highway actually bypasses the town of Big Bend and provides good views of the river curving through the green sugar fields, especially in the late afternoon when the spray from the irrigation sprinklers sparkles in the setting sun. A tall bridge over the river, just on the outskirts of town, is a good place to stop and take in the scene. A short distance further along the road, towards Lavumisa, is the Riverside Complex with shops, restaurants and a hotel. This site has a good view of the river, and is adjacent to the large Crookes Brothers citrus farm.

Nearby, there is the Van Eck Dam and Mhlosinga Conservancy, a 400-hectare wildlife sanctuary jointly established by Ubombo Sugar and other landowners. The dam has a camp site and is stocked with fearsome tiger fish, barbel and bream. You can also sail or water-ski on the dam, but watch out for the crocs.

From Big Bend, the Usuthu River heads inexorably east as it cuts its way through the Lubombo Mountains to form the dramatic, eight-kilometre-long Usuthu Gorge. This is the start of the proposed Usuthu-Tembe-Futi Transfrontier Conservation Area which will extend through South Africa, Swaziland and Mozambique. It's a huge project that seeks to link Usuthu Gorge, Ndumo Game Reserve, Tembe Elephant Park, the Futi Corridor, Kosi Bay and the Maputo Elephant Reserve into a single, contiguous area which will allow the elephants to resume their natural east-west migration pattern for the first time in over a century.

- Bend Inn: 268-363 6725
- Lebombo Villa: 268-603 6585; www.swazilive.com/thelebombovilla. htm
- Lismore Lodge and Restaurant: 268-363 6019
- Riverside Restaurant and Hotel: 268-363 6910
- Big Bend Country Club and Golf Course: 268-363 6288
- www.peaceparks.org
- www.noboundaries.co.za
- www.sntc.org.sz/programs/usututembefuti.asp

Nsoko

About 30km south of Big Bend, on the MR8 highway, is the little village of Nsoko. The main attraction here is a privately-run conservation area called Nisela Safaris, which offers guided game drives, walking trails, two fishing dams, a lion enclosure and a well-equipped reptile house that has over 200 specimens of 70 species (feeding time is on Saturdays). The birding is also very highly regarded by twitchers.

Nisela has a restaurant, conference facilities, a craft shop, and traditional dancing displays can be arranged if you ask in advance. Accommodation is in a colonial-style guest house, reed cabins, rondavels or traditional beehive huts. There is also a caravan park and campsite.

East of Nsoko is the Maloma Colliery, the only official mine in Swaziland. This underground operation produces around 40,000 tons of anthracite a month, which is mostly exported to South Africa. Maloma is operated by the South African company Xstrata which has a 75 per cent interest in the venture (the Swazi Government owns the other 25 per cent). The mine is doing well, and they are currently investigating plans to develop a local coal-burning power plant to reduce Swaziland's electrical dependence on its neighbour.

- Nisela Safaris: 268-303 0318; www.niselasafaris.co.za

Lavumisa

Thirty-five kilometres south of Nsoko is the town of Lavumisa/Golela, which is split through the middle by the Swaziland/South African border. This is the closest border post into Swaziland from Durban, and it is often crowded with truckers hauling their loads from the harbours of KwaZulu to Mozambique. It is also an important stop on the north-south rail link between Komatipoort and Richard's Bay. There are currently plans to make the border into a 24-hour crossing.

The story of the Lavumisa/Ngwavuma area stretches far back into the roots of Swazi history. Many of the early battles that defined the Swazi nation took place hereabouts and the town is thought to be named after the wife of King Sobhuza I, whose name translates as 'arbitrator'.

This region was once part of the Hlatilkhulu Reserve, declared in the early 1900s and deproclaimed in 1919. The land was then split up and sold off as cattle farms. Soldiers returning from World War I were also settled on the land, but the area was isolated and conditions were tough. The Natal railway reached the town, then called Gollel, in 1927 and the famous Gollel Hotel was opened in 1930. With the arrival of the railway, a company called Cotton Plantations bought up many of the soldiers' farms and began producing tobacco and cotton. The area is still a productive agricultural centre, with fertile soil and good rainfall.

Lavumisa is located right next to the massive Jozini Dam, which was created by blocking the Phongolo River at the head of a narrow poort. The dam straddles the border between Swaziland and South Africa, and is a haven for fishermen and boating enthusiasts.

A huge multi-billion-rand development is now being constructed on the Swazi side of the dam, where 14,000 hectares of land have been secured on a renewable 99-year lease and plans include the establishment of a game reserve with the Big Five, a casino, hotel, equestrian centre, golf course, boating marina, jetty and slipway. A large private residential estate is also being built, as well as a new commercial centre in Lavumisa town. The name of this ambitious development is the Royal Jozini Big 6 Estate because, in addition to the Big Five game reserve, the reserve will have tiger fish in the dam. The reserve will be part of the new Nsubane-Pongola Transfrontier Conservation Area between South Africa and Swaziland, and has already been stocked by Big Game Parks with wildebeest, zebra, waterbuck, impala and kudu.

Nearby, you will also find Border Cave, an important archaeological site where human skeletons and implements dating back 100,000 years have been uncovered. Although the site was known for many years, the full extent of human involvement with the site was only fully uncovered by a guy who was collecting bat guano for fertilizer, back in 1940. Border Cave can only be explored as part of a guided tour from Ndumo Game Reserve in South Africa.

- Royal Jozini Private Big 6 Estate: 268-602 3325; www.royaljozini.com

Suggested itineraries

Swaziland is so small that practically anywhere is within a day's drive from anywhere else. As such, you can simply choose a nice place to stay and just go exploring. Nevertheless, you don't want to spend the whole day in the car, so it's better to choose a region that interests you and check out the attractions in the surrounding area.

If you have two nights: Pick an area and stick to it. For first-timers, I would suggest the Ezulwini Valley or the Malolotja/Pigg's Peak area— my personal favourite. If you want to venture deeper into the country, Mlawula/Hlane is well worth a visit, and so is Mahamba/Nhlangano/ Grand Valley. If you've seen it all before, try Big Bend/Lavumisa, or check out one of the Community Tourism camps at Khelekhele, Ngwempisi or Shewula.

If you have four nights: There's plenty to do and see in any of the regions listed above, so either spend more time getting to know your surroundings, or pick two regions and spend a bit of time in each.

If you have seven or more nights: If you really want to get to know Swaziland, might I suggest a grand tour around the circumference of the country? Starting at Mbabane, this route would go as follows: Ezulwini Valley, Malkerns, Mliliwane, Manzini, Grand Valley, Nlhangano, Lavumisa, Big Bend, Hlane, Mlawula, Tshaneni, Pigg's Peak (with a side trip to Bulembu), Malolotja, Ngwenya and back to Mbabane. This journey will cover just about all the major attractions and plenty of rural splendour besides. The entire route is tarred, and measures only 535km from start to finish.

Volunteer tourism

If you are interested in taking a gap year or a career break, the newly emerging concept of volunteer tourism could be just the ticket. So, instead of lazing around on a beach and slurping down cocktails with little paper umbrellas in them, why not get involved in one of the many cultural, social and environmental projects in Swaziland? You'll be making a difference, meeting cool people, experiencing new cultures and having fun, all at the same time.

In Swaziland, one of the pioneers of volunteer tourism is All-Out Africa. They are affiliated to a number of important initiatives, such as orphan care, savannah conservation, teaching, sports development, wildlife training and home-building. They also have several marine conservation projects on the go in Mozambique.

Rhino eco-volunteer projects are run at Mkhaya Game Reserve where hands-on conservation work is undertaken—patrolling, game counts, alien vegetation control, night watch, game capture and control—if they happen to coincide with your visit.

- All-Out Africa: 268-550 4951; www.all-out.org
- Mkhaya Game Reserve: 268-528 3943; www.biggameparks.org

Adventure tourism

Swaziland has an amazing diversity of natural landscapes that will appeal to adrenaline junkies and fitness freaks alike. Whitewater rafting, tubing, caving, abseiling, rap jumping, quad-biking, extreme marathons, rock climbing, you name it, there is a tour operator who can deliver what you want.

- Raw Africa: 268-416 2180; www.swazi.travel
- Swazi Xtreme Adventure Race: 268-416 2180; www.swazixtreme.co.sz
- Whitewater Rafting Festival: 268-416 2180; www.rawafrica.com/wwf
- Swazi Trails (Mantenga): 268-416 2180; www.swazitrails.co.sz
- Adventure Sports Cycle Race and Tours (Mbabane): 268-404 9609; www.adventuresport.co.sz
- Chubeka Trails – overnight horse trailing: 268-528 3943; www. biggameparks.org

Tour operators and cultural guides

One of Swaziland's greatest assets is its long and unbroken cultural tradition. There are few countries in the world where ancient rituals and ceremonies are still so much part of everyday life, and there's no better way to experience this continuity with the past than through a cultural tour with a well-informed guide.

There are many operators offering cultural tours in Swaziland, and these can be customized to fit your itinerary and interests. Personally, I spent a day driving around with Mandla Masuka of Ekhaya Cultural

Tours, and it was a revelatory experience. Dressed in his traditional skins, Mandla really made an impression; pointing out things I had missed, explaining things I had seen but misunderstood, fleshing out the nuances of a culture that I didn't really understand. A good guide can really enhance your experience in the kingdom—so take advantage of one of the practitioners listed below, and make Swaziland come alive.

- Cheetah Holiday Travel: 268-505 9100
- Ekhaya Cultural Tours: 268-405 0017
- Enkhaba Adventure Centre: 268-602 0578; www.enkhabaadventures.co.sz
- Inyatsi Tours and Safaris: 268-604 0224,
- Karibu Travellers Solution: 268-404 8462
- Mngoma Tours: 268-623 0653, www.mngomatours.com
- Myxos Cultural Tours: 268-505 8363; www.earthfoot.org/sz.htm
- Sibebe Tours: 268-614 5396, www.sibebetours.com
- Swazi Trails: 268-416 2180; www.swazitrails.co.sz
- Swazi Defined (Pigg's Peak): 268-641 3580
- Tana Tours and Travel Services: 268-604 8152
- The Travel Centre: 268-505 2983
- Themba's Tours: 268-658 9801
- Tour Swaziland: 268-617 5175; www.tourswaziland.com

Cultural festivals

Incwala

Although it's usually translated as the 'first fruits ceremony', *incwala* is much more than a harvest festival. It is a sacred celebration of kingship, incorporating a series of ceremonies that extend over a month or so. When there is no king, as is sometimes the case in the Swazi tradition, there is no *incwala*. It is high treason for anyone other than the king to convene an *incwala*—so don't get any ideas!

Incwala takes place during December/January, depending on the lunar cycle. The main day of the festival, a public holiday, is a spectacular pageant that culminates with the king tasting certain fruits from the new harvest. This event takes place in the royal kraal four days after the full moon nearest the summer solstice, December 21, and members of the public are welcome to attend. However, photographs are not allowed unless you get written permission from the Swaziland National Trust Commission.

The whole thing kicks off at full moon in November when the *bemanti* (people of the water) meet at the Queen Mother's (*ndlovukhati*) home. They are then divided into two groups. The larger group is sent to kaTembe (Catembe, south of Maputo) to collect water from the sea, a task sometimes poetically described as catching 'foam off the waves'. The smaller group is sent north to collect water from the rivers. When the *bemanti* return to the royal capital with their 'holy water', the two-day *little incwala* ceremony takes place. This must happen before the full moon in December.

About two weeks later, the big *incwala* begins. According to the Swaziland National Trust Commission, the festival breaks down as follows:

Day 1 – Fetching the *lusekwane*

A group of young, unmarried men meet at *Ndlovukhati's* residence. They then march off to cut branches of the *lusekwane* (sickle bush/ *Dichrostachys cinerea*)—the biggest they can carry. Traditionally, these are collected under the light of the full moon at Gunundvweni in the Sidvokodvo area, about 50km away. The *lusekwane* boys must be relatively chaste, as tradition states that the leaves of the *lusekwane* branch will wither in the hands of anyone who has been intimate with a married woman or impregnated a young maiden.

Day 2 – Dropping the *lusekwane*

The next day, the boys return to the royal kraal (cattle byre) with their *lusekwane* branches. The elders then weave these branches between upright poles to create the *inhlambelo*—the king's private sanctuary.

Day 3 – Day of the bull

In the morning, young boys who wish to participate in *incwala* but are too young for the *lusekwane* are sent into the hills around Lobamba to cut branches of the black *imbondvo* (red bushwillow/*Combretum apiculatum*). The *imbondvo* are then added to the *inhlambelo*. In the afternoon, a black bull is slaughtered by the *lusekwane* boys and the remains are made into ritual medicines which are given to the king in his *inhlambelo*. This phase of the ceremony is said to encourage solidarity, discipline, valour and loyalty to the nation.

Day 4 – Eating the first fruits and throwing the gourd
On the main day of the festival, hundreds of people in traditional dress assemble at the royal kraal. This includes the king (*ngwenyama*) and his regiments, the Queen Mother, royal wives and children, governors (*indunas*), chiefs and any other Swazi people who wish to participate. Visitors are welcome as long as they conform to tradition (no shoes or cameras in the kraal—ox hides and leopard skins are optional).

In the afternoon, with various guests of honour assembled on a grandstand, the king inspects his warriors. *Ngwenyama* then retreats into his *inhlambelo* where he bites and spits out certain plants from the first harvest. The crowd now begins a low, hypnotic chant, surging forwards and backwards, entreating the king to come out and rejoin his people. According to David Johnson, writing in 1983, "after pretending reluctance, the king emerges from his retreat. His face is smeared with black medicines, his body draped in bright green grass, his head dressed with big black plumes. His waist is belted with silver monkey skin. He then dances before his regiments and his people in a dance that he improvizes and is never copied".

The king then throws the sacred gourd, *luselwa*, which is caught on a black shield by one of the *lusekwane* boys. Until that moment, it is forbidden for any Swazi to eat from the new harvest.

Day 5 – Day of abstinence
This is a solemn day of taboos (*kutila*). People may not have any sexual contact and they may not wash. Wearing decorations, sitting on chairs or mats, shaking hands, scratching, singing, dancing and all other forms of merriment are not allowed. On this day, the king remains in seclusion while the *bemanti* patrol the royal capital to ensure that no one is breaking the rules.

Day 6 – Day of the log
On the final day of the festival, the regiments go out and collect firewood. The elders then stack the wood in the middle of the kraal and

certain ritual objects are placed on the pyre, representing the old year. As the crowd sings and dances, the huge bonfire is lit and left to burn. It is considered a good omen if the rains fall and extinguish the flames. The king will now remain in seclusion until the next full moon, when the *lusekwane* branches are removed and burnt.

Umhlanga

The *umhlanga*, or reed dance, is a colourful social ritual that takes place in late August or early September, depending on the lunar cycle. It is largely secular in nature, aimed at encouraging solidarity, chastity and loyalty to the Queen Mother (*ndlovukazi*). You could say it's the Swazi equivalent of a 'coming out' party for debutantes which gives the girls, as David Johnson puts it, somewhat sensually, "a heavenly chance of parading their nubility".

The week-long festival begins when girls from across the kingdom gather at the *ndlovukazi's* residence, currently Ludzidzini. Traditionally, every eligible maiden in the country was expected to attend. Now, it's more voluntary but I was told that about 80 per cent of the female population will do *umhlanga* at least once in their lives.

And so, on the appointed date, girls from many of Swaziland's 200 or so chiefdoms travel to the royal kraal with an escort of around four men, appointed by the local chief. Only childless, unmarried girls under 21 years old (the Swazi age of 'spinsterhood') can take part.

The girls are met by a female *induna* (captain), a commoner selected by the royal family as the 'head girl' of the ceremony. Being the *induna* of *umhlanga* is a great honour, and only someone with a thorough knowledge of dancing and royal protocol will be chosen. One of the king's daughters will work together with the *induna* to ensure everything goes according to plan.

On the second day, the girls are separated into two groups according to their age (one group about eight to 13 years old; the other about 14 to 22). They then walk to the reed-beds to collect the longest reeds they can find. The older girls often go to Ntondozi (about 30km away) while the younger girls usually go to Bhamsakhe near Malkerns (about 10km). Sometimes the older girls are sent to Mphisi Farm on government-supplied lorries. That night, the girls sleep in specially-erected tents or marquees. Formerly, the local people would have accommodated them.

On the third day, the girls cut the reeds and tie them into bundles of around ten or 20. Nowadays plastic strips are used to secure the bundles, but those who are particularly thorough will cut grass and plait it into traditional rope.

The following afternoon, the girls return to the *ndlovukazi's* kraal. They are supposed to arrive at night 'to show they travelled a long way'.

On the fifth day, the girls admire each other's bundles and make themselves look beautiful. Their costumes consist of decorative short skirts (*indlamu*), anklets (*emaqakala*), bracelets (*tigcizo*) and necklaces (*emagcebesha*).

Finally, on the afternoon of the sixth day, the girls dance into the kraal with a sweeping motion. They place their bundles outside the Queen Mother's quarters; these will later be used to repair the *ndlovukazi's* reed screens. Several hours of dancing and singing follow, with each group singing a different song at the same time.

The dancing and singing continues throughout the seventh day, when the king and Queen Mother are present. The idea is to win royal approval for their performance, but there is but no formal competition element—although the king always has his eyes open for attractive new brides. Visitors are welcome to attend the ceremony, but photographs are not allowed without permission from the SNTC.

On the eighth day, the king orders a number of cattle to be slaughtered, around 20 to 25 of them. The girls collect their pieces of meat and return home.

The modern Reed Dance is not an ancient ceremony. Instead, it developed out of the old *umcwasho* custom, in which young girls were placed in age-regiments and forbidden from interacting with men until they reached a suitable age. Once they had matured, the girls would celebrate their eligibility for marriage by performing labour service for the Queen Mother. Under *umcwasho*, if any girl fell pregnant outside of marriage, her family would have to pay a fine of one cow to the local chief.

Recently, the king revived *umcwasho* for a set number of years to promote abstinence and thus stem the rise in HIV infections. This traditional attempt to fight the AIDS pandemic swamping the country met with mixed reactions, both in Swaziland and abroad.

In its modern incarnation, *umcwasho* (the name of the headgear that is worn by the participating girls) is characterized by a long tassel that runs down the back: gold and blue wool for girls up to 18 years, and red and black for 19-year-olds and upwards. Any girls wearing the *umcwasho* were thus proclaiming their abstinence and could not be approached by men with impure intentions.

General information

Driving in Swaziland

South African drivers' licences are valid in Swaziland. Foreign drivers' licences and international drivers' licences (available through the Automobile Association) are also valid, as long as they display a photograph of the driver. All traffic laws and regulations are consistent with South Africa, and vehicles drive on the left-hand side of the road (which everyone knows is the right side). There are currently no toll roads in Swaziland, but there are plans to erect toll booths on the Ngwenya/Mbabane road and the Mbabane/Ezulwini route. This is to recoup some of the money that has been spent on the revamped MR3 highway. Petrol (unleaded and lead replacement) and diesel are freely available throughout Swaziland. I was able to use my South Africa petrol card at most filling stations, but it's a good idea to have cash on you, just in case there are no card facilities available.

Telephony

The international dialling code for Swaziland is +268. If you are calling from South Africa, dial 00268 and then the number. There are an estimated 44,000 landlines and 380,000 mobile phones in the country. Travellers who want to use their own cell phones should be aware that Swaziland is considered an international territory, and you will not be able to utilize your South African network unless you activate international roaming. This is expensive, however, and the best way to stay in touch is to buy a pre-paid card from MTN Swaziland once you are across the border. This will let you make calls from your cell phone within Swaziland, and it also opens up a text message channel to South Africa or overseas.

If you are coming in through the Oshoek border post, here's how to do it: pull into the first petrol station, just after you cross the border, and buy a starter pack and air-time voucher at the kiosk. This will give you a Swaziland phone number, which people can use to contact you while you are in the kingdom. Starter packs cost around E40 and air time starts at E30, so just E70 will get you connected. Now, here's the clever bit—since you are so close to South Africa, you can still use your South African SIM card to make calls on your South African network. So, while you are at the petrol station, call your loved ones and give them your Swazi number. You can even phone into your voicemail service and change your message so that people calling you on your regular number will get your new Swazi number. Then, when you're done, switch SIM cards and you're connected to MTN Swaziland. Nifty, hey?

Malaria

The western half of Swaziland is malaria-free, and no precautions are necessary. The low-lying bushveld region, east of Manzini, is a malaria-endemic area. Thankfully, the Lubombo Spatial Development Initiative (LSDI – www.malaria.org.za/lsdi) has made great strides in its malaria-control programme with incidence reduced from 250 to less than 20 per 1,000. Nevertheless, you should take the appropriate precautions. Mosquitos are essentially nocturnal, so try to stay indoors at night and make sure that your accommodation has screens and nets. Use a good insect repellent, especially at night and in the summer. Products with citronella and khakibos seem to be effective. Cover up by wearing long pants and thin sweatshirts that come down to your wrists. To make absolutely sure, take one of the recommended anti-malarial medications that are available—check with your doctor what is suitable for you.

Crime and safety

As any Swazi will tell you, this is a peaceful country with a relatively low crime rate—especially when compared to South Africa. One guy said that this is because everybody is related to one another, and you don't want to steal from your own family. Others have pointed out that Swaziland is a more equitable society than many others and people who fall on hard times are supported by their community, thus preventing a descent into crime. Nevertheless, there is some petty crime around (such as pick-pocketing), and there are even occasional murders (but these are usually the result of a specific betrayal or feud). All in all, however, Swaziland is a safe destination for travellers. On a related topic, as you drive around the country, you will see many pedestrians asking for lifts. Picking up hitchhikers is a matter of personal choice, but I found myself doing it quite often, especially in the remote parts of the country where distances between towns are long and dusty. I also enjoyed chatting to the people I picked up, if their English was up to it, and learnt a lot about local opinions in this way.

As an illustration of this, allow me to relate the experience I had with Ngabisile and Dudu, two young girls I shuttled from the mountains to Manzini. After chatting for a bit, one of them asked if I was a Christian. I asked "Why?" and she replied that white people normally don't pick up black people in their cars. Feeling a bit defensive, I explained that people from South Africa are scared of picking up a criminal and getting robbed. Ngabisile calmly replied that that kind of thing doesn't happen in Swaziland. Again, I asked "Why?" and she said, "Because we have a good king, who keeps the people good." Makes you think ...

Photography

Swaziland is a very photogenic country, so bring along plenty of batteries and memory cards (who uses film anymore?). Photographic supplies are available in the main centres, but may be pretty scarce in the more remote areas. If you like taking portraits, it is usually a good idea to ask before you take a picture of someone. Some Swazi are a bit touchy about getting snapped without permission, especially the elderly, and the occasional refusal should be accepted graciously. You may not take photographs inside the royal kraal without a permit from the Swaziland National Trust Commission.

As is usually the case, the best time for photographs is in the late afternoon. This 'golden hour' is much beloved by photographers for its warm light that infuses everything with a soft glow. Interestingly, the Swazi have a specific expression that refers to this period between three and five; *selibantu bahle* which means 'everyone looks beautiful'.

Public holidays

1 January	New Year's Day
March / April	Easter Friday and Monday
19 April	King's Birthday
25 April	National Flag Day
1 May	Workers' Day

17 May				Ascension Day		
22 July				public holiday		
August				*Umhlanga* Reed Dance Day (depending on the position of the moon)		
6 September				Independence / Somhlolo Day		
25 December				Christmas Day		
26 December				Boxing Day		
December / January				*Incwala* Day (depending on the position of the moon)		

Border posts (clockwise, starting from the northeast)

Swazi name	South African name	Open	Close	Nearest town in Swaziland	Nearest town in South Africa	Tar
Mananga	Bordergate	08:00	18:00	Tshaneni	Komatipoort	Y
Matsamo	Jeppe's Reef	07:00	20:00	Pigg's Peak	Nelspruit	Y
Bulembu	Josefdal	08:00	16:00	Pigg's Peak	Barberton	N
Ngwenya	Oshoek	07:00	22:00	Mbabane	Ermelo	Y
Lundzi	Waverley	08:00	16:00	Mbabane	Ermelo	Y/N
Sandlane	Nerston	08:00	18:00	Bhunya	Amsterdam	Y
Sicunusa	Houtkop	08:00	18:00	Sicunsa	Piet Retief	Y
Gege	Bothashoop	08:00	16:00	Sicunsa	Piet Retief	N
Mahamba	Mahamba	07:00	22:00	Nhlangano	Piet Retief	Y
Nsalitje	Onverwacht	08:00	18:00	Nhlangano	Pongola	N
Lavumisa	Golela	07:00	22:00	Big Bend	Pongola	Y
Mhlumeni	Goba Frontiera	07:00	20:00	Siteki	**Maputo**	Y
Lomahasha	Namaacha	07:00	20:00	Simunye	Maputo	Y

Banking

- Central Bank of Swaziland: 268-408 2000; www.centralbank.org.sz
- First National Bank: 268-404 5401
- Nedbank Swaziland: 268-408 1000; www.nedbank.co.sz
- Standard Bank: 268-404 1540; www.standardbank.co.sz
- Swazi Bank: 268-404 2551; www.swazibank.co.sz
- Swaziland Building Society: 268-404 2107

Post and telecommunication

- Swaziland Post & Telecommunication:
  - Hhohho region: 964
  - Manzini region: 965
  - Lubombo region: 963
  - Shiselweni region: 962
  - Enquiries: 901
  - Faults: 971
  - International assistance: 941
- Swazi MTN: 922; www.mtn.co.sz

Embassies and agencies

- British Consulate: 268-404 9727
- Consulate of The Netherlands: 268-404 4006
- Cyprus Consulate: 268-404 2650
- Embassy of the Republic of China (Taiwan): 268-404 4740
- Embassy of the United States of America: 268-404 6441; http://swaziland.usembassy.gov
- High Commission of the Republic of Mozambique: 268-404 3700
- High Commission of the Republic of Singapore: 268-404 2661
- Italian Consulate: 268-404 44371
- Portugal Consulate: 268-404 6780
- Royal Danish Consulate/Norwegian Consulate: 268-404 3547
- South African High Commission: 268-404 4651
- United Nations Developement Programme (UNDP): 268-404 2301
- World Health Organization: 268-404 0913
- UN High Commission for Refugees (UNHCR): 268-404 4314

Emergency

- Police emergency: 999
- Assist 911: 268-404 8911
- Fire department: 933 or 268-404 3333
- Army: 990
- Trauma link 24hrs: 268-606 0911
- Police Stations:
  - Airport Police: 268-518 5222
  - Bhunya: 268-452 6113
  - Big Bend: 268-363 6322
  - Bulembu: 268-437 3222
  - Ebuhleni: 268-437 3272
  - Hlatikulu: 268-217 6222
  - Hluti: 268-227 5222
  - Kaphunga: 268-207 9222
  - Lavumisa: 268-207 9121
  - Lobamba: 268-416 1221
  - Lomahasha: 268-323 6221
  - Lubuli: 268-303 0222
  - Mafutseni: 268-505 6343
  - Mahlalini: 268-207 9032
  - Mahlangatsha: 268-531 5017
  - Malkerns: 268-528 3011
  - Mananga: 268-323 2050
  - Mankayane: 268-538 8222
  - Manzini: 268-505 2221
  - Matsapha: 268-518 7111
  - Mbabane: 268-404 2221
  - Mlawula: 268-383 8930
  - Mliba: 268-383 8022
  - Nhlangano: 268-207 8222
  - Pigg's Peak: 268-437 1222
  - Sidvokodvo: 268-505 4180
  - Simunye: 268-383 8966
  - Siphofaneni: 268-344 1222
  - Siteki: 268-343 4222
  - Tshaneni: 268-323 2074

Hospitals and medical services

- Mbabane Government Hospital: 268-404 2111
- Mbabane Clinic: 268-404 2423
- Raleigh Fitkin Memorial Hospital (Manzini): 268-505 2211
- Imphilo Clinic (Manzini): 268-505 7430
- Good Shepherd Hospital (Lubombo): 268-343 4133; www.goodshepherdhosp.org
- Hlatikulu Government Hospital: 268-217 6111
- Mankayane Government Hospital: 268-538 8311
- Pigg's Peak Government Hospital: 268-437 1111
- TB Hospital (Manzini): 268-505 5170

Tourism offices
- Ezulwini Tourism Office: 268-416 2180
- Ngwenya Tourism Information Office: 268-442 4206
- Swazi Plaza Information Office (Mbabane): 268-404 2531
- Ziggy's Internet Cafe & Tourist Office (Malkerns): 268-528 3423

Distance table in kilometres

	Piet Retief	Nelspruit	Maputo	Manzini	Mbabane	Johannesburg
Nelspruit	258					
Maputo	374	182				
Manzini	193	214	181			
Mbabane	236	171	224	34		
Johannesburg	329	358	540	407	364	
Durban	422	689	796	539	582	598

Websites

Tourism

- Swaziland Tourism Authority: 268-404 9693/75; www.welcometoswaziland.com
- www.experienceswaziland.com
- www.swazi.com
- www.swazi.travel
- www.swaziland-direct.com
- www.swazilandhappenings.co.za
- www.swaziland-travel-guide.com
- www.swazilive.com
- www.swazilodgings.com – Hotels and Tourism Association of Swaziland
- www.swaziplace.com
- www.swaziplace.com
- www.swaziwhatson.com
- www.swaziweb.net
- www.visitswazi.com

Environmental

- www.ecs.co.sz – Environmental Centre for Swaziland
- www.environment.gov.sz – Swaziland Environmental Authority
- www.naturalhistorysociety.org.sz
- www.sntc.org.sz – Swaziland National Trust Commission
- www.swazimet.gov.sz – Swaziland Meteorological Service

Newspapers and media

- www.observer.org.sz – The Swazi Observer
- www.swala.sz – Swaziland Library Association
- www.swazitv.co.sz
- www.times.co.sz – The Times of Swaziland

Government and agencies

- www.gov.sz – Official Swaziland Government website
- www.seb.co.sz – Swaziland Electricity Board
- www.sptc.co.sz – Swaziland Post and Telecommunications
- www.swazirail.co.sz – Swaziland Railway
- www.swade.co.sz - Swaziland Water and Agricultural Development Enterprise
- www.swsc.co.sz – Swaziland Water Services Corporation
- www.undp.org.sz – United Nations Development Programme
- www.uniswa.sz – University of Swaziland

Business

- www.business-swaziland.com – Swaziland Chamber of Commerce
- www.sidc.co.sz – Swaziland Industrial Development Company
- www.sipa.org.sz – Swaziland Investment Promotion Authority
- www.ssa.co.sz – Swaziland Sugar Association
- www.ssx.org.sz – Swaziland Stock Exchange
- www.swazibusiness.com
- www.swaziyellowpages.com
- www.tibiyo.com – Tibiyo Taka Ngwane Development Agency

Sports

- www.nfas.org.sz – National Football Association of Swaziland
- www.sportscouncil.org.sz – Swaziland National Sports Council
- www.swazilandrugby.com

Social, cultural, health and religious

- www.breastcancernet.org.sz
- www.flas.org.sz – Family Life Association of Swaziland
- www.friendsofswaziland.org – volunteer website
- www.nercha.org.sz – National Emergency Response Council on HIV/AIDS
- www.savethechildren.net/swaziland
- www.scouting.org.za/swazi - Swaziland Scout Association

- www.swagaa.org.sz – Swaziland Action Group Against Abuse
- www.swazicoalition.org.sz – Swazi Coalition of Concerned Organizations
- www.swaziland.anglican.org – Swaziland Anglican Diocese
- www.swazimission.co.za – Swaziland Reformed Church
- www.unicef.org/swaziland - United Nations Children's Fund
- www.youngheroes.org.sz

References / further reading

- Bonner, Philip. 1983. *Kings, Commoners and Concessionaires—the evolution and dissolution of the nineteenth-century Swazi state.* Ravan Press.
- Boycott, R.; Forrester, B.; Loffler, L.; Monadjem, A. 2007. *Wild Swaziland—common animals and plants.* Natural History Society of Swaziland, Conservation Trust of Swaziland.
- Bulpin, T. V. 1965. *Lost Trails of the Transvaal.* Thomas Nelson and Sons.
- Bulpin, T. V. 2001. *Discovering Southern Africa* (sixth edition). Tafelberg Publishers.
- Campbell, Alec; Ambrose, David; Johnson, David. 1983. *A guide to Botswana, Lesotho and Swaziland.* Winchester Press.
- Forsyth-Thompson, Cynthia. 2007. *Swaziland Business Year Book* (16th edition). www.swazibusiness.com/sbyb
- Forsyth-Thompson, Cynthia. *Swaziland Discovery—official guide of the Swaziland Tourism Authority.* www.swazibusiness.com/discovery
- Gosnell, Peter J. 2001. *Big Bend—a history of the Swaziland Bushveld.*
- Harrison, David. 1995. *Development of tourism in Swaziland.* Annals of Tourism Research, Vol. 22, No. 1, pp. 135-156.
- Matsebula, J. S. M. 1988. *A history of Swaziland* (third edition). Longman.
- Mountain, Alan. 1999. *The rise and fall of the Zulu empire.* kwaNtaba Publishing.
- Norman, Nick & Whitfield, Gavin. 2006. *Geological Journeys.* Struik.
- Taylor and Francis Group. 2003. *Africa south of the Sahara* (33rd edition). Routledge.
- Viljoen, M. J. & Reimold, W. U. 1999. *An introduction to South Africa's geological and mining heritage.* Mintek, Geological Society of South Africa.

Index

INDEX

King
Makhosini, Prince 118, 119, 122, 123
Makosine Valley 203
Makundwe River 68
Malambule, Prince 52, 55-57-59
Malandela 172, 173
Malangwane Pass/hills 85, 156, 157
malaria 13, 207, 212, 222, 235
Malelane 106
Malelane Gate 180
Malkerns Valley Meander 171-176
Malkerns/Valley 21, 135, 155, 157,
    166, 172, 201, 205, 222, 227, 232
Malolotja 148
Malolotja Falls 184
Malolotja Nature Reserve 22, 24,
    26-29, 138, 145, 147, 180-188, 227
Malolotja River 184
Maloma Colliery 225
Maloyi, Councillor 42, 70, 80, 93
Malunge, Councillor 70, 80
Malunge, Prince Regent 105, 109
Mamahato, Queen 125, 126
Mamba 42
Mampuru, Prince 68
Mananga 79, 140, 218, 219
Mananga College 211, 212
Mandela, Nelson 130
Mankanyane 205
Mantanga, Sylvia 199
Mantenga Falls 163, 164
Mantenga Nature Reserve 163-166,
    228
Manzimnyame 32
Manzini 21, 85, 102, 135, 136, 138,
    152, 156, 159, 174, 176-179, 201,
    202, 205, 207, 220
Manzini district 17, 21, 118, 201
Manzini Motha, Chief 85, 177
Maputaland Centre of Plant Diver-
    sity 24
Marais, Mr 97
Margaret, Princess 125

Maritz, Ignatius 81, 88
Marlborough House Independence
    Conference 120
Martin, Col Richard 98, 100
Marwick, A. G. 80
Maseko tribe 43
Masire, Quett 125
Masuku, Mandla 229
Masundvwini 112
Matabele tribe 45
Matsafeni, Prince Mdluli 74, 85, 87
Matsamo 138, 180, 199, 200
Matsapha 176, 177
Matsebula clan 129
Matsebula, Dr 41, 45, 46
Matsemo 140
Mavimbela tribe 43
Mavuso I, King 37
Mawewe, Prince 64, 65, 74, 87
Maziya tribe 43
Mbabane 21, 23, 85, 108, 111, 125,
    135-139, 143, 149-155, 159, 180,
    227, 234
Mbabane River 108, 156
Mbabane, Chief Kunene 151
Mbandzeni, King 70-77, 80-86, 88-
    97, 99, 109, 177, 208
Mbandzini Convention Party 117
Mbekelweni 85, 89, 90, 177
Mbeki, Thabo 124
Mbhabha, Chief 102, 103
Mbilini, Prince 66-68, 72, 76
Mbuluzi Game Reserve 212-214
Mbuluzi River 23, 26, 181, 213, 217
Mbuyazi, Prince 61, 67
McCorkindale, Alexander 69
McLachlan, Tom 84, 85, 191
McMillan, Harold 203, 204
McNab, Bob 87, 92, 94, 207
Mdzabuko, Prince 81, 82
Mdzimba Mountain 42, 95, 103,
    105, 156
Merensky, Alexander 66

public holidays 236, 237

Rathbone, T. B. 89
Reagan, Maureen 129
Red Data Book 27
Reed Dance *see Umhlanga* festival
Reilly, Ann 28
Reilly, Liz 29
Reilly, Mickey 28, 170
Reilly, Ted 27-32, 168, 209, 221
Rhodes, Cecil John 98, 99
Ripon, Lord 101
Robinson, Sir Hercules 84
Rogers, Bob 85, 177
Rorke's Drift, Battle of 77
Rovos Rail 136
Royal Council 40, 66, 67, 69, 74, 76,
    80-82, 86, 87, 90, 91, 95, 101, 109,
    115, 126
Royal Swaziland Sugar Corporation
    (RSSC) 211, 212, 218
Rudolph, Magistrate 72, 80
Rutherford, Secretary 83, 84

Sabie River 48
Saddleback Pass 138, 192, 196-197
Sand River Convention 62
Sand River Dam 218
Sandhlana, Chief 93
Sandlane 140
Sandlane, Councillor 70, 80, 81
Sara Camp 216
Save River 65
Sayler, Horst 159
Schriener, Oliver 98
Schwab, Gustav 106
Sekhukhune, King 68, 71, 74, 75,
    78, 96
Sekwati, King 56, 68
Selborne, Lord 109
Senzangakona, Chief 46
Shaka, King 41, 42, 44-48, 51, 53
Shaw, Rev William 57

She Mine 183
Sheba's Breasts 166
Shepstone Jnr, Theophilus 'Offy'
    89-91, 95, 96, 98, 101
Shepstone, Arthur 85
Shepstone, Sir Theophilus 59-63,
    72, 75, 76, 85
Shewula Mountain Camp 217-218
Shewula Nature Reserve 32, 212,
    217-218, 227
Shiselweni district 17, 21, 38, 41, 42,
    44, 118, 201, 203, 205
Sibebe 32
Sibebe Rock 23, 153-155
Sibhaca dancing 169
Sicunusa 139, 140, 201
Sikhunyana, Chief 45
Sikhupe International Airport 207
Silenana, Chief 50
Simunye 21, 211, 212
Sinceni 32
Siphiso shelter 34, 216
Siphiso Valley 214
Siphofaneni 207, 220
Sisile, Queen 70, 71, 80-82
Siteki 139, 208, 209, 216
Smuts, Gen Tobias 107
Smuts, Johannes 109
Sobandla, Councillor 80
Sobhuza I, King 16, 17, 28, 29, 39-
    48, 51, 57, 225, 226
Sobhuza II, King 110-126, 128, 129,
    147, 167, 184, 209
Somcuba, Prince 56, 59, 60-63, 68
Somdlalose 81, 82
Somhloho *see* Sobhuza I, King
Sondeza 184
Songimvelo Nature Reserve 22, 146,
    184, 196
Songimvelo-Malolotja TFCA 32
Soshangane, King 45, 48, 64
South African National Parks (SAN-
    Parks) 209, 210

Author's note

A final note on accommodation

Apart from the Southern Sun's casino hotels in the Ezulwini Valley and Orion Pigg's Peak resort, there are no major hotel chains in Swaziland. Instead, most accommodation providers are independently run and each establishment tends to have its own personality and charm. This idiosyncrasy should be embraced by holiday-makers and I encourage you to look around for a spot that suits your personal taste.

At the moment, there is no star-grading system for accommodation providers in Swaziland. Rod de Vletter of Phophonyane is currently working with the tourism authorities to get a system in place, and he wants to include a special category for ecolodges. As Rod points out, in South Africa, natural environment counts for only 2% of the evaluation and, as such, the tiles in the bathroom are more important than environmental management. That just aint right!

Thanks

I wish to thank Sipho Simelane, Mandla Masuku and all those people who gave so generously of their time and knowledge. The Swazi reputation for friendliness is totally justified. Thanks also to Jaydon Immerman, Anthony Rosmarin and all my other travelling companions who have made all my visits to Swaziland so memorable. And most of all, I want to thank my publishers who were extraordinarily patient with me during my wobbly. Finally, a customary shout out to my ever-supportive family and friends—you know who you are ...

***

Disclaimer: Although the publisher and author have done their best to ensure that all facts contained in this book are accurate and up to date, they accept no responsibility for any loss, injury or inconvenience caused to any person, resulting from information contained herein.

The views expressed in this book are the author's. The publisher, advertisers and people/organizations mentioned in the book do not necessarily subscribe to these views.

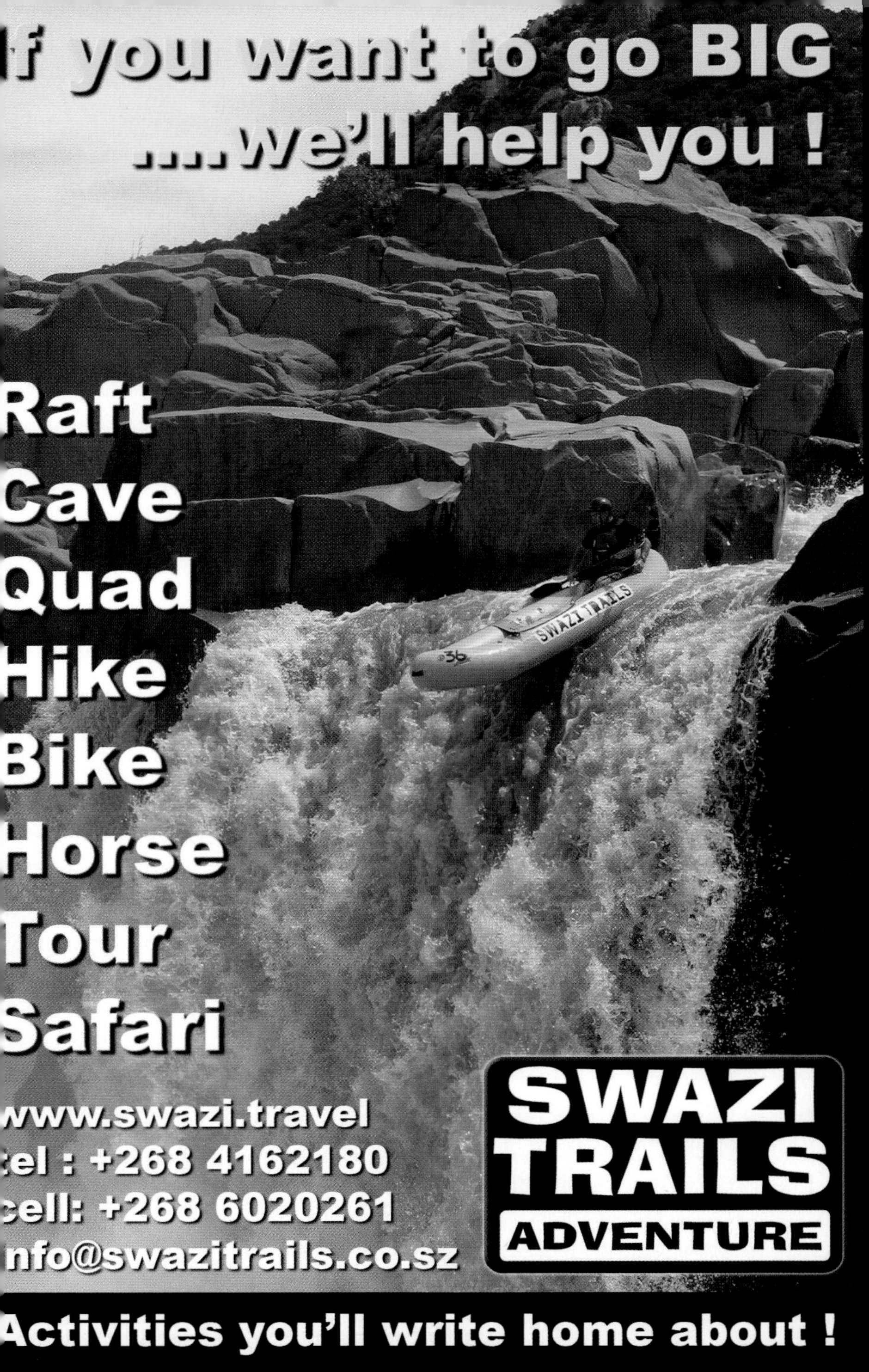
If you want to go BIG
....we'll help you !
Raft
Cave
Quad
Hike
Bike
Horse
Tour
Safari
SWAZI TRAILS
www.swazi.travel
tel : +268 4162180
cell: +268 6020261
info@swazitrails.co.sz
SWAZI
TRAILS
ADVENTURE
Activities you'll write home about !

Ngwenya Glass
Swazilands HOTTEST tourist attraction Est. 1987

This charming complex at Ngwenya Glass, set in large indigenous gardens, is one of Swaziland's major tourist attractions.

- Witness first-hand, the magical art of glassblowing, from an overhead balcony. Each item is handmade from 100% recycled glass! Browse around the adjoining well stocked showroom and purchase your little memento of a truly African visit to our Kingdom.
- Relax in the sunny coffee shop overlooking the imaginative play park for children, which serves a variety of light meals.
- The on-site Craft Market offers rare African weapons, artifacts, craft and clothing.
- Visit African Temptations to sample and witness the creation of delicious handmade Belgian chocolates. Witness the carving of exquisite traditional hard wood rocking horses, zebras and other wonderful toys at the Rocking Horse Co.

Ngwenya Glass (Pty) Ltd, P O Box 45, Motshane, H104, Kingdom of Swaziland
Tel: +268 442 4053 or +268 442 4142 /
Fax: +268 442 4588
Email: ngwenya@ngwenyaglass.co.sz /
web: www.ngwenyaglass.co.sz
Ngwenya Glass (Pty) Ltd, Red Shed, V&A Waterfront, Cape Town
Tel: +27 21 418 0654

All facilities are wheelchair friendly
Ngwenya Glass complex is open 7 days a week (closed some public holidays)
Pre booking for tour bus lunches recommended

NGWENYA GLASS

bulembu
Country Lodge

Bulembu Country Lodge is situated in a tranquil setting among magnificent mountain scenery in a historic mining village, at the foot of Swaziland's tallest mountain, Emlembe.

Bulembu Country Lodge once housed senior mine staff and now has 12 enchanting and comfortable en-suite bedrooms . Village houses can be rented on self-catering or full board basis.

Come and enjoy our various hikes and trails, cooling off in rock pools and secluded waterfalls.

1 Chinda Place, Bulembu, Swaziland
t +268.437.1998/3888
c +268.602.0501 • **f** +268.437.1580
e reservations@bulembu.org • www.bulembu.org

Tambankulu Club/Guesthouse

Tel: (00278) 373-7193 Fax: (00268) 373-7193
jenny@swazi.net
C/O Tambankulu Estates,
P/B Mhlume, L309, Swaziland

Nestling amongst the sugar cane fields in Swaziland, lies the unique Tambankulu Club/ Guesthouse. Set in a tranquil garden with two lovely swimming pools are 14 en-suite bedrooms; of which one is a honeymoon suite. When visiting us, you can relax in our spacious lounge. Delicious breakfast can be enjoyed either in the Breakfast room or on the patio. Within walking distance, you will find a tennis court, restaurant and 3 conference facilities. The more adventurous traveler can enjoy bass fishing with a professional guide. Bass fishing weekend packages are available on request. Tambankulu Guesthouse is a suitable stop over for all tourists, company reps and guests. We are only 3km off the main road. A grass runway is available for small Lear jet aircrafts.

Credit Card Facilities Available
Children Welcome
We are waiting for your call!

King and Queen Tours and Coaches

.. the fleet you want to explore in ...

... the places you want to explore ...

King & Queen Tours and Coaches started on 14 May 2003 and operate as a sole proprietor. Sanet Clarke has been in the tourism industry since 1998. It was during May 2003 that Sanet decided to start her own business and apply the skills, contacts and knowledge gained the past 4 years. A small touring company based in Gauteng South Africa. The founders of King & Queen Tours and Coaches created the company to seek meaningful tourism to make use of our experience and interest in travel within the South Africa tourism industry and most of all client service. Our approach is informed by a commitment to responsible tourism and meaningful cultural exchange. We strive to share our knowledge and learn from our clients, providing an exceptional service and developing mutual beneficial relationships. Only in 2007 we came to the point of deciding to purchase a small fleet of Quantums. In 2009 King & Queen Tours and Coaches became a fully BEE Company with a Level 4 Grading

Tel. 011-412-3407; Fax. 0866-198-245

PHOENIX STEAK HOUSE
AT THE RIVER @ THE MALL MBABANE
TEL: 00268-4049103

Open 7 days a week breakfast, lunch and supper from 9am till late.
Phoenix's swanky new retro décor gives you a chance to wine and dine in a intimate atmosphere. Experience our scrumptious & mouth watering selection from the grill, our Mexican dishes, a variety of fresh salads and decadent new desserts. The restaurant is fully licensed with a variety of wine, beers and spirits
Kids birthday parties are our speciality. Check the menu for our weekly specials.

Mountain Inn

The Preferred Hotel
Located along the main Mbabane Manzini road a warm and personal welcome awaits you at Swaziland's most prominent family owned hotel. Relax in Mountain Top spender with unbeatable views of the Ezulwini Valley- From here you are perfectly positioned to discover all Swaziland has to offer.

Enjoy total room comfort including Free Wireless Access. Superb Al a Carte cuisine at our cozy Friar Tucks Restaurant or dine al fresco under an African Sky. Enjoy the Swimming Pool with unbeatable views, Croquet, Boulez, Chess and Residents Gym All this with secured parking your rest is assured.

www.mountaininn.sz
info@mountaininn.sz
+268 4042781

Hawane Resort

Hawane Resort

Hawane
RESORT
Swaziland

For Bookings:

infohawane@realnet.co.sz   Tel+268 442 4744   Cell+268 6276714

CATHMAR COTTAGES

Self Catering / Bed & Breakfast
Accommodation in Mbabane, Swaziland

Good value-for-money accommodation and relaxed, comfortable living. Each self-catering cottage or room has private entrance with patio or deck. Facilities include televsion in every room, wireless internet access, braai facilities, swimming pool, and large beautiful garden with stunning views. Breakfasts and dinners, utilizing our home-grown fresh vegetables and herbs, are available upon request.

Cottages start from R250 sgl, R300 cpl (quoted in South African Rand). Self-catering cottages and rooms. B&B and dinners available upon request.

Tel: (+268) 404-3387/1165   Fax: (+268) 404-6072
Cell: (+268) 608-6229; 608-0820 email: cathmar@visitswazi.com
website: www.visitswazi.com/cathmar

SHIELD GUEST HOUS

Self-catering or B & B accommodation in Mbabane, Swaziland

Shield Guest House offers self-catering or bed and breakfast accommodation, ideal for busines visitors to Mbabane, Swaziland.

The guest house is five minutes walk from the city centre and has a large garden, combining convenience with a tranquil setting.

Shield Guest House is located at 173 Tsekwane Street, between Panasonic and Prince Flats.

Tel/Fax: (+268) 404 6072
Mgr: (+268) 607 1337
Cell: (+268) 608 0820
Email: shieldguest@yahoo.com
www.visitswazi.com/shield

PHOPHONYANE FALLS

ECOLODGE AND NATURE RESERVE

A unique and private ecolodge set in a place of legendary romance and magical beauty. A stunning combination of mountains, waterfalls, sub-tropical indigenous forest and lush gardens, situated just 70 km south of Kruger Park (Malalane Gate) and 12 km north of Pigg's Peak. We accommodate a maximum of 24 people in our private paradise and offer you a choice of comfortable safari tents on decks over the river, luxurious Swazi beehives with spectacular views, and comfortable double-storey thatched cottages in large private gardens. Our spacious and stylish restaurant offers an extensive a-la-carte menu and fine wines. Activities include great swimming, mountain drives, and hiking trails in the biodiversity rich 500 ha nature reserve (small game and 230 bird species). You are assured a warm welcome and personal service from our friendly staff. We are highly recommended by all the best travel guides.

lungile@phophonyane.co.sz
www.phophonyane.co.sz

T:+268 437 1429
F: +268 437 1319
C: +268 602 2802